To Daniel

Keep in touch!

Janice

SELVES, PERSONS, INDIVIDUALS

Selves, Persons, Individuals

Philosophical Perspectives on Women and
Legal Obligations

JANICE RICHARDSON
University of Leicester, UK

ASHGATE

Published by
Ashgate Publishing Limited
Gower House
Croft Road
Aldershot
Hants GU11 3HR
England

Ashgate Publishing Company
Suite 420
101 Cherry Street
Burlington, VT 05401-4405
USA

Ashgate website: http://www.ashgate.com

British Library Cataloguing in Publication Data
Richardson, Janice
  Selves, persons, individuals : philosophical perspectives
  on women and legal obligations
  1.Obligation (Law) 2.Feminist jurisprudence 3.Women - Legal
  status, laws, etc. 4.Women - Identity
  I.Title
  346'.0134

Library of Congress Control Number: 2003063934

ISBN 0 7546 2398 X

Printed and bound by Athenaeum Press, Ltd.,
Gateshead, Tyne & Wear.

Contents

Acknowledgements

I would like to thank Christine Battersby and everyone from Warwick University Feminist Philosophy Society for a fascinating few years. Thanks also to Austin and Ali and everyone who made my life more interesting in the Arts Centre bar and Earlsdon pubs and to Jon Rubin for everything, including the way that you proved that Deleuzians can actually use computers. I am very grateful for the formatting. Thanks also to Tom Huggon and Glenys Rogerson for being around.

Chapter 1

Introduction

The aim of this book is to examine some of the contested meanings of what it is to be a self, a person or an individual in relation to the law of obligations. There is a political issue at stake: a concern with the way in which the question of what it is to be a woman has been problematised within recent feminist legal theory. In order to overcome what appears to be a block in this area, I turn to areas of philosophy that, with some exceptions, are not usually discussed within feminist legal theory. I draw these together from disparate areas of philosophy in support of a new view of selfhood through which to examine both legal personhood and individualism.

An important move in feminist philosophy has been to show that the supposedly neutral, universal terms: self, person and individual, have actually referred to males; male bodies and traditional lifestyles, as the paradigmatic case. In legal theory, the fact that these supposedly neutral terms actually took men as the norm has given rise to, what is known as, 'the equality/difference debate'. The terms of this debate describe a dilemma that is faced by women upon entering political institutions, workplaces and social organisations that were initially made by and for men. They can either gain rights by appearing to be like men or can argue that they should be treated differently. Luce Irigaray,[1] amongst other feminist philosophers, has argued that men should not be the neutral measure against whom women are judged. The dilemma posed by the equality/difference debate can therefore be understood as operating in practice, when women enter the male dominated legal profession for example, and within philosophy when theoretical structures are shown to be built upon the assumption that men represent the universal category of what it is to be a self, person or individual.

The dilemma of equality/difference debate has been explored in ways that cut across both theory and practice.[2] Scott,[3] for example, has traced the way in which the equality/difference problem has dogged feminist activists in French history. She illustrates how the theoretical terms of the debate have changed. Sometimes the faculty of imagination was viewed as important, sometimes it was the ability to reason, but whatever was viewed as the defining characteristic of personhood, it is males who were deemed to be proficient and women as lacking this ability. Scott draws an interesting conclusion, one which provides a challenge to feminist theory

---

1 L. Irigaray, *Je, Tu, Nous* (London: Routledge, 1993b) p. 12.
2 Feminism generally and feminist legal theory in particular has been conscious of the need to hold together concerns about both theory and practice. See, for example, C. McGlynn, *Legal Feminisms: Theory and Practice* (Aldershot: Dartmouth, 1998); A. Bottomley and J. Conaghan, *Feminist Theory and Legal Strategy* (Oxford: Blackwell, 1993).
3 J.W. Scott, *Only Paradoxes to Offer: French Feminists and the Rights of Man* (London: Harvard University Press, 1996).

and marks the starting point for this book. It is Scott's view that the paradox of
women's position, that is summed up within the equality/difference debate, is not
one that can be resolved; not even by changing the conceptual framework in which
the debate has arisen. It is implicit within the position of feminism as an historical
movement. She concludes,

> [I]n the case of feminism, the problem that has been deemed so central (equality
> versus difference) cannot be resolved as it has been posed. But can it be resolved
> otherwise? Would there be a feminism without the discourse of individual rights that
> represses sexual difference? I think not. Can there be a feminist politics that exploits
> that tension without expecting finally to resolve it? I think so; the point of this book
> has been to say that feminists have been doing just that for at least two centuries.[4]

I agree that the equality/difference debate cannot be resolved as it is posed. The
question of whether this can be resolved by employing different frameworks is
partly what this book is about. Whilst both have been described as paradigmatically
male, it is necessary to distinguish between the self and legal personhood. What it
is to be a self is an ontological concept, whereas 'personhood' denotes a moral and
legal concept. Historically, women have been denied legal personhood, the ability
to sue and be sued in the courts. I want to explore different ways of thinking about
the self (starting in Chapter 2) and legal personhood (starting in Chapter 3) that do
not take men as the norm against whom women are measured. This involves
thinking about a model of selfhood that takes the bodies and lives of women as the
norm rather than as an aberration. I will also examine a model of legal personhood,
provided by the work of Drucilla Cornell, that aims to move beyond the
equality/difference problem.

The paradoxical position of women with regard to individualism, and the
problems with individualism, are examined in Chapters 5 and 6 in the light of these
earlier chapters. My reference to individualism and 'possessive individualism'
focuses upon the ontological and political arguments of Thomas Hobbes and
Robert Nozick. They share a perspective that views the self as the owner of his
(and her?) abilities and owing nothing to society for them. This image of the self is
associated with the arguments in political theory about 'self-ownership' and
'property in the person', which are discussed in the final two chapters in relation to
employment contracts and marriage contracts.

Recent History of Feminist Legal Studies

An Australian work by Ngaire Naffine and Rosemary J. Owens,[5] *Sexing the Subject
of Law*, initially appears to have some similarities to my project of looking at the

---

4   Scott (1996) pp. 174-175.
5   N. Naffine and R.J. Owens, *Sexing the Subject of Law* (London: Sweet and Maxwell,
     1997).

question of the self and of the person in a legal context. In their introduction, Naffine and Owens state,

> This book reflects a central concern of modern social theory, which is the nature of identity. What does it mean to be a human subject or self? What is the nature of (legal) personhood?...The legal person, or legal subject, plays an absolutely critical role in law. The attributes accorded by law to its subject serve to justify and rationalise law's very forms and priorities. If feminists are to change the law, then, it is vital that they deal with the implicit as well as explicit sexing of the legal person. The aim of this book, then, is to bring together for the first time a diverse group of legal scholars whose task is to engage in a sustained critique of the legal person.[6]

However, after examination, it is clear that we are employing very different theoretical perspectives. As I will discuss below, it is my aim to try to open up more promising philosophical frameworks in order to move beyond the discomfort about talking about women that pervades *Sexing the Subject of Law*. Before outlining my response to current problems in feminist legal theory, I want to sketch its history to draw out these concerns.

To situate their work, Naffine and Owens[7] trace the following recent history of feminist legal theory. They point out that well into the 1980s the discipline of law was resistant to feminist theory because of law's history of being viewed as 'autonomous, self-defining and possessed of its own internal logic'.[8] Legal formalists continue to view law as merely a description of rules drawn from cases and statutes. When these rules are viewed as autonomous and as abstracted from their social context, law is cast as a type of quasi-mathematics that involves the search for the right rule.[9]

Although Naffine and Owens are writing from an Australian perspective, the points that they make about the background of feminist legal theory have general application. Inevitably any attempt to draw out a brief history of feminist legal theory is contentious. I will continue to follow Naffine and Owens' account because it is written with a view to thinking about the self, person and individual, which is the focus of my own project, but will point to particularly English concerns where relevant.

When feminism did have an impact upon legal theory it took the form of liberal feminism, which Naffine and Owens link with an acceptance of the nature/culture divide:

---

6   Naffine and Owens (1997) pp. 6-7.
7   Naffine and Owens (1997) pp. 3-14.
8   Naffine and Owens (1997) p. 3.
9   For a discussion of legal method, see for example, M.J. Mossman, 'Feminism and Legal Method: The Difference It Makes', *Australian Journal of Law and Society*, Vol. 3, 1986, pp. 30-52. Reprinted in M.A. Fineman and N.S. Thomadsen, eds., *At the Boundaries of the Law: Feminism and Legal Theory* (London: Routledge, 1991) pp. 287-388.

Humanity was regarded as naturally and self-evidently divided into two sexes: the ordering of human life into men and women was part of nature, not culture, and so the concern of feminists was necessarily limited to the treatment of women once they had entered the cultural order.[10]

They sketch this version of 'liberal feminism' as taking for granted a split between nature and culture. The sex/gender distinction – one that has been undermined in recent years[11] – was mapped onto this split such that 'gender' was viewed as a social construct whereas 'sex' was viewed as biological. Here 'biology' was viewed as something that could not easily be altered – a point that is now contentious within feminist legal theory. In Chapter 2, I take the unusual step of drawing upon the work of Susan Oyama and those biologists who employ developmental systems theory to consider the nature/culture dichotomy in more detail. As well as concerns about the relationship between sex and gender, in the UK early feminist legal theory highlighted some of the problems women encountered with the operation of the law.[12]

Naffine and Owens[13] detect a major shift away from the dominance of liberal feminist legal theory in the 1980s with the influence of the US lawyer, Catherine MacKinnon. MacKinnon's radical feminism has also been an important influence upon English feminist legal theory. Central to her argument is an analogy with Marxism that,

> sexuality is to feminism what work is to marxism: that which is most one's own yet most taken away.[14]

---

10 N. Naffine and R.J. Owens, 'Sexing Law' in Naffine and Owens (1997) p. 4.

11 For the way in which this nature/culture split has been challenged by poststructuralism with the argument that the way that we think about nature is also socially constructed, see J. Butler, *Gender Trouble: Feminism and the Subversion of Identity* (London: Routledge, 1990); J. Butler, *Bodies that Matter: On the Discursive Limits of 'Sex'* (London: Routledge, 1993). This nature/culture split has also been subject to a more compelling challenge from within the philosophy of biology, see S. Oyama, *Evolution's Eye: A Systems View of the Biology-Culture Divide* (Durham: Duke University, 2000a); S. Oyama, *The Ontogeny of Information: Developmental Systems and Evolution* (Durham: Duke University Press, 2000b).

12 See for example, A. Sachs and J.H. Wilson, *Sexism and the Law: A Study of Male Beliefs and Judicial Bias* (Oxford: Martin Robertson, 1978); S. Atkins and B. Hoggett, *Women and the Law* (Oxford: Blackwell, 1984); J. Brophy and C. Smart, eds., *Women in Law* (London: Routledge and Kegan Paul, 1985). In the area of sexuality, see for example: S. Edwards, *Female Sexuality and the Law* (Oxford: Martin Robertson, 1981); Z. Adler, *Rape on Trial* (London: Routledge and Kegan Paul, 1987).

13 Naffine and Owens (1997) pp. 5-6.

14 C.A. MacKinnon, 'Feminism, Marxism, Method and the State: An Agenda for Theory', *Signs: Journal of Women in Culture and Society*, Vol. 7, No. 3, 1982, pp. 515-544. See also C.A. MacKinnon, 'Feminism, Marxism, Method and State: Towards Feminist Jurisprudence', *Signs: Journal of Women in Culture and Society*, Vol. 8, No. 4, 1983, pp. 635-658.

For MacKinnon, sexuality is central to identity such that the way to reconstruct what it means to be a 'woman' is to use 'consciousness raising' to show the way in which women are oppressed. Despite the fact that MacKinnon's work appears to position women as always exploited, she has taken legal cases and influenced the development of the law in areas such as sexual harassment[15] and, more contentiously amongst US feminists,[16] the regulation of pornography.[17]

MacKinnon's inclusion in Naffine and Owens' outline of the recent history of feminist legal theory works to pinpoint areas of particular concern for their position. They argue that MacKinnon produces a shift in thinking about sex/gender, or nature/culture, by viewing the category of 'woman' as a matter of social construction.

> There was nothing natural or positive about the female sex: the meaning of woman was very much the cultural work of men who had crafted women according to their sexual interests.[18]

As they point out, this is subject to the criticism that it reduces women to a debased sex.[19] This criticism has been linked with a further attack upon MacKinnon: that she produces a 'universal' view of women. It is this point that is central to much of contemporary feminist legal theory. I will return to this argument in the next section.

Naffine and Owens argue that MacKinnon's work questioned the 'naturalness and fixity of the idea of sexual identity'.[20] They then cite the work of US feminist legal theorist Cornell, as 'producing a deeper fracture' in the category of 'woman'. The reference to 'fracture' presumably means that there is a further attack on the idea that there can be a universally accepted view of what it is to be a woman – as Cornell does not view what it is to be a self or a person as fractured. Cornell is described as influenced by Derrida. She is characterised as making the move that,

> The masculine language, through which women were constructed, was always open to subversion because it was, of its very nature, metaphorical, contingent and fluid.

---

15 C.A. MacKinnon, *The Sexual Harassment of Working Women* (New Haven: Yale University Press, 1979).
16 For the debate about pornography see, for example, D. Cornell, ed., *Feminism and Pornography* (Oxford University Press, 2000b).
17 A. Dworkin and C.A. MacKinnon, *Pornography and Civil Rights: A New Day for Women's Equality* (Minneapolis: Organising Against Pornography, 1988).
18 Naffine and Owens (1997) p. 5.
19 For UK criticisms of MacKinnon, see for example S.L. Roach Anleu, 'Critiquing the Law: Themes and Dilemmas in Anglo-American Feminist Legal Theory', *Journal of Law and Society*, Vol. 19, No. 4, 1992, pp. 423-440; E. Jackson, 'Catherine MacKinnon and Feminist Jurisprudence: A Critical Appraisal', *Journal of Law and Society*, Vol. 19, No. 2, 1992, pp. 195-213.
20 Naffine and Owens (1997) p. 6.

It did not have the power to encapsulate women because it could always be undermined and manipulated by such strategies as irony, satire and mimesis.[21]

It is understandable that Cornell's engagement with Derrida and with Lacan should mean that she is characterised as 'poststructuralist', particularly in 1997. Whilst this was written after Cornell had published *The Imaginary Domain*,[22] in which she develops her own theoretical framework from which her legal principles are derived, it was written before her further development of this approach in her later books.[23] Cornell's developed conceptual framework is more complex and original than is implied in the above quotation. She also produces many more practical arguments than are captured by the reference to strategies of 'irony, satire and mimesis'. Despite the fact that Cornell engages at length with Derrida and Lacan, she avoids being confined by them. On the contrary, Cornell is also in conversation with many of her other contemporaries, including Ronald Dworkin and John Rawls. She takes what she wants from her contemporaries, aware of their conflicting positions, in order to create a unique philosophical framework. In Chapter 3, in which I discuss Cornell's legal proposals drawn from her framework developed from *Imaginary Domain* onwards, I argue that the standard description of Cornell as 'poststructuralist' or 'psychoanalytic' does not capture the clearly acknowledged debt that she has to Hegel.[24] However, this should not be overstated. As I will discuss below, she is anxious not to be viewed as a 'follower of a particular man'.[25] She accounts for her eclectic approach as providing a way to avoid such identification whilst recognising that her work has come out of German Idealism.[26]

In their historical sketch, Naffine and Owens then point to the influence of Luce Irigaray. Irigaray's radical reworking of Lacan and her work as an analyst clearly position her within a psychoanalytic tradition. I believe that Irigaray, at least in her earlier work, also overcame this Lacanian influence. I am interested in one aspect of her work, drawn from *Speculum of the Other Woman*:[27] the way in which she radically rethinks the relationship between self and other, such that the self is not defined by what is not-self. I will return to explain this move in more detail in Chapter 2.

---

21 Naffine and Owens (1997) p. 6.
22 D. Cornell, *The Imaginary Domain: Abortion, Pornography and Sexual Harassment* (London: Routledge, 1995).
23 D. Cornell, *At the Heart of Freedom: Feminism, Sex and Equality* (Chichester: Princeton University Press, 1998); D. Cornell, *Just Cause: Freedom, Identity and Rights* (Oxford: Rowman and Littlefield, 2000a).
24 'I identified myself as a left Hegelian with strong socialist commitments from the time I was a teenager...' Cornell (2000a) p. 2.
25 P. Florence, 'Towards the Domain of Freedom: Interview with Drucilla Cornell', *Women's Philosophy Review*, No. 17, 1997, p. 24.
26 Florence (1997) p. 25.
27 L. Irigaray, *Speculum of the Other Woman* (New York: Cornell University Press, 1985d).

A history of the literature would not be complete without mentioning the 'ethics of care' that has developed from the influential work of Carol Gilligan.[28] This work has been used to attack perspectives that view social relations in terms of contract, both social contract theory and actual contracts, in favour of thinking about the relationship between mother and child as a potential model for social interaction.[29] Gilligan links empathy and caring with the 'feminine'. She tries to invert the priority attributed to traditionally 'female' and 'male' positions, as 'relational' and 'isolated' selves, respectively. The process of separating self and other is viewed as taking place within childhood to produce these 'relational' or 'isolated' selves. This can be contrasted with the theoretical frameworks that I will be looking at in Chapter 2.[30]

One work that is not mentioned by Naffine and Owens is that of Carol Smart. In the UK, the influential work of Carol Smart[31] draws upon her reading of Foucault to illustrate how women are 'constructed' by the way in which they are discussed in legal cases. Smart raises two different theoretical issues: whether it is worth feminists trying to engage with law at all and whether there should be such a discipline as feminist jurisprudence. Smart's analysis has some common features with that of Naffine and Owens and I will respond to these points below.

Naffine and Owens' emphasis upon language and upon, what they describe as, the 'open' meaning of what it is to be a 'woman' brings them up to date and is used to situate their own work: they are concerned with 'the meaning or construction of law's subject – the legal person'.[32] Throughout their book there is a tension between: (1) what they call 'sexing the law', the phrase used to describe their 'method' of recognising the way in which sexist assumptions about women permeate the operation of law; and (2) ensuring that, in employing this 'method', they do not perpetuate sexism by reinforcing such stereotyping in their analysis.

A Problem with the Dominant Approach to Feminist Legal Theory

In her review of the current state of feminist legal theory, Joanne Conaghan expresses concern about the influence of poststructuralism.[33] She argued that,

---

28 C. Gilligan, *In a Different Voice: Psychological Theory and Women's Development* (Cambridge Mass: Harvard University Press, 1982).
29 V. Held, 'Non-Contractual Society: A Feminist View' in S.M. Okin and J. Mansbridge, eds, *Feminism: Volume One* (Hants: Edward Elgar Publishing Ltd., 1994).
30 See also C. Battersby, *The Phenomenal Woman: Feminist Metaphysics and the Patterns of Identity* (Cambridge: Polity, 1998a) pp. 206-208.
31 C. Smart, *Feminism and the Power of the Law* (London: Routledge, 1989).
32 Naffine and Owens (1997) p. 6.
33 This is a broad term that includes a number of different theoretical perspectives. My aim is not to focus upon different positions that come under this umbrella term.

The political implications of what has become known as 'the critique of essentialism' in feminism are potentially far-reaching. Not only does it produce disillusionment within feminism with what has proved to be a valuable political asset, woman-centredness, it also threatens to strip feminism of its political constituency because it appears that no shared identity exists to unify women and justify their political grouping.[34]

This echoes some earlier responses to poststructuralism within feminist theory.[35] In contrast with the theoretical position that I want to develop, I do not believe that Lacanian psychoanalysis or Derridean deconstruction, in particular, offer sufficient resources to open up the way in which the self can be thought. This is because of the way in which 'woman' has been positioned within their conceptual frameworks.[36] However, my aim is not to assess the limits of these positions but to use a different point of departure in order to examine other ways of thinking about the self and personhood and to critically examine individualism. 'Poststructuralism' is such a broad term that some of the contemporary continental philosophy which I find useful, such as the middle and late work of Foucault, is sometimes included within it. Rather than arguing that Foucault should not be labelled in this way, I have selectively used aspects of his work, which is discussed in Chapter 4.

It is interesting to note how often feminist legal theorists who employ Derridean or Lacanian perspectives manage to circumvent their constraints. This has been achieved by the adoption of the following strategies: firstly, some writers continue with some very useful work – for example, analyses of legal cases which show injustice to women – whilst simply couching their arguments in the language of poststructuralism, with warnings that the term 'women' is used strategically.[37] In particular, there have been some fascinating discussions about the way in which the sexed body is treated within law, which do not rely upon their broadly stated philosophical position.[38] Secondly, there are theorists who engage with Lacan and Derrida and who radically reuse their work to produce original positions of their own. I would maintain that both Cornell and Irigaray, in different ways, fall within this category and I will be considering Cornell's response to the equality/difference debate in detail in Chapter 3.

---

34 J. Conaghan, 'Reassessing the Feminist Theoretical Project in Law', *Journal of Law and Society*, Vol. 27, No. 3, 2000, p. 367.

35 See for example, C. Di Stefano, 'Dilemmas of Difference: Feminism, Modernity and Postmodernism' in L.J. Nicolson, ed., *Feminism/Postmodernism* (London: Routledge, 1990); S. Bordo, 'Feminism, Postmodernism and Gender-Scepticism' in Nicolson (1990) pp. 133-156. For a useful analysis of these perspectives see A. Phillips, *Democracy and Difference* (Cambridge: Polity, 1993).

36 A.A. Jardine, *Gynesis: Configurations of Woman and Modernity* (Cornell University Press, 1985); Battersby (1998a) pp. 81-102.

37 For example, K. O'Donovan, 'With Sense, Consent or Just Con: Legal Subjects in the Discourse of Autonomy' in Naffine and Owens (1997) pp. 47-64.

38 For example, A. Hyde, *Bodies of Law* (Princeton: Princeton University Press, 1997).

The main theme of many of the chapters in Naffine and Owens' book take the form of the worry that Conaghan detects in other work: that when they describe women's interaction with law they will be read as perpetuating a particular view of women as a category or committing the sin of essentialism. Naffine and Owens express this central theme in the following way:

> many of these essays are explicitly concerned about feminism's apparent limitations, especially its tendency to work with simple oppositions (male and female; masculine and feminine) which feminism often condemns and yet reproduces in the very act of condemnation.[39]

As I will explain in the next section, I do not believe that this is a necessary limitation, neither within feminism nor within philosophy. I think that it is a trap that occurs because of the adoption of a particular theoretical perspective derived from deconstruction. This can be illustrated by looking at O'Donovan's[40] uneasy distinction between the feminist method of 'sexing the law' – i.e. by showing the assumptions about men and women that are made within legal cases – and the endorsement of these categories of male and female as natural and fixed. O'Donovan produces an interesting analysis of the meaning of 'consent' in legal caselaw by examining a paradox: under the doctrine of coverture, women were viewed as able to consent to enter into the marriage contract, which then removed their ability to refuse to consent to have sex with their husbands. She links this to a consideration of contemporary medical caselaw in which women's consent was deemed to be unnecessary by the courts.

This consideration of the way in which consent has been viewed as problematic with regard to women has much in common with Carole Pateman's earlier analysis of women's position within contemporary liberalism,[41] which I will discuss in Chapters 5 and 6. However, O'Donovan frames this useful analysis with the cautious note that,

> My substantive position is that a methodology of distinguishing ['sex' and 'gender'] may be useful for certain purposes. I accept, however, the views of theorists who refuse such a distinction and argue that persons, regardless of biology, are cultural products.[42]

---

39 Naffine and Owens (1997) p. 7.
40 O'Donovan (1997) pp. 47-64.
41 Pateman has addressed the issue of consent in much of her work. She addresses O'Donovan's concerns in an earlier paper, C. Pateman, 'Women and Consent', *Political Theory*, Vol. 8, 1980, pp. 149-168. Reprinted in C. Pateman, *The Disorder of Women* (Stanford: Stanford University Press, 1989a) pp. 71-89.
42 O'Donovan (1997) p. 49. It is this approach to 'biology' and 'culture' that Oyama takes issue with, to be discussed in the next chapter.

O'Donovan cites a paper by Nicola Lacey,[43] who similarly describes herself as wishing to contribute to,

> a feminism which recognises the problematic status of the category 'woman' without making her disappear; which engages with the feminine as a construct, yet as a construct which has enormous social power.[44]

By separating 'feminist method' from her substantive arguments O'Donovan makes a move that is effectively the same as that of Gayatri Spivak.[45] Spivak argues for the employment of 'strategic essence'. This is the assumption that it is necessary to talk about women as a category in order to make claims on behalf of women, whilst recognising that there is no fixed identity that can be described as pertaining to 'woman'. In an interview[46] she describes a conflict between wanting to be a 'pure deconstructionist' and to attack sexism. In other words, the only way that she felt that she could attack sexism was to put aside her theoretical purity. I do not believe that this choice is a necessary one. Philosophy holds more resources than deconstruction in order to address this problem.

My Response

It is important to separate the different strands of the argument, that there is a danger in discussing women as a group, because the less convincing positions are shielded from criticism by inclusion with more compelling arguments, which carry with them less drastic implications for thinking about women as a category. Firstly, I want to outline the uncontentious argument. Naffine and Owens point out that feminists, such as Angela Harris[47] and Patricia Williams,[48] argue that this 'universal' view of women does not recognise the experience of black women. This is a powerful critique, not least because it employs the same argument – that the universal position marginalises difference – that feminists have used to critique both law and philosophy. From the 1980s, the concern has been that the experiences of white, middle-class, able-bodied, heterosexual women have been

43 N. Lacey, 'Feminist Legal Theory Beyond Neutrality', *Current Legal Problems*, Vol. 48, 1995, pp. 1-38.
44 N. Lacey, *Unspeakable Subjects: Feminist Essays in Legal and Social Theory* (Oxford: Hart Publishing, 1998) p. 14.
45 G.C. Spivak, 'Criticism, Feminism and the Institution' in S. Harasym, ed., *The Post-Colonial Critic* (London: Routledge, 1990) pp. 1-16. Spivak's position has subsequently changed, see G.C. Spivak, 'In a Word' in G.C. Spivak, *Outside in the Teaching Machine* (London: Routledge, 1993) pp. 1-23.
46 Spivak (1990).
47 A. Harris, 'Race and Essentialism in Feminist Legal Theory', *Stanford Law Review*, Vol. 42, 1990, pp. 581-616.
48 P. Williams, *The Alchemy of Race and Rights* (Massachusetts: Harvard University Press, 1991).

viewed as the paradigm case within feminism, just as men have been viewed as the universal example of selfhood. It was argued that this has the effect of closing down the space in which women's differences could be expressed. I think that this is a compelling argument but that it tends to be confused with arguments that do not follow from it. For example, Naffine and Owens run a number of arguments together when they comment that 'Such feminists destabilise the category of "woman"'.[49] I will argue that there are alternative models, from diverse areas of contemporary philosophy, that avoid the current concerns about talking about women as a group. This does not mean that sensitivity to women's differences is not important when discussing women, merely that there are some concerns that women have in common at a particular time.[50]

In Chapter 2, I will expand upon the argument that it is unnecessary to move from a position in which only the universal category of selves or persons can be discussed, of which men are the best example, to the view that it is impossible to talk of any category. Again, it is necessary to stress that this does not mean that the marginalisation of differences does not remain potentially problematic. However, the response to this problem must be one of historical sensitivity to the question of which differences are politically relevant in a particular practical situation. This cannot be predicted theoretically before hand.

A similar point can be made with regard to Carol Smart's arguments, derived from her reading of Foucault. She argues that feminist effort to reform the law may be misplaced. This follows from Smart's analysis of the discourse about, and treatment of, women within legal judgments and within the broader legal process, for example by lawyers and police. She argues that these are so detrimental to women that caution is needed when seeking a legal solution and that it may be more constructive to focus upon direct action. Whilst I have some sympathy with her position, I think that it is important to stress that the question of law's usefulness is not one that can be dictated in advance by theory.[51] For example, Women's Aid supports battered women in practical ways rather than appealing to law. This is because of contingent problems with the English law and there are empirical studies to indicate how law could be improved.[52] Women's Aid, in

---

49 Naffine and Owens (1997) p. 5.
50 For the argument that the insights of second wave feminism, such as the challenge to the public/private distinction and the insistence that housework is real work, are useful despite the concerns about difference that are emphasised by feminists who are worried by talk of women's 'essence' see, S.M. Okin, 'Families and Feminist Theory: Some Past and Present Issues' in H.L. Nelson, ed., *Feminism and Families* (London: Routledge, 1997) pp. 13-26.
51 See also R. Sandland, 'Between "Truth" and "Difference": Poststructuralism, Law and the Power of Feminism', *Feminist Legal Studies*, Vol. 3, No. 1, 1995, pp. 3-47. I agree with Ralph Sandland's response to Smart when he argues that it is necessary to be strategic about the engagement with law.
52 See for example, H. Johnson, 'Rethinking Survey Research' in R.E. Dobash and R. Dobash, eds., *Rethinking Violence Against Women* (London: Sage, 1998) pp. 23-51.

common with standpoint feminists, argue that those who have suffered from domestic violence may well be in a better position than theorists to suggest practical changes – a line of argument that Foucault echoes in his concern for 'subjugated knowledge'.[53]

In conversation, Deleuze and Foucault[54] argue against the 'common sense' view of the relationship between theory and practice: the idea that theory sets up a blueprint to be followed in practice or that practice is then used to produce or amend theory.[55] They argue that sometimes it is impossible to theorise further about a political issue and that the only way forward is action. This does not involve following a blueprint for action but is carried out on the ground. Conversely, Foucault's 'history of the present' can be understood as an attempt to challenge assumptions about the inevitability of certain accepted practices, such as incarceration, in order to remove blockages from practical action in particular areas. This can be contrasted with the idea of an intellectual producing a blueprint for action, which is then carried out by others. It does not imply that those 'on the ground' do not have beliefs, the history and philosophical implications of which must opened up to analysis.

Deleuze and Foucault's views about the relationship between theory and practice both challenge – and perform the same work as – the Hegelian/Marxist view of 'praxis', which informed aspects of feminist theory. Their work marks a shift away from a dialectical model to a concern to trace the actual 'relays' or links between specific areas of thought (not all of which is carried out by 'intellectuals') and practice. To understand this argument it is useful to think of it as a theoretical response to feminism. The feminist movement with its emphasis upon situated knowledge – gained by women who compared their own experiences (and how these differed from the supposed 'reality' provided by male experts) – challenged assumptions about what was inevitable. In fact, I would argue that it is this feminist questioning of the position of the intellectual (or expert) that prompted Foucault's position with regard to subjugated knowledges. However, as I argue in the next section, it is impossible to have pure practice or experience that is without theoretical understanding – examination of the historical and philosophical background of which is important. The idea of pure experience is the other side of the coin to the image of pure theory produced by the knowing intellectual. Both envisage a split between a knowing subject and passive object, which is challenged

---

53 M. Foucault, *Society Must be Defended* (London: Penguin Press, 2003) pp. 6-12.
54 M. Foucault and G. Deleuze, 'Intellectuals and Power: A Conversation between Michel Foucault and Gilles Deleuze' in D.F. Bouchard, ed., *Language, Counter-Memory, Practice: Selected Essays and Interviews by Michel Foucault* (London: Cornell University Press, 1980) pp. 205-217. See also A. Bottomley and J. Conaghan 'Feminist Theory and Legal Strategy' in Bottomley and Conaghan (1993) pp. 1-5.
55 This has some similarity with Andy Clark's position on the self that I draw upon in Chapter 2. I return to compare these positions in more detail in Chapter 4.

by the images of self that I wish to develop in Chapter 2. They also envisage a split between the body (linked traditionally with women) and mind (linked with men) that has been the subject of much feminist critique.[56]

Feminists in Philosophy

Feminist philosophers work within a traditional which has been hostile to women, a fact that is equally true in law and in the sciences. Within the discipline of philosophy today, feminist theory is more marginal and controversial than it is within other disciplines in the social sciences. The response to this cannot be to have women refuse to take part in philosophy after years of exclusion, nor can women philosophers once involved in the discipline ignore the way in which women have been positioned within philosophical frameworks. Feminist philosophy has had to work within this tradition whilst undermining, and moving it forward, from within. It is impossible to stand outside a culture and to start again. Failure to address philosophical questions would not mean that we could live without theoretical assumptions because practice cannot avoid the use of concepts. To reject philosophy would simply mean that these theoretical beliefs were not being questioned.

One way in which women have been marginalised within philosophy has derived from the way in which they have been positioned as commentators on some masters' work rather than as theorists working within and yet reworking this tradition. Penelope Deutscher[57] has traced the way in which particular women philosophers, such as Clémence Ramnoux and Sara Kofman, were described as commentators upon a man's work. She points to a further twist. Given that these women actually produced their own original work, they were then described as 'bad commentators' rather than recognised as original. As Cornell comments,

> I think part of what we are up against is the historical fact of the exclusion of women from philosophy, which has nothing to do in my mind with any natural characteristics of the feminine mind, but simply with imposed, brutally imposed, exclusion. As we get to the point – if we are getting to the point – where women can place themselves in philosophy, then what we would hopefully see is more women engaging enough in disidentification, so that we will no longer have to spend our whole life labelled as a follower of a particular man.[58]

I defend the view that both continental and analytic political/legal philosophy can provide resources for feminism – just as both need feminist theory to show up

---

56 See for example G. Lloyd, *The Man of Reason: 'Male' and 'Female' in Western Philosophy* (London: Methuen, 1984).
57 P. Deutscher, '"Imperfect Discretion": Interventions into the History of Philosophy by Twentieth-Century French Women Philosophers', *Hypatia: A Journal of Feminist Philosophy*, Vol. 15, No. 2, 2000b, pp. 160-180.
58 Florence (1997) p. 24.

historical (and contingent) blind spots within their theoretical frameworks. In this respect, I agree with the view of Fricker and Hornsby,[59] as expressed in their introduction to an anthology of analytic philosophy,

> People sometimes suppose that 'feminist philosophy' must either name a subject area – as, say, 'political philosophy' does – or else stand for something that is meant to supplant philosophy. But at least as we understand 'feminist philosophy', it stands for philosophy informed by feminism; and feminism has different sorts of relevance as it impinges on different philosophical subject areas.[60]

As I will illustrate by examining contemporary theory, the fact that the position of women produces a blind spot for a number of theoretical frameworks can be viewed constructively. The question: 'what would it be to think of the self in ways that do not view women as an aberration?' can open up new ways of thinking. In other words, I believe that feminist philosophers can improve philosophy, not simply by highlighting the way in which women provide a weak point for certain views of ourselves and law, but by producing better concepts and better models. This does not merely involve adding women into already existing frameworks. This is not possible if the framework depends upon either the exclusion or the ambivalent treatment of women. It is also necessary to avoid the opposite error: producing an image of a self or of personhood that renders male bodies as monstrous or unintelligible. This would be to invert the mistake of those perspectives which have viewed women in such a way.

Chapter Summaries

I start by discussing the concept of self, by bringing together the work of three philosophers from different areas of contemporary philosophy: Oyama, Clark and Battersby. This allows me to draw out common threads which I view as useful to think about the self. I return to these broad themes in later chapters to compare them with other views of self. In addition, I examine the meaning of 'essentialism' to consider potentially more productive frameworks for feminist legal theory than that of poststructuralism.

In Chapter 3, I turn from ontological views of self to legal personhood, in particular the work of Cornell. This is considered in the context of her arguments regarding tort law, the civil obligations that we are deemed to owe each other. Whilst Cornell has been classified as a poststructuralist, her conceptual framework, which radically reworks Kant and Rawls, incorporates the work of Lacan whilst not relying upon it. Cornell suggests an answer to the problem of equality/difference,

---

59 M. Fricker and J. Hornsby, 'Introduction' in M. Fricker and J. Hornsby, *The Cambridge Companion to Feminism in Philosophy* (Cambridge: Cambridge University Press, 2000).

60 Fricker and Hornsby (2000) p. 4.

arguing that women must be added into law as persons with rights. To avoid the problem that this 'person' will be viewed as traditionally male she argues that what it is to be a person should be left open.

The starting point for Cornell's work is the use of rights, which has been attacked by a number of feminists.[61] I do not focus upon this objection but draw out the implications of her work for a legal test. I agree with Cornell, rather than Irigaray, that women should not be added into law *as women*, a move which I view as potentially regressive.

In Chapter 4, I continue the discussion of tort law, by employing the work of Ewald. I argue that, despite the fact that his work is focused upon the implications of insurance within France, his broader analysis of the techniques employed in the management of risk and use of the Foucauldian concept of governmentality (the 'conduct of conduct')[62] provide important ways to think about the actual operation of English tort law. I adapt Ewald's work to the common law and examine it from a feminist perspective. Again, the paradoxical position of women can be used constructively. I draw a link between 'possessive individualism' – the view of the self as initially separate from others, owner of his/her abilities and owing nothing to society for these abilities – and the image of the self that Ewald criticises: the prudent self-regulating individual. I then return to consider the extent to which Cornell can avoid assimilation into this view of personhood, such that her 'open' view of personhood is understood merely as the possessive individual.

The historically paradoxical position of women with regard to possessive individualism is then considered in more detail in the rest of the book. In Chapter 5, I focus upon Carole Pateman's reading of Hobbes in *The Sexual Contract*,[63] which brings together an analysis of the social contract, the marriage contract and employment contracts. I want to take up Pateman's concerns with the 'traditional' marriage contract, which she characterises as operating between 1840-1970, in order to consider the contemporary position of marriage contracts, employment

---

61 For example, E. Kingdom, *What's Wrong with Rights? Problems for Feminist Politics of Law* (Edinburgh: Edinburgh University Press, 1991); Smart (1989) pp. 138-159. Cornell recognises that, 'rights are only as good as the people who enforce them' Florence (1997) p. 14.

62 M. Foucault, 'The Subject and Power' in H.L. Dreyfus and P. Rabinow, eds., *Michel Foucault: Beyond Structuralism and Hermeneutics* (Sussex: The Harvester Press, 1982) pp. 220-221. 'Perhaps the equivocal nature of the term *conduct* is one of the best aids for coming to terms with the specificity of power relations. For to "conduct" is at the same time to "lead" others (according to mechanisms of coercion which are, to varying degrees, strict) and a way of behaving within a more or less open field of possibilities.' The translator notes that 'Foucault is playing on the double meaning of *conduire* – to lead or to drive and *se conduire* – to behave or conduct oneself, whence *la conduite*, conduct or behaviour' Foucault (1982) p. 220.

63 C. Pateman, *The Sexual Contract* (Cambridge: Polity Press, 1988).

contracts and welfare. Pateman's critique takes on a contemporary relevance in the context of feminist calls for the extension of contractualism[64] and the development of further medical opportunities for the use of parts of women's bodies.

This discussion is continued in Chapter 6 which looks in more detail at the meaning of possessive individualism (self-ownership or property in the person). In Chapter 6, I place Pateman's work alongside Marxist concerns about possessive individualism. The historical reason for women's paradoxical position with respect to possessive individualism is examined. Again, the aim is to use women's ambivalent position productively at a time when the government has discussed the 'work/life balance'[65] and the traditional models of employment contracts and marriage contracts have broken down.

Finally, I draw upon previous chapters to think about the future development of the 'sexual contract' in the context of the proposed 'new contractualism': the employment of 'contract' as a technique of government, and the relationship between women and the welfare state. I return to the link that was drawn between possessive individualism and the image of what it is to be a self/person envisaged within Ewald's work on risk. This entails an examination of the ways in which women's tradition position fails to fit, neither within possessive individualism nor within Ewald's analysis of it. I consider the extent to which women are now treated as possessive individuals and whether their traditional position allows for the rejection of this model, for example by being resistant to treatment as a commodity.

Cutting Across Disciplines

Much of this work cuts across different subject boundaries, not simply those of philosophy and law, in order to discuss the self, person and individual in the context of the law of obligations. This is a move which I defend on the grounds that it is productive to be able to transplant a problem in order to think about it differently. Whilst this does hold the potential danger of misreading a tradition or of drawing together broad terms that have different meanings within those different approaches, I think that it is worth the risk. As Oyama[66] points out, in her analysis of the key terms employed in the nature/culture debate within the philosophy of

---

64 For example, D. Dickenson, *Property, Women and Politics: Subjects or Objects?* (Cambridge: Polity, 1997); D. Dickenson, 'The New Contractualism?', *Women's Philosophy Review*, No. 20, 1998, pp. 108-111; A. Yeatman, 'Contract, Status and Personhood' in G. Davis, B. Sullivan, A. Yeatman, *The New Contractualism?* (Melbourne: MacMillan, 1997) pp. 39-56; A. Yeatman, 'Interpreting Contemporary Contractualism' in M. Dean and B. Hindess, *Governing Australia: Studies in Contemporary Rationalities of Government* (Cambridge: Cambridge University Press, 1998) pp. 227-241.

65 http://www.dti.gov.uk/er/fairness/fore.htm.

66 See for example, Oyama (2000b) p. 2.

biology, the ability to talk at cross purposes is not confined to interdisciplinary theory.

Within Chapter 2, the relationship between self/other arises from within the traditions of continental philosophy but is also discussed employing arguments from philosophy of science. This in turn can be subdivided into the philosophy of biology (Oyama) and philosophy of cognition (Clark). In Chapter 3, Cornell's complex analysis of personhood itself engages with both continental philosophy and contemporary Anglo-American political theory. In Chapter 4, Ewald's Foucauldian analysis is employed to think about tort law, Cornell's work and possessive individualism.

Issues of possessive individualism raise concerns that have been widely debated within the Anglo-American tradition. In Chapter 5, Pateman's reading of Hobbes is considered in the rich context of the contemporary feminist theory from Australia[67] and, in Chapter 6, this continues to be discussed in the context of Anglo-American debates between analytic Marxism and libertarianism, in the work of Cohen and that of Nozick.

The legal process involved in the law of obligations sets the context for this examination of the self, person and individual. The focus is initially upon tort law and then upon contract law; upon the practical impact of the operation of contemporary English law. Many of the theorists whose work is used have discussed law from the perspective of other jurisdictions: the US, in the case of Cornell, and France, in the work of Ewald. I discuss their insights and the extent to which they are applicable to English law.

To concentrate upon an area that has been classified as 'private' law, the law of tort and contract, I have ignored traditional legal subject demarcations where I have found it fruitful to do so. For example, I have highlighted some of the curiosities that emerge when comparing the marriage contract with the employment contract.[68] I am lead by my theoretical discussion of selves, persons and individuals, with law merely setting the context. My aim has not been to write an analysis of law or to produce particular recommendations for legislation. Instead, I want to intervene in a theoretical debate. Given that practice is always theory-laden, my aim has been to find resources within philosophy that are productive of better ways of thinking about the self.

Tort law[69] is concerned with those duties that persons are deemed to owe each other, whereas contract law is concerned with obligations to which the parties have agreed, or to which the parties are deemed to have consented. There are often

---

67 For a collection of, and discussion on, contemporary Australian feminist philosophy, see *Hypatia: A Journal of Feminist Philosophy, Special Issue: Going Australian Reconfiguring Feminism and Philosophy*, Vol. 15, No. 2, 2000.

68 A special issue of *Feminist Legal Studies* on the law of obligations drew a similarly broad view of what were involved in obligations. *Feminist Legal Studies Special Issue: Law of Obligations*, Vol. 8, No. 1, 2000.

69 I have employed the term 'tort law' rather than the 'law of torts' for ease of reference. I am not discussing the question of which term is more appropriate.

obligations that overlap between tort and contract. So, for example, the parents in so-called 'wrongful birth' cases, in which a faulty sterilisation operation leads to the birth of a child, have sued using the tort of negligence. However, when the operation took place in a private hospital, there has been litigation for breach of contract arising out of the same circumstances. I have not discussed in detail the potential overlap between tort law and contract law,[70] nor the law of restitution.[71]

Cornell's legal principles, that are derived from her theoretical position, imply more legal changes than those discussed in the area of tort law in Chapter 3. However, tort law can be used to illustrate her general theoretical approach. I have focused upon Cornell's proposals for tort law, to be able to position them within a particular context in Chapter 4. This opens up a different understanding of the practical operation of the law, in order to consider Cornell's principles, which are intended to have practical effect.

Pateman draws a link between the social/sexual contract and her discussions of marriage contracts and employment contracts. I follow her in this regard, particularly because I think it is useful to juxtapose these contracts. It is necessary to view them as interrelated in order to think about the ways in which they are changing after the breakdown of the breadwinner/wife model.

---

70 See, J. Wightman, *Contract: A Critical Commentary* (London: Pluto Press, 1996) pp. 137-142.
71 Restitution is concerned with the reversal of undue enrichment, for example if someone is paid more money than they should have received. For arguments regarding the division between tort, contract and restitution see A.S. Burrows, 'Contract, Tort and Restitution: A Satisfactory Division or Not?', *Law Quarterly Review*, Vol. 99, pp. 217-267. For a critical discussion of Burrows' position see Wightman (1996) pp. 25-26.

Chapter 2

Emergence, Dynamic Systems and Identity

In this chapter I want to illustrate what is at stake in Christine Battersby's view of the self by juxtaposing her contemporary feminist philosophy with work that is taking place within the philosophy of science, in particular the work of Andy Clark and of Susan Oyama. This does not purport to be a definitive account of such debates but is used simply to draw out some of general approaches to the self that I think these theorists have in common, despite the fact that they do not engage with each other's work. I highlight those themes which are potentially useful for feminist legal theory.

To contextualise this aspect of Battersby's work has some parallels with her own discussion of contemporary science within her book, *Phenomenal Woman: Feminist Metaphysics and the Patterns of Identity*. In the chapter 'Her Body/Her Boundaries',[72] she asks why she does not experience herself as being like a container, with clear boundaries between her body and the outside world.[73] This question arises because this way of looking at oneself as a container with inputs and outputs into the separate external world continues to be taken for granted, as illustrated by those working within the field of 'cognitive semantics'.[74]

Battersby considers a number of possible explanations. Amongst these, she discusses the idea that her experience reflects a change in attitudes and experience of the self that took place in the West in the twentieth century. This has arisen, she speculates, because our views of ourselves have been influenced by a move away from reductionism within contemporary science. She points out that, since the 1914–1918 war, there has been a shift away from the privilege given to solidity and also from the view of space as a container. The mathematics of fluidity has become more central to the scientific tradition.[75] In particular, Battersby cites the development of the mathematics of topology as precipitating a rethinking of the distinction between matter and form. This is in keeping with her attack on the traditional assumption, that can be traced back to Plato, that matter is inactive, unable to change itself unless imprinted upon by form. Battersby's concern is with the metaphysics that underlies many of these recent topological models, which

---

72 Battersby (1998a) pp. 38-60.
73 This is a framework evoked by Kant's description of the sublime in which the boundaries of the (male) self are threatened by the might of nature but are then re-established by the use of reason. I. Kant, *Critique of Judgment*, trans. W.S. Pluhar (Indianapolis: Hackett, 1987) pp. 97-140.
74 M. Johnson, *The Body in the Mind* (Chicago: University of Chicago Press, 1987); G. Lakoff, *Women, Fire and Dangerous Things* (Chicago: University of Chicago Press, 1987) both cited in Battersby (1998a) pp. 40-43.
75 Battersby (1998a) p. 50.

allows us to think of forms, not as fixed things but as temporarily stable points in a continuous flow. So, she gives the example of a book falling on the ground as being temporally stable because the ground acts as 'an attractor' within the topographical field. The book will stay there unless there is another attractor (such as me picking it up) or unless the first attractor goes (for example, the floor collapses).

The topological model allows us to view fixed forms as only temporarily stable and as interrelated. This allows Battersby to rethink the boundaries of her body in a way that is not that of the standard model and more in keeping with her experience:

> If we think about boundaries, then, from the point of view of the new sciences, the boundaries of our bodies need not be thought of as 'three dimensional containers into which we put certain things...and out of which other things emerge'. The boundary of my body can be thought of as an event-horizon, in which one form (myself) meets its potentiality for transforming itself into another form or forms (the not-self).[76]

This is a self that emerges with otherness and is not cut off from it. She goes on to attack the image of the self with fixed boundaries, defined against otherness.

Firstly, I want to compare her work with some of the work of Andy Clark, a researcher in the area of 'philosophy/neuroscience/psychology' at Sussex University and then with that of Susan Oyama, researcher in psychology in the College of Criminal Justice, New York University. The implications of this for law will also be drawn out both during the comparison and in more detail at the end of the chapter.

'Being There'

Andy Clark is concerned with the area of cognition rather than the self.[77] There is an important distinction here, which will be discussed more fully below. To avoid confusion, it is worth underlining at this stage that Battersby's project is to rethink the self in a way that treats the body and traditional lives of women as the norm rather than as an aberration. It is not some 'essential' underlying self that is discovered. The way that we view ourselves emerges within different cultures.[78] As discussed in the last chapter, contemporary feminists, including Battersby, have detailed the ways in which Western history has taken male bodies and lifestyles as the norm. However, by reading history 'against the grain' it is possible to produce other ways of viewing ourselves.

---

76 Battersby (1998a) p. 52.
77 See, for example, A. Clark, *Being There: Putting Brain, Body and World Together Again* (Massachusetts: MIT, 1997); A. Clark, *Mindware: An Introduction to Philosophy of Cognitive Science* (Oxford: Oxford University Press, 2001).
78 For discussion of the reworking of the nature/culture debate see 'Feminism, Essentialism and Law' later in this chapter.

One of the central themes of Clark's work is resonant with Battersby's reworking of the subject/object divide. To sum up some subtle arguments very crudely, he argues that cognition is not 'all in the head'. He describes an emergence of cognitive processes in which it is no longer appropriate to talk about a mind/environment split. In an article written with David Chalmers, he makes the following argument:

> Where does the mind stop and the rest of the world begin? The question invites two standard replies. Some accept the demarcations of skin and skull, and say that what is outside the body is outside the mind. Others are impressed by arguments suggesting that the meaning of our words 'just ain't in the head', and hold that this externalism about meaning carries over into an externalism about mind. We propose to pursue a third position. We advocate a very different sort of externalism: an *active externalism*, based on the active role of the environment in driving cognitive processes.[79] (Italics are in the original.)

He illustrates his argument by examining the way in which successful players of a computer game (Tetris) manipulate their environment in order to think faster. This approach can be compared to that of Battersby. For Battersby, the importance of the fact that the self is embodied foregrounds sexual difference. For Clark, concerned with cognition, embodiment is important in producing messy real-time solutions to problems. Counting on your fingers, manipulating your environment to play scrabble – rather than having to spend time imagining change in your head – are all important and yet traditionally ignored aspects of our cognition.

> First and foremost, we must recognize the brain for what it is. Ours are not the brains of disembodied spirits conveniently glued into ambulant, corporeal shells of flesh and blood. Rather, they are *essentially* the brains of embodied agents capable of creating and exploiting structure in the world.[80] (Italics are in the original.)

The fact that Clark is concerned with an organ that has evolved to produce real-time messy solutions to problems, rather than disembodied rational thought, means that he describes the ways that we rely heavily upon what he calls 'scaffolding', our ability to use the 'external' world so that it is integral to our ability to think. He draws an analogy with dolphins. Dolphins are not physically strong enough to swim at the speeds that they can in fact reach. The trick is that they exploit aquatic eddies, and further, that they actually create pressure gradients in order to do so. This description should not be read as a description of a controlling subject who simply manipulates an external object. It is clear that Clark wants to think about a dynamic system, which does not involve such a straightforward separation of mind and environment (or, in other words, subject and object).

---

79 http://www.nyu.edu/gsas/dept/philo/courses/concepts/clark.html.
80 Clark (1997) p. 220.

By analogy with the dolphin, people who suffer from Alzheimer's disease manage to exist in environments in which they should not, in theory, be able to cope. They rely upon external prompts to memory such as diaries and photographs. This suggests that they are not merely being reminded about the dates of meetings but are also reminded 'who they are' – or their place within an 'external' system that is not straightforwardly separate from themselves – by photographs of friends etc. In this context, when there is a permanent available aid to memory that is relied upon, Clark supports a remark of Daniel Dennett,[81] that to steal a diary which acts as part of someone's memory has more in common with offences against the person than against property.

In a more ambitious move, Clark extends this view of 'scaffolding' to consider the broader institutions in which we work. This raises questions about the extent to which he can legitimately move from a discussion about the manipulation of the immediate environment (for immediate problem solving) to what appears to be, in Clark's framework, a potentially politically neutral – or at least undeveloped – approach to institutions. Nevertheless, to be fair, this is not the central focus of his work, which is worth considering in detail because of the extent to which it resonates with that of Battersby.

I have drawn out the following points to show, very broadly, the areas of overlap between Clark's analysis of cognition and Battersby's radical reworking of the Kantian self:

1. both approaches emphasise the embedded,[82] embodied nature of cognition/self;

2. this results in an image of cognition or behaviour/self that tends to focus upon their emergent properties;[83]

---

81 A. Clark, 'Where Brain, Body and World Collide', *Journal of Cognitive Systems Research*, Vol. 1, 1999, p. 14

82 The term 'embedded' should not be confused with the use of the term by communitarians, within recent Anglo-American political theory, who talk about individuals being 'embedded' in culture and tradition, generally produced by and for white men. Clark, in contrast, is working within the philosophy of science to discuss the relationship between self and environment in problem solving. For a discussion of the 'liberal communitarian debate' from a feminist perspective see E. Frazer and N. Lacey, *The Politics of Community: A Feminist Critique of the Liberal-Communitarian Debate* (London: Harvester Wheatsheaf, 1993). Battersby's work can be understood as thinking about embeddedness that brings in social context but does not lead to communitarian conclusions. This is discussed below in the section on agency.

83 Clark argues that 'the notion of emergence is itself still ill understood' in Clark (2001) p. 112. I am employing the term as Battersby uses it to evoke the idea of self and other coming into being gradually through patterns of relationality that do not occur simply as a result of a split between self and other.

3. linked with this, both are concerned with thinking of cognition/the self as dynamic rather than fixed. The idea of dynamic, temporary stability is illustrated by Battersby's analogy of the self/other in dynamic equilibrium as being like the water level in a sieve that is dynamically stable because the amount of water that runs out is equal to that running into it;

4. there is an attack upon the subject/object divide (in Clark's work this is a cognition/environment split) as traditionally conceived and a move to characterise the emergent process as one which involves rethinking this divide;[84]

5. within the work of both theorists there is a shift away from the importance of envisaging cognition, or the self, in terms of centralised control. This is illustrated by Battersby's[85] reference to the emergence of self through patterns, through repeated habits, for example. It is explicitly implicated in Clark's view of the messy real-time solutions that we produce in response to problems that involve using the environment to such as extent that it cannot be separated from the thought process itself.

These five points are interconnected within the work of both writers. Clark's emphasis upon the way in which cognition should be viewed as 'real-time embodied cognition' leads him to emphasise our use of the environment to solve problems. His analysis undermines the idea of a distinct boundary between our thought processes and our environment. He illustrates his argument about the need to consider cognition as 'embedded and embodied' by a scathing attack upon attempts to teach robots to think by simply giving them huge amounts of information. He argues that our (men's?)[86] traditional image of ourselves, as exhibiting disembodied reason, has been misguided and is to blame for such an approach to robotics. His alternative approach is to try to produce 'thinking' robots by getting them to try to find real-time solutions to embodied problems. This move prompts a different approach both to the way in which problems are solved and to the way that cognition is understood.

He considers three different ways of thinking about cognition: what he calls a componential approach; the 'catch and toss' approach; and, finally, the one that is prompted by embodied, embedded thinking, that of 'emergence'. The componential approach is the traditional way of thinking about cognition, which attempts to understand the complex whole of cognition by looking at its parts to examine how they work. He does not reject this approach on the pragmatic basis that he would

---

84 This move is also central to Oyama's attack upon the nature/culture divide, to be discussed below.

85 See for example Battersby (1998a) p. 184.

86 For the argument that reason was traditionally viewed as male, see G. Lloyd, *The Man of Reason: 'Male' and 'Female' in Western Philosophy* (London: Methuen, 1984).

attempt to use any approach to see what results it will yield. The 'catch and toss' approach goes some way to recognising that cognition is embodied and that it takes place within an environment. However, it continues to consider this in a traditional way by focusing upon 'inner processing, inner computation and representations'.[87] The 'catch and toss' approach continues to envisage a firm and fixed boundary between the brain and the world. So, the world throws up problems and we catch and throw them back. Clark argues that this only makes sense when considering very simple feedback situations. As soon as the number of feedback processes increase, as in our messy real world when we need immediate solutions to problems, then this model breaks down.

He then turns to an 'emergent explanation' of cognition which he illustrates using an example from robotics from Steels.[88] To consider a sexless robot may seem some way removed from thinking about Battersby's reworking of Kant to think of a view of self that considers woman as the norm rather than an aberration. Indeed, the example of the robot is useful in illustrating what is missing. Robots do not share those aspects of embodiment that Battersby seeks to foreground: those that have been historically linked with the female and both degraded and viewed as superfluous. There is nothing fleshy, for example, about a robot. It does not have the 'flab' that Battersby wants to mobilise to think about embodiment in our culture and within the history of Western philosophy; to start to view women as typical rather than an aberration.[89]

However, I think that there are some useful comparisons to be made in this area of 'emergence'. To illustrate this, consider Clark's use of Steels' work, cited above. Steels is concerned with the problem of a robot that needs to position itself between two poles in order to recharge itself. The poles are both lit. The non-emergent solution would be to give the robot light sensors that can measure its position relative to the poles and a programme to tell it to stand between them. An emergent solution would be to programme it with the following two 'behaviour systems': 1) a phototaxis system that yields a zigzag approach to any light source; 2) an obstacle avoidance system that makes it turn away from anything it hits. With this in place then the required behaviour simply emerges out of the programme after a few tries.

To characterise 'emergence', Steels suggests that what is required is the use of vocabulary that does not look at components but at the behaviour of aggregates of these components. This is rejected by Clark on the grounds that this would include the feedback of a hi-fi when this system would be better approached by a componential explanation. In his attempt to characterise 'emergence', Clark substitutes a definition that relies upon the distinction between: (1) 'controlled variables' which track behaviours that can be directly manipulated and which represent the componential approach or 'catch and toss' approaches to the system;

---

87 Clark (1997) p. 106.
88 L. Steels, 'The Artificial Life Roots of Artificial Intelligence', *Artificial Life*, Vol. 1, No. 1-2, 1994, pp. 75-110 cited Clark (1997) p. 108.
89 Battersby (1998a) p. 14.

and (2) 'uncontrolled variables' which track behaviours or propensities that arise from the interaction of multiple parameters and tend to resist direct and simple manipulation and represent the emergent approach.[90]

This move away from the 'catch and toss' model to an image of emergence, which acknowledges the complexity of the dynamic systems, has parallels with the way in which Battersby shifts the Kantian image of the self. A distinction must be drawn between this analysis of cognition and of the self. It is important that, whilst these positions do produce similarities, they are not confused. It is necessary to be careful about the overlap in vocabulary, coming as it does from within different areas of philosophy. In the example drawn from Steels' work in robotics, Clark is talking about the emergence of a particular form of behaviour. Battersby employs the term 'emergence' to describe a self that emerges out of modes of relationality. Battersby's self is described as emerging out of patterns of relations and mutual or interlocking dependencies which, over time, come to mark out the boundary between self and non-self. This involves a rejection of the move that we define ourselves against others (or otherness). What we are, as a self, emerges out of repetition or habits in which the boundary between self and other (including other selves but also anything that is not-self) is not fixed; yet a distinct self emerges from this process. Clark's model is also dynamic, to be discussed in more detail below.

Clark does ask the question:

> Does the putative spread of mental and cognitive processes out into the world imply some correlative (and surely unsettling) leakage of the self into the local surroundings?[91]

Here, Clark appears to assume the existence of a pre-existent self that then merges with its environment rather than Battersby's image of a self that emerges along with otherness, by patterns of relationality (rather than by a direct split). To be fair to Clark, he is not focusing upon the concept of self in detail. This can also be read as a humorous choice of phrase.

It is worth considering the difference between Battersby and Clark on this point in more detail. As Battersby is reworking Kant's analysis of the transcendental self from within the Kantian framework, to explain this point it is necessary to return to Kant's framework itself. For Kant, the transcendental self is that which persists through time from moment to moment. For Kant, the transcendental self must be presumed to exist along with the transcendental object, as the 'I' that orders the world in Euclidean space and linear time. So, to suppose that we have a transcendental self is a logical move rather than a psychological description. Battersby attacks the kind of disembodied, persistent 'I' that Kant's philosophy requires by showing that the position of women provides a weak point within this system. Kant's assumption that matter is inactive, permanent and no more than the

---

90   Clark (1997) p. 110.
91   Clark (1997) p. 216.

counterpole to the transcendental self, makes it impossible to think of matter that can actively reproduce itself. She uses this weakness as the point of departure from which to rethink the opposition between the transcendental self and transcendental object so as to undermine the image of the body as dead inactive matter. She envisages an embodied self that persists through time but is not constructed in a top-down manner by an 'I' that imposes a space-time structure on matter and the world. Linked with this is the image of an emergence of this self with its other, the boundaries of which are not fixed.

Clark seems to ask an analogous kind of question about the relationship between self and not-self:

> Does the putative spread of mental and cognitive processes out into the world imply some correlative (and surely unsettling) leakage of the self into the local surroundings?[92]

His answer to his own question is as follows:

> ...'Yes and No.' No, because (as has already been conceded) conscious contents supervene on individual brains. But Yes, because such conscious episodes are at best snapshots of the self considered as an evolving psychological profile. Thoughts, considered only as snapshots of our conscious mental activity, are fully explained, I am willing to say, by the current state of the brain. But the flow of reason and thoughts, and the temporal evolution of ideas and attitudes, are determined and explained by the intimate, complex, continued interplay of brain, body and world.[93]

At a superficial level, the reference to the self as a 'psychological profile' would worry those, like Nikolas Rose,[94] who draw upon Foucault to historically situate such terminology. In keeping with the anti-psychiatry movement, Rose is cynical about the role of psychology in shaping the way that we view ourselves, employing psychological terms and analysis. However, it is important to focus upon the point of Clark's argument, which in the last sentence, resonates with Battersby's position in its rethinking of the traditional subject/object boundary. To summarise, Clark argues that in complex real world situations, we use the environment to such an extent that it is part of the thinking process. It becomes 'part of ourselves' as illustrated by his view that its theft should be viewed as akin to an offence against the person. The circumstances involve having to 'use an artefact' that is 'reliable, present, frequently used and deeply trusted'.[95] This is a psychological description of how we think which then challenges conventional images of what it means to be a

---

92 Clark (1997) p. 216.
93 Clark (1997) p. 216.
94 See, for example, N. Rose, 'Assembling the Modern Self' in R. Porter, ed., *Rewriting the Self: Histories from the Renaissance to the Present* (London: Routledge, 1997) pp. 224-248 and the postscript in N. Rose, *Governing the Soul: The Shaping of the Private Self* (London: Free Association Books, 1999a) pp. 263-272.
95 Clark (1997) p. 217.

self. In contrast, Battersby works with a logical system to show that Kant cashes out his framework in such a way as to make the transcendental self stable but which renders him incapable of thinking an 'I' that is embodied – and selves that are born (to women) in a material (fleshy) way. However, in keeping with Clark's view of cognition, Battersby's reworking of the self also involves rethinking the boundaries between what is to be classed as part of the self and what is other to the self. A distinct self does emerge but through patterns of relationality rather than in opposition from its other. Battersby asks:

> what would happen if we thought identity in terms that did not make it always spatially and temporally oppositional to other entities?[96]

Clark argues that the best way of viewing emergent phenomena is through the use of Dynamical Systems theory. This is an approach which treats any source of variance (here, the environment and the organism) together as one system and looks at their mutual evolution. It is this approach, that mathematically describes patterns of actual and potential unfolding, that Battersby discusses in her reference to topology.

Clark outlines the best way of thinking about the question of emergent cognition, in which the subject/object boundary is problematised, in the following way:

> In such cases [of emergence]…we ideally require an explanatory framework that (1) is well suited to modelling both organismic and environmental parameters and (2) models them both in a uniform vocabulary and framework, thus facilitating an understanding of the complex interactions between the two. A framework that invokes computationally characterized, information-processing homunculi is not, on the face of it, an ideal means of satisfying these demands.[97]

This emphasis upon the creation of a uniform vocabulary and framework, in which to discuss the thinking self and environment, starts with the assumption that a subject/object split is not useful. It radically undermines the notion of a fixed boundary between subject and object and between self and its other. Whilst Battersby's image of the self does have boundaries, these emerge, along with the self and its other, from patterns of relationality. As part of the same move, Battersby attacks the image of a self with the body as a container providing a fixed boundary against its environment.

Although she is not cited by Battersby, this move can be illustrated by considering the work of Polly Matzinger.[98] Matzinger is a biologist whose work on immunology has successfully undermined the simple idea that there is a self/other

---

96 Battersby (1998a) p. 2.
97 Clark (1997) p. 113.
98 P. Matzinger, 'The Real Function of the Immune System: or Tolerance and the Four Ds (Danger, Death, Destruction and Distress)'
    http://cmmg.biosci.wayne.edu/asg/polly.html.

boundary that is policed by the immune system. Such a straightforward split would have to explain how the body could change, for example, in adolescence, and still recognise what is to be classified as 'self'. Instead, Matzinger has argued for a model in which the immune system responds to unnatural cell death. This model does not depend upon a rigid self/other boundary, whilst recognising that there is such a thing as the self that emerges, along with its other. This is analogous to Battersby's move in refusing to view the (embodied) self as something that has fixed boundaries that are defined by what is excluded. From this perspective both Kant and Lacan are attacked for setting up models in which the self can only emerge by setting boundaries against the outside world, or by rejection of the mother/other. This approach is also echoed in Oyama's work in the context of her radical reworking of the nature/culture debate, to be discussed below.

Battersby and Oyama

Before discussing Oyama's work, it is useful to return to the points that Battersby and Clark have in common, whilst repeating the health warning that they are focusing upon different things: the self and cognition respectively. I argued that the following points represent broadly common themes within Clark's analysis of cognition and Battersby's reworking of the Kantian self:

1. there is an emphasis upon the embedded, embodied nature of cognition/self;

2. this results in an image of cognition/self that tends to focus upon their emergent properties;

3. linked with this, both are concerned with thinking of cognition/the self as dynamic rather than fixed;

4. there is an attack upon the subject/object divide (in Clark's work this is cognition/environment split) as traditionally conceived and a move to characterise the emergent process as one which involves rethinking this divide;

5. there is a shift away from the importance of centralised control.

To discuss the relationship between Battersby's approach to the self and that of Oyama to the radical rethinking of the nature/culture debate, it is useful to bear in mind these general points of overlap in approach. Oyama shares a broadly similar framework, in a different area of concern. This can be characterised as an attack upon the boundaries between subject and object; a move which involves rethinking this relationship in a way that is attentive to the emergence of a self (and a subject)[99] whose boundaries are not defined by what is outside it. This approach

---

99 As outlined in Chapter 1, I want to keep apart the terms self, subject, person and individual because they are used in different contexts.

attempts to produce a theoretical framework in which due weight is given to the complexity of the emergence of the self.

Further, both Battersby and Oyama share an explicit rejection of hylomorphism and the form/matter distinction. They make the point that the image of 'form' as the active ingredient that works upon 'matter' – which has been viewed as passive and unable to change itself – has been linked with sexual difference and images of women's passivity from the start. Battersby[100] critiques Plotinus' Aristotelian reading of Plato in which the *chora* is (female) passive matter that can only be imprinted by the male form.

Oyama argues that the terms in which the nature/culture debate has been played out have been misconceived. The opponents within the debate have tended to counter genetic determinism with environmental determinism. Oyama argues that the subtlety of development of any organism over time cannot be understood by simply viewing nature as a fixed entity represented by genes that have built in instructions for development. The novelty of her approach, which she describes as 'developmental systems theory', is that she is also critical of those who argue that the environment, and not nature, causes our behaviour. She argues for a more radical understanding of the debate and a different understanding of what is meant by 'nature'.

Recall that Clark makes the following point with regard to the best way of thinking about the question of emergent cognition in which the subject/object boundary is problematised:

> In such cases [of emergence]...we ideally require an explanatory framework that (1) is well suited to modelling both organismic and environmental parameters and (2) models them both in a uniform vocabulary and framework, thus facilitating an understanding of the complex interactions between the two. A framework that invokes computationally characterized, information-processing homunculi is not, on the face of it, an ideal means of satisfying these demands.[101]

Although she is not concentrating upon cognition but upon development in general, Oyama also considers the ways in which the reworking of the boundaries of subject and object (self and environment) result in a reconceptualisation of the emergent process. Strikingly, she speaks in similar terms, rejecting the image of a centralised control system – in this context envisaged by the genes (or even, through what is envisaged as a 'different channel': memes). She asks,

---

100 Battersby (1998a) pp. 108-109. This is also developed by Butler: Butler (1993) p. 14. For my discussion on the relationship between Butler and Cavarero on this point see, J. Richardson, 'Beyond Equality or Difference: Sexual Difference in the work of Adriana Cavarero', *Feminist Legal Studies*, Vol. VI, No. 1, 1998b, p. 117. For a detailed discussion of the nuances of Aristotle's biology and feminist critiques, see C.A. Freeland, 'Nourishing Speculation: A Feminist Reading of Aristotelian Science' in B.A. Bar On, ed., *Engendering Origins: Critical Feminist Readings in Plato and Aristotle* (New York: State University of New York, 1994) pp. 145-187.
101 Clark (1997) p. 113.

Why should there be such striking parallels between the problem of the subject in developmental psychology and the problem of conceptualizing biological, especially genetic, processes? In both cases, a single source of organizing (information-processing) power seems necessary, so that the cognitivist subject and the homunculoid gene play similar roles in the dramas of cognitive and ontogenetic formation.[102]

In attacking both models, she undermines both the notion of centralised control and a hylomorphic approach that envisages the top-down imprinting of selves by their genes or by society. This model of genes, as producing a top-down imprint is not the only model of genes available. In her edited collection *Cycles of Contingency*,[103] Oyama brings together papers from geneticists and others who work broadly within 'developmental systems theory' and reject the idea that genetics concerns the passing on of 'master molecules'.[104] Again, she points out that there are multiple causes for development, the subtleties of which are not captured by drawing a distinction between genes and everything else, which is lumped together as 'environment'. In different ways, Eva Neumann-Held[105] and Lenny Moss[106] discuss the change in the way in which the gene is understood in biology and the philosophy of biology. Both, in different ways, provide accounts which move the debate forward by rejecting the image of the gene as a mechanism of top-down imprinting that is necessary to give form to matter, a move that is unnecessary when matter is no longer viewed as inert.

Agency

Whilst not wishing to neglect the fact that Battersby, Oyama and Clark are addressing different issues in different areas of philosophy, and whilst not wishing to collapse the distinctions between them, I think that they share a very broad, generalised approach – as indicated by the list of five central themes within this framework. This suggests a useful perspective on the legal practice of obligations that I want to discuss. The question of agency is relevant here.[107] Battersby and Oyama explicitly deal with this question in similar ways. This derives from their concern to think of the emergence of the self that questions what has previously been designated as 'inside and outside', self and non-self or person and

---

102 Oyama (2000a) pp. 172-173.
103 S. Oyama, P.E. Griffiths and R.D. Grey, eds., *Cycles of Contingency: Developmental Systems and Evolution* (Massachusetts: The MIT Press, 2001).
104 Oyama et al (2001) p. 1.
105 E.M. Neumann-Held, 'Let's Talk about Genes: The Process Molecular Gene Concept and Its Context' in Oyama et al (2001) pp. 69-84.
106 L. Moss, 'Deconstructing the Gene and Reconstructing Molecular Developmental Systems' in Oyama et al (2001) pp. 85-97.
107 For arguments that agency may become less relevant to the law of tort as a result of potential moves to no fault compensation, see Chapter 4.

environment. This challenge to these generally accepted boundaries produces a different way of conceptualising the question of agency, amongst others. It is linked to the rejection of the form/matter distinction and the image of a centralised command structure.

One of the central arguments made by critical legal theorists has been aimed at undermining the way in which lawyers have employed the technique of abstracting individuals from their social circumstances. Alan Norrie,[108] for example, has pointed to the way in which the criminal law has operated so as to exclude discussion of the social context by, for example, separating 'direct intention to perform an act' from 'the motivation to perform it'. This means that the court is concerned only with the question of whether or not the defendant 'intended' to act, i.e. that it was not an accident. It rules out any discussion of the social context which motivated the accused, for example stealing bread because of hunger. This social context is only considered relevant to the question of mitigation of punishment and not of whether or not the offence was committed. Norrie, drawing upon work of E.P. Thompson[109] and Douglas Hay,[110] traces this to the role of the courts in trying to stifle – or at least avoid inciting – civil unrest in the eighteenth century. He argues for a reworking of a Kantian framework in order to discuss social context without simply dismissing personal agency or blame.

My concern is not with crime but with the law of obligations. Nevertheless, this question of agency is relevant. The refusal to delineate fixed boundaries between the self and its supposed 'outside' offers a new approach to the law of obligations. It is therefore worth considering how the relationship between the person and his/her social circumstances can be reframed using this perspective. Battersby describes agency in terms of feedback structures. She argues that it is possible to think of agency within her model. This is no longer to be considered as the will of the subject (at least if 'will' is conceived of as autonomous) but involves thinking of a 'feedback loop' between the self and environment, such that they are considered as open systems. She clearly envisages this as complex and capable of producing unpredictable changes.

Oyama focuses upon the relationship between nature/culture that addresses the question of agency and of the politics involved in the attribution of behaviour to genes or to the environment. One point to come out of this work is an attack on the idea that there is a centralised command structure in the brain that produces images

---

108 A. Norrie, 'Criminal Law' in I. Grigg-Spall and P. Ireland, *The Critical Lawyers' Handbook* (London: Pluto Press, 1992) pp. 76-83; A. Norrie, *Punishment, Responsibility and Justice: A Relational Critique* (Oxford: Oxford University Press, 2000).

109 E.P. Thompson, *Whigs and Hunters: The Origin of the Black Act* (Harmondsworth: Penguin, 1977).

110 D. Hay, 'Property, Authority and Criminal Law' in D. Hay, P. Linebaugh, J.G. Rule, E.P. Thompson and C. Winslow, eds., *Albion's Fatal Tree* (Harmondsworth: Penguin, 1977).

and co-ordinates our responses. This attack upon a centralised command structure is central to recent debates within developmental and evolutionary science. As Oyama puts it,

> To see the organism-niche complex as both source and product of its own development is to acknowledge the role of activity in the life process – not genes organising raw materials into beings, and not environments shaping or selecting passive bodies and minds, but organisms assimilating, seeking, manipulating their worlds, even as they accommodate and respond to them.[111]

This is similar to the way in which Battersby talks about feedback loops:

> The subject that I will posit is neither completely free nor autonomous, but is also not simply passive. It is both marked –'scored' – into specificity by its relationship with 'otherness', and yet is itself also capable of agency and of resisting modes of domination. This self is not only shaped by 'the other', it is also self-shaping as potentiality is transformed into actuality via echo and the feedback-loops of memory.[112]

Both are concerned to think about agency in a manner that takes into account the embodied nature of the self and the way that agency does not simply involve a removal or abstraction from the particular circumstances in which the self finds her/himself. This derives from the five general points that these theorists have in common. In particular, it involves thinking through the implications of matter not being inert. A corollary to this is the rejection of the image of a centralised organising structure, such as that envisaged as the self that decides upon her/his actions in a vacuum. As Oyama puts it,

> If matter is inert, then organized processes can be explained only by reference to a structuring intelligence. But if it is interactive (think of any chemical reaction) under changing, interdependent constraints, such outside direction is not needed.[113]

Legal judgments in the law of obligations depend upon attributions of the causes of human behaviour. This is familiar territory for feminists who have challenged the many crass assumptions about the inevitable nature of women that continue to be used to justify a status quo in which women are subordinate. What is innovative about Oyama's approach is that, like Battersby in the context of metaphysics, she responds by changing the framework in which the debate is carried out. Using the example of a type of genetic disorder which can be controlled by environmental changes, she points out that it is not the case that this should be understood only as genetically caused – employing a traditional model of genetics. She is critical of biologists who ignore the environment simply because it appears to be constant.

---

111 Oyama (2000a) p. 95.
112 Battersby (1998a) p. 12.
113 Oyama (2000a) p. 173.

It is possible to illustrate this with an analogy from political, or critical legal, theory. Oyama's move is analogous to that of Marx,[114] who argued that the point of departure for political theory should not be to consider the nature of selves or individuals but of the society which produces such an emphasis upon individualism. It is impossible to study an individual outside of society. It is the nature of this society that allows the study of individuals, in a vacuum, to appear as a natural point of departure. It is precisely this image of a rigid, fixed boundary, between the 'outside' environment both physical and social, and the 'inside' self that is challenged in the work of both Oyama, Battersby and Clark.

Similarly, Oyama attacks a simplistic view of 'biology' as an external force that structures, and permanently fixes, inert matter. Oyama attacks the root of the political argument, that women's subordination, for example, is inevitable if it can be shown to be 'natural' or 'biological'. She argues that, even if a type of behaviour previously had some evolutionary value in certain circumstances then there is no reason why this should continue to be the case.

Battersby's metaphor, derived from Kierkegaard, is of the wind that is effected by and yet also shapes the landscape,

> Self-shaping (or becoming an individual) is like an alien wind that gradually takes on a familiar pattern as it blows across an unfamiliar landscape...
>
> Although in the end, a pattern emerges and the wind plays a melody that remains 'unaltered day after day', this sequence only emerges slowly.[115]

Battersby suggests a similar move to Oyama, here. Oyama points to the inadequacies of the metaphors of transmission – in the sense of genetic or cultural transmission which, she argues, do not capture the subtlety of the developmental process. They fail to show the ways in which the embedded organism is able to rework, what is viewed as, both biological and social 'inheritance'. Oyama is also sensitive to the ways in which this use of the term 'inheritance' is also deeply problematic. There is a link between this view of inheritance and the way in which property was seen as a thing that could be owned and transmitted.

The Marxist historian, E.P. Thompson[116] analyses the history of this view of property which dovetails with the image of genetic property that Oyama attacks. He points out that in feudal societies it is difficult to think of land ownership as anything other than in terms of relations between people. People were born to a

---

114 K. Marx, 'Thesis on Feuerbach' in K. Marx, *The German Ideology* (New York: Prometheus Books, 1988) p. 573. He states, 'But the essence of man is no abstraction inherent in each single individual. In its reality it is the ensemble of the social relations'.
115 Battersby (1998a) p. 184. I will return to discuss this further in Chapter 3 in the context of legal theory.
116 E.P. Thompson, 'Custom, Law and Common Right' in E.P. Thompson, *Customs in Common* (London: Penguin, 1991). See also C.B. Macpherson, ed., *Property: Mainstream and Critical Positions* (Oxford: Basil Blackwell, 1978b).

certain position, within a hierarchy based upon different rights and obligations around land. Thompson argues that it is only with the *Enclosure Acts*, and the extinguishing of feudal rights below copyhold, as in *Gatewards Case*[117] that a property owner could think of his land as his object, a commodity, rather than as representing rights against other persons. In different ways, a number of contemporary feminist legal theorists[118] have explored the link between sex/gender and sexuality, the image of a bounded self and the ability of property owners to exclude others. This ceases to be simply a metaphor when the term 'inheritance' is used to describe the passing on of both genetic and *environmental* material. As discussed above, Oyama attacks this usage (for both types of material) along with its implication that there is a fixed, stable object, a gene or part of the environment, that is passed between generations.[119] Her aim is not to argue that the environment alters how we develop, as much as do genes, but to move away from this approach to development altogether. This is achieved by looking at *interacting systems and processes*, many aspects of which are ignored simply because they are stable enough to allow such development to take place.

Feminism, Essentialism and Law

The question of 'essentialism' has been widely debated within the feminist movement and has been described by Schor[120] as a defining feature of feminism in the 1980s. Within feminist legal theory it continues to be debated.[121] As discussed in Chapter 1, there has been a perceived contradiction between the way in which the feminist movement has challenged the view that women have a particular nature (which has been used to justify the status quo) and the view that there is some property (or quality) that all women have in common that forms the basis of the feminist movement itself. There has also been a strong challenge to the distinction, drawn by second wave feminism, between sex – said to represent natural and fixed attributes – and gender – which was employed by second wave feminists to

---

117 *Gateward's Case* (1603) 6 Co. Rep.
118 Dickenson (1997); J. Nedelsky, 'Law, Boundaries and the Bounded Self' in R. Post, ed., *Law and the Order of Culture* (California: California University Press, 1991) pp. 162-189; N. Naffine, 'The Legal Structure of Self-Ownership: Or the Self-Possessed Man and the Woman Possessed', *Journal of Law and Society*, Vol. 25, No. 2, 1998, pp. 198-212; M. Davies, 'The Proper: Discourses of Purity', *Law and Critique*, Vol. IX, No. 2, 1998, pp. 141-173; M. Davies, 'Queer Property, Queer Persons: Self-Ownership and Beyond', *Social and Legal Studies*, Vol. 8, No. 3, 1999, pp. 327-352.
119 Oyama (2000a) p. 194.
120 N. Schor, 'Introduction' in N. Schor and E. Weed, *The Essential Difference* (Indiana University Press, 1994) p. vii.
121 For example, A. Barron, 'Feminism, Aestheticism and the Limits of the Law', *Feminist Legal Studies*, Vol. 8, 2000, pp. 275-317; M. Drakopoulou, 'The Ethic of Care; Female Subjectivity and Feminist Legal Scholarship', *Feminist Legal Studies*, Vol. 8, 2000, 199-226.

emphasise the belief that that many behaviours are learned and not fixed. It is precisely this latter approach that Oyama seeks to undermine by arguing against the idea that 'biology' is fixed in the first place. As discussed above, she also challenges the idea that either environment or genetics can be analysed as discrete, centralised, control mechanisms.

A more influential challenge to the sex/gender distinction, within the feminist movement, has come from 'postmodern' or 'poststructuralist' feminism. However, it is important not to lump together all approaches that draw from contemporary continental philosophy. Poststructuralists, such as Judith Butler,[122] have pointed to the way in which biology is viewed as something that is pre-discursive and yet can only be understood in terms of language. At its least politically useful, poststructuralist feminism has been characterised as assuming that women's political claims cannot be discussed; that they represent merely a position of difference within a psychoanalytic or deconstructive framework. In the area of feminist legal theory, Barron describes the central theme of postmodern legal theory in the following terms:

> Postmodernist legal theory, including postmodernist-feminist legal theory, imagines law to be founded on a repression of the desiring, embodied, particular (female) other, thus bringing into view what is excluded or denied in the elevation of this abstract reason as the source of law's authority.[123]

As discussed in Chapter 1, a suspicion of 'essentialism' has lead to the argument that there can be no voice of the women's movement because the only voice that is heard tends to be that of white, middle-class, able-bodied, heterosexual women. This is analogous to the feminist criticism of the way in which a universal image of selfhood actually takes male bodies and traditional lifestyles as the norm. (This argument can be distinguished from the more abstract claim that 'woman' represents 'the other' or 'the position of difference' within psychoanalytic or deconstructive frameworks.) The feminist criticism can be illustrated using a couple of examples taken from the law of obligations. Firstly, the law of tort relies upon establishing negligence by the adoption of the 'reasonable man test', which in recent years has been renamed as the 'reasonable person' test. In practice, this remains the same because the judges adopt the test of what they view is reasonable, irrespective of the fiction of the man, or person, on the 'Clapham omnibus', whose view they are supposedly expressing. The question of whether the person's behaviour has fallen below that of the reasonable person does raise issues about personal differences. For example, how a 'reasonable person' perceives the behaviour of another is relevant in sexual harassment cases. Women tend to perceive a threat – in situations when men do not think such perception is reasonable – because women in our culture are taught to fear rape and are

---

122 Butler (1990); Butler (1993); Butler (1997).
123 Barron (2000) p. 276. Here Barron registers the way in which the question of women's subjectivity has been linked with an 'ethic of care' within legal theory.

concerned that a situation could escalate, whereas men are often insensitive to this interpretation of events. The argument is that male judges would not be able to view the situation through women's eyes and would therefore employ a male standard from which to judge the situation. In *R v A (2001)*[124] the (all male) House of Lords was asked to weigh up the rights of women rape victims not to have evidence of their sex lives introduced within a rape trial (as stated in *Youth Justice and Criminal Evidence Act 1999 s. 41*) against the rights of the male defendant to a fair trial (under *Human Rights Act 1998 Sch. 1*). They found in favour of the male defendant, leaving the decision of whether on not to admit this evidence to the trial judge in individual cases, thereby doing nothing to undermine concerns of bias.

Another example raises similar issues. The question of who should sit on a jury and whether race or sex should be taken into account has been argued with regard to both race and sex cases. Although the Runciman Royal Commission on Criminal Justice[125] recommended that there should be some representation from ethnic minorities on the jury when race is an issue, the position has not been amended since the Court of Appeal turned down the objection of a black defendant tried by an all white jury.[126]

In both the above examples, the legal system relies upon the assumption that it should be possible for judges to imagine themselves in the position of others. However, Gatens,[127] drawing upon Spinoza, undermines this assumption by arguing that imagination derives from bodily experience. Spinoza uses the example of our perception of the sun as seeming close to us. Even when it is discovered that this is false, the initial bodily experience does not disappear but continues to have an effect. Gatens applies this to her feminist concerns about the judiciary. Given that most male judges are unlikely to have experience of women in roles other than those that are subservient then, she reasons, they are less likely to be able to even recognise this as an important issue let alone attempt to view themselves within the position of women. I will return to this question in the next chapter.

These examples appear, at first blush, to pose a problem for the feminist movement which has been sensitive to the way in which men purport to represent a universal position which silences women's perspective. Given that this has been extended to the question of differences between women, such as class, race, disability and sexuality, the question is asked, how can feminists ground claims on behalf of women without committing the same mistake? As we have seen, Spivak,[128] although she has moved away from this position, once suggested that

---

124 *R. v A* (Complainant's Sexual History); also known as: *R. v Y* (Sexual Offence: Complainant's Sexual History) (2001) 2 W.L.R. 1546; (2001) 3 All ER 1. The Lords found in favour of protection of the male defendant.

125 Lord Runciman (chair), *Royal Commission on Criminal Justice*, Cmnd 2263 (London: HMSO, 1993).

126 *R v Ford* (1989) 3 WLR 762; *R v Smith* (2003) 1 WLR 2229.

127 M. Gatens, *Imaginary Bodies: Ethics, Power and Corporeality* (London: Routledge, 1996) pp. 135-141.

128 Spivak (1990) p. 12.

feminists should take the desperate measure of adopting a 'strategic essentialism'. This involves both accepting the claim that there is no essential female quality from which to make feminist demands, but that we should act as if there is such a thing in order to ground political claims. I want to argue that Battersby offers a way out of this problem, which is in keeping with the general approach of Oyama.

To introduce this reworking of essentialism, Battersby starts by historically situating the meaning of the term 'essence' which she seeks to reframe. It is worth considering her method, at this stage, before looking at her analysis of essentialism. Her approach to the question of essentialism employs a similar technique to the way in which she considers the work of female artists and poets, such as Karoline von Günderode.[129] She demonstrates that these artists' work can be reactivated within a contemporary feminist context. This can feedback to redefine the artistic traditions which had initially excluded these artists. Similarly, Battersby's search for a better way of conceptualising the essentialist debate for feminism involves a recognition that this concept has a history, the underside of which can provide resources for feminism.

This method or approach to history is itself implicated in the way that she thinks about essentialism. It draws from, and alters, Adorno's image of an object, such as an art object, that can shock the subject into a different conceptual framework. Further, for Adorno, objects that do not fit within the frame of reference of the subject do not fall outside any possible view, as in Kant's framework. They might be seen (or be seen differently) at a later date when the subject has a different frame of reference. Adorno, as a Marxist, envisaged this switch in terms of a change in the mode of production. In Battersby's work, it is the social change and questions raised by the feminist movement that allow the work of the female artists to be viewed differently. In this way, her work accounts for its own position.

Considered in this way, it has some similarities with the project of another contemporary feminist philosopher, Adriana Cavarero,[130] who aims to rework historical narratives to show how the position of women undermines their theoretical framework from within. Both are concerned with the ways in which women's bodies and traditional lifestyle disrupt different 'modern' and 'postmodern' views of the self. However, whilst their method of attack may have similarities, the important constructive aspects of their work differ. Cavarero's work draws more from Hannah Arendt to describe the importance of the telling of one's story whereas Battersby is more focused upon bodily habit and the daily ambiguities of power relations through which the self emerges.

---

129 C. Battersby, 'Unblocking the Oedipal: Karoline von Günderode and the Female Sublime' in S. Ledger, J. McDonagh and J. Spencer, *Political Gender: Texts and Contexts* (London: Harvester Wheatsheaf, 1994b) pp. 129-43.

130 A. Cavarero, *In Spite of Plato* (Cambridge: Polity, 1995); A. Cavarero, *Rethinking Oedipus: Stealing a Patriarchal Text.* Paper at the UK Society of Women in Philosophy Conference 1996; A. Cavarero, *Relating Narratives: Storytelling and Selfhood* (London: Routledge, 2000).

Battersby makes two important points that are central to her work. Firstly, in *Gender and Genius*[131] she distinguishes between the meaning of the 'feminine' and 'female'. It is clear from her historical analysis that men who were classed as fitting the definition of the romantic genius could be classified as 'feminine', as having feminine attributes. However, they were valued in a way that women, whether viewed as having feminine or masculine attributes, were not. It was therefore possible to call a man 'feminine', but to call him 'female' would be a category mistake – with the possible exception of post-operation transsexuals. So, it was the state of being female (and not the possession of 'feminine' attributes) that was degraded.

Secondly, Battersby concentrates upon thinking what it would mean to take the female subject position as norm rather than as an aberration. She develops this to provide a philosophical answer to the feminist problems of essentialism discussed above. This is done by challenging the assumption that the only way to talk about essence is as a fixed, unchanging, underlying characteristic. As Battersby points out, this interpretation of Aristotle is subject to disagreement, but what is relevant is the definition of essence that has influenced Western philosophy.[132] The Aristotelian view of essence is such that the essence of x is that property which all examples of x have in common. This involves ignoring the particularity of something and looking for common features which are said to define the essence of the universal category or species. This model therefore blocks any attempt to discuss a female essence because it is only at the level of the species that an essence can be discerned.

This can be illustrated in more detail by discussing the way in which Aristotle then instantiates his view of essence in biology, such that both men and women have human essence. However, according to Aristotle's biology, women are viewed as failed males – who would have developed into males had they not been subject to cold and damp conditions in the womb. So, in this strangely influential model, although women have human essence, they are not the perfect example of this essence. In other words, there is a universal species essence, of which the male is the best example. The female is viewed as failing to reach her full potential (to be male).

Given that this makes Aristotelian essentialism an inauspicious place to start to think of the specificity of women, Battersby turns to alternative views of essence within the history of philosophy. In particular, she considers Locke's[133] distinction between 'nominal essence' and 'real essences', the latter of which he associated with Aristotle. Nominalists maintain that names are simply that which people give to things and that these things have nothing else in common. The 'nominal essence'

---

131 C. Battersby. *Gender and Genius: Towards a Feminist Aesthetics* (London: The Women's Press. 1989) pp. 10-15.

132 Battersby (1998a) p. 211.

133 J. Locke. 'Of the Names of Substances' in *An Essay Concerning Human Understanding* (London: Collins. 1969) pp. 283-296.

is the abstract idea of things of that sort. The universal therefore attaches to the name of the thing in language rather than to the thing itself.[134] It is the way in which we label the thing, rather than any property within the thing itself, that counts as its 'nominal essence'. These things are linked by the way in which the ideas are built up by a process of abstraction, using simple ideas to derive complex ideas, rather than by some internal property. Locke rejects Aristotle's view of essence by arguing that we cannot categorise things in terms of their real essence because we simply do not know what its 'real essence' is.[135]

Battersby employs a Kantian framework in order to improve Locke's account of essentialism. Rather than rely upon a top-down approach in which language is viewed as labelling things in the world, she uses the Kantian schemata to describe a process in which the data about x impinges upon the way in which they are labelled. The empirical image of x is then understood within a set of rules in which it is classified. However, this set of rules can alter within different cultures and at different times. This allows the term 'women' to be discussed in terms of its meaning at a particular point in history in a particular culture. This is informed, not only by the way in which the term is used, but also by the way in which the world of which we are a part imposes itself upon us. In other words, Battersby employs a Kantian framework to find an alternative to Lockean nominalism on one side and Aristotelian essentialism on the other.

Battersby's argument can be illustrated further by addressing some criticisms of Battersby made by Linda Alcoff.[136] Alcoff argues that there is a tension in Battersby's work between: 1) the materially real and 2) the image or representation of women as objects. Alcoff ignores the post-Kantian framework which informs Battersby's work, a point that is clear in the way in which she discusses the influences upon Battersby earlier in the paper.[137] Hence, Alcoff describes Battersby in the following terms,

> Battersby, like other feminists, looks to Benedict Spinoza...Nietzsche and John Dewey: more originally and surprisingly, she also looks to Søren Kierkegaard, in whose aesthetic works she finds a conception of selves as ambiguous and relational, patterned by habits and 'repetitions' rather than an inner stable core.[138]

As a result of ignoring the central role of Kant in Battersby's work, Alcoff wrongly characterises Battersby as viewing women as 'objects of representation' and as hence emphasising language, putting her into the 'postmodern feminist' camp. As described above, Battersby uses a Kantian move to view essence – not simply as

---

134 Battersby (1998a) p. 29.
135 Locke (1969) p. 287.
136 L.M. Alcoff, 'Review Essay: Philosophy Matters, A Review of Recent Work in Feminist Philosophy'. *Signs: Journal of Women in Culture and Society*, Vol. 25, No. 3. 2000 p. 856.
137 Alcoff (2000) p. 856.
138 Alcoff (2000) p. 856.

the way in which something is talked about (which she discusses in term of Lockean nominalism) – but as something that is informed by the way in which the world impinges itself upon our senses, viewed through sets of rules which can alter in response to, for example, different ways of viewing the world produced by the empirical sciences.

As outlined above, this does not collapse into Aristotelian essentialism because essence is not viewed as an immutable underlying characteristic of a thing. It changes with cultural understanding which is itself informed by empirical science but, as I will discuss below, always involves power.

Further, Battersby cannot be viewed as ignoring materiality because it is precisely an attempt to think of matter as active that is pivotal to her reworking of Kant. In Battersby's later discussion of the transcendental self and transcendental object, she uses the question of what it would be to think of the female body as typical, to show how the Kantian framework makes it impossible to think of active matter – for example, of bodies that can become two.

Battersby uses this reworking of essence, from the 'underside of philosophy' to return to her question of thinking female specificity. It is possible to think about the 'essence' of woman when it is no longer assumed that essence refers to a fixed underlying characteristic that defines the group. Neither is the essence of woman simply a name attached to 'women', without any bottom-up input from the data, for example, from biological research. In addition, there is no neutral value-free analysis. It is worth quoting Battersby on this point to show how she carves out a definition of essentialism that differs from both Aristotle and from Locke:

> For the supporter of extreme nominalism, the question is only which characteristics in our culture act as linguistic definers. However, for paradigms of human sexual difference to evolve there have to be perceived similarities – and discrepancies – between the class of entities compared. To maintain this is 'just' linguistic and social plays down the capacity of data to disturb the definition in a 'bottom-up' way. To allow that empirical 'evidence' might play a role in dislocating and redrawing current paradigms of sexual difference does not entail that linguistic and social practices do not also enter into the current definitions. Nor does it entail that there might not also be social reasons why the markers for sexually differentiated bodies should change. Opposing extreme nominalism does not entail positing underlying, unchanging, 'real truths' about female bodies and forms.[139]

There is also an acknowledged debt to Foucault in Battersby's work at this point. It is clear that there is no neutral description of a female essence, in her use of the term. What is classed as essential in the definition of the female differs at different times. This may be influenced by the 'data' about sexual difference but it is never 'neutral'. Power is always involved in this view of essence, even though it is acknowledged that not any story will do.

---

139 Battersby (1998a) p. 30.

To return to the problem within feminist legal theory of making claims on behalf of women – claims that then silence the voices of racial, sexual and other minorities – this does offer an approach that is more pragmatic. There is no fixed definition of women at stake because the possibility of such a move is closed by the emphasis upon an essence that is subject to change. As Battersby puts it,

> Remodelling identity in terms of a metaphysics of becoming allows us to register differences and changes occurring within a single category, and allows us to register power differentials and differences amongst women themselves. As such, an identity politics need not entail homogenizing 'woman' or 'women'...Instead, we will need to ally a metaphysics of becoming with an account of the historical and cultural factors that help configure the female subject-position in its diverse specificities.[140]

To Clark and Oyama, with their particular concerns, it is obvious that not any story will do and neither will the image of an underlying Aristotelian essence. It is precisely this Aristotelian approach that Oyama attacks in her rethinking of development. Battersby's insistence on thinking both sexual difference and 'the self' may appear an odd pursuit when compared to the more 'scientific' aims of analysis of cognition or development. This rethinking of 'essence' suggests an answer to this objection. The meaning of what it is to have, or be, a self – or to be a person – in our culture will continue to affect the way in which we live, including the practical operation of law of obligations. It is not that we can simply change the stories about ourselves at will. They emerge from complex social histories. However, these histories are not without an underside that can allow the meaning of what it is to live as a woman to be discussed. Importantly, this does not mean that there is only a top-down imposition of images of ourselves. Oyama's attack upon the reduction of complex interactions into separate canals of 'social' and 'biological' is useful here.

As Irigaray[141] has argued, to refuse to discuss sexual difference would be to leave it unthought. There is an argument here that is akin to Battersby's[142] argument for the need to rework, rather than simply abandon, the notion of genius in her earlier work. In both cases, we will continue to employ the term, or some equivalent, because it is actually doing some work in practice. The way to challenge it is to reveal the assumptions that go with it and to try to rework its meaning from within. Similarly, to exchange Aristotle's definition of human essence for a position that does no more than reject all images of the self would be to fail to register the way that the meaning of what it is to be a self works in

---

140 Battersby (1998a) p. 124.
141 'Sexual difference is probably the issue in our time which could be our "salvation" if we thought it through.' L. Irigaray, *An Ethics of Sexual Difference* (London: Athlone Press, 1993a) p. 5. For discussion of this point see J. Richardson, 'Jamming the Machines: "Woman" in the Work of Irigaray and Deleuze', *Law and Critique*, Vol. IX, No. 1, 1998a, p. 90.
142 Battersby (1989) p. 225.

practice, including in legal practice. It would be to block a discussion of what it means to be a woman, a move that has produced the current problems within feminist legal theory.

I will return to the broad framework of the self that I have drawn out of the work of these contemporary theorists, Battersby, Clark and Oyama working within different areas of philosophy. In the next chapter, I want to consider what it is to be a person, or be or have a self within the law. In particular, I will focus upon the legal theorist Drucilla Cornell, whose work can more easily be characterised as imposing top-down stories upon the world but in a manner that is distinct from Alcoff's misreading of Battersby.

Chapter 3

Cornell's 'Imaginary Domain'

This chapter focuses upon the legal framework proposed by feminist legal theorist Drucilla Cornell, whose practical proposals for changes in law are derived from her theoretical analysis of personhood. Cornell's work has a wide application but I will focus upon her contribution to the law of tort. Whilst Cornell is writing in the US, her legal claim for particular rights based upon personhood is intended to have universal application. In particular, she provides answers to the equality/difference debate and to feminist concerns that in making claims for (or analysing the position of) women as a group they may thereby reinforce stereotypes of women. These were the worries that prompted ideas around strategic essentialism, that were introduced in Chapter 1.

In the last chapter, I looked at different ways of thinking about the self, drawn from diverse areas of contemporary philosophy in order to argue against the need for 'strategic essentialism'. In this chapter I consider personhood, a legal rather than an ontological concept. Whilst Cornell discusses personhood, linked with a claim for legal rights to be explained below, her view of personhood derives from her view of what it means to be a self and from her broader view of 'the project of becoming a person', in which what it means to be a self is linked historically with the law.

Before discussing Cornell's view of personhood it is worth considering the legal context of the term 'person', in the UK. The meaning of the term 'person' has a legal, as well as a philosophical, history.[143] Women were not classified as 'persons' until the 'Persons Case': *Edwards v Attorney General of Canada (1930)*.[144] In a series of cases over the previous sixty years women challenged their position as non-persons that prevented them from voting, taking part in government or the professions or receiving an education.[145] Women were denied these rights, because the courts failed to classify them as 'persons', at the the same time as companies began to be viewed as legal persons.[146] This not only allowed companies to sue and

---

143 For my discussion of this see J. Richardson 'A Refrain: Feminist Metaphysics and Law' in J. Richardson and R. Sandland, *Feminist Perspectives on Law and Theory* (London: Cavendish. 2000) pp. 119-134.

144 *Edwards v Attorney General of Canada* (1930) A.C. 124 at 128. For a discussion of the case see J. Bridgeman and S. Mills, *Feminist Perspectives on Law: Law's Engagement with the Female Body* (London: Sweet and Maxwell, 1998) p. 18.

145 For a discussion of these cases see Sachs and Wilson (1978); Bridgeman and Mills (1998) pp. 11-26.

146 For an analysis of the development of the doctrine of separate personality of companies see I. Grigg-Spall. P. Ireland and D. Kelly, 'Company Law' in *The Critical Lawyers Handbook* (London: Pluto. 1992) pp. 98-105.

be sued in the courts, as if they were men, but also facilitated the development of limited liability in the 1860s so that for the first time the resources of business were separate from that of the household.[147]

Rethinking the concept of personhood is central to Cornell's position. Cornell's project is aimed at fully extending rights to women by thinking about ways in which the law can give expression to practical feminist concerns. For example, in tort law she has made proposals for employment rights (a tort of wrongful discharge),[148] protection from sexual harassment[149] and Spanish language rights.[150] She has also applied her framework to the redefinition of the family, adoption,[151] and in support of abortion rights.[152]

In addition, she suggests a legal test to replace the 'reasonable man test' that is central in tort law. I will therefore outline the reasonable man test, mentioned in the last chapter, and then turn to Cornell's proposals to replace it and the way in which she links together a philosophical system with a practical legal principle. These are positions that she has developed since 1995, starting with *The Imaginary Domain.*[153]

The Reasonable Man

As mentioned in the last chapter, the 'reasonable man' is a central concept in tort law. To decide if someone has been negligent judges must decide whether the defendant's actions fell below the standard of the hypothetical 'reasonable man'. As Conaghan and Mansell point out,

> Traditionally, the reasonable man has been invoked to represent an objective standard of care against which all are measured. He is thus devoid of all characteristics which make him human. By so denuding him of those 'idiosyncrasies of the particular person whose conduct is in question' (*Glasgow Corporation v Muir* (1943), *per* Lord MacMillan at 457) the reasonable man poses as the average man,

---

147 L. Davidoff, M. Doolittle, J. Fink and K. Holden, *The Family Story: Blood Contract and Intimacy 1830-1960* (Harlow: Addison Wesley Longman Ltd, 1999) pp. 106-7.

148 D. Cornell, 'Worker's rights and the Defence of Just-Cause Statutes' in Cornell (2000a) pp. 83-117.

149 D. Cornell, 'Sexual Freedom and the Unleashing of Women's Desire' in Cornell (1995) pp. 167-227.

150 D. Cornell, 'Spanish Language Rights: Identification, Freedom and the Imaginary Domain' in Cornell (2000a) pp. 129-153.

151 D. Cornell, 'Adoption and its Progeny: Rethinking Family, Gender and Sexual Difference' in Cornell (1998) pp. 96-130; D. Cornell 'What and How Maketh a Father: Equality Versus Conscription' in Cornell (1998) pp. 131-149.

152 D. Cornell, 'Dismembered Selves and Wandering Wombs' in Cornell (1995) pp. 31-91.

153 Cornell (1995); Cornell (1998); Cornell (2000a).

thereby providing a single and universal standard purporting to correspond with reasonable behaviour.[154]

There have been a number of feminist arguments[155] that the reasonable man test relies upon a male perspective which differs from women's attitudes, particularly in areas such as sexual harassment. The feminist debate about the reasonable man test is therefore a version of the equality/difference debate – that women either have to appear to be like men in order to gain the same rights (thereby problematising pregnancy, for example) or they have to appear different from men and risk affirming traditional oppression. This is a topic introduced in the first chapter and developed further below. In the area of sexual harassment, for example, it has been argued that sensitivity between the sexes differs and therefore a universal test as to how the 'reasonable man' would behave is inappropriate.[156] Cornell's critique of the reasonable man test leads her to argue that it should be replaced by her own test,[157] and that, more broadly, her approach to personhood resolves the paradox of the equality/difference debate in its many guises.

---

154 J. Conaghan and W. Mansell, *The Wrongs of Tort*, 2nd edition, (London: Pluto Press, 1999) pp. 52-53.

155 For example, R. Martin, 'A Feminist View of the Reasonable Man: An Alternative Approach to Liability in Negligence for Personal Injury', *Anglo-American Law Review*, Vol. 23, 1994, pp. 334-374. For a summary of the arguments regarding tort law, see Conaghan and Mansell (1999) pp. 52-53. There is also work on the way in which the reasonable man is raced. For an historical analysis of the way that the rise of the use of the 'reasonable man' test coincided with the heyday of British Imperialism (and how the meaning of 'reasonable man' test was adapted so the 'primitive reasonable man' was not viewed as having the same sense of restraint as British men) see the Sindh Criminal appeal case of *Ghulam Mustafa Gahno (1939) AIR Sind 182*, cited and discussed in K. Laster and P. Raman, 'Law for One and One for All: An Intersectional Legal Subject' in Naffine and Owens (1997) pp. 193-212.

156 The EU Code of Practice includes reference to 'conduct that is unwanted, **unreasonable** and offence to the recipient': Recommendation 92/C 27/04. For a discussion see M. Rubenstein, 'Sexual Harassment: European Commission Recommendation and Code of Practice', *Industrial Law Journal*, Vol. 21, 1992, p. 70; J. Dine and B. Watt, 'Sexual Harassment: Moving Away From Discrimination', *Modern Law Review*, Vol. 58, 1995, pp. 355-362. The possibility of the development of tort law to provide a remedy for sexual harassment more generally has been traced by Joanne Conaghan. See, J. Conaghan, 'Enhancing Civil Remedies for (Sexual) Harassment: s3 of the Protection from Harassment Act 1997', *Feminist Legal Studies*, Vol. 7, 1999a, pp. 203-214; J. Conaghan, 'Equity Rushes in Where Tort Fears to Tread: The Court of Appeal Decision in *Burris v Asadani*', *Feminist Legal Studies*, Vol. IV, No. 2, 1996, pp. 221-228; J. Conaghan, 'Harassment and the Law of Torts: *Khorasandjian v Bush*', *Feminist Legal Studies*, Vol. I, No. 2, 1993, pp. 189-197.

157 See, Cornell (1995) pp. 14-16 for her discussion of the reasonable man test.

Cornell's Approach to Tort: Free and Equal Persons

Cornell's analyses of different torts – as well as her broader arguments about law – all work by concentrating on the idea of freedom. She wants to keep in play the question, 'would free and equal persons agree to this decision?' and this question is to act as a legal principle. She proposes that this question should be asked whenever legislation is passed or a judicial decision made. She argues that,

> We judge public law by the 'as if' of a postulated original contract. The rightfulness of a law is one that all citizens, regarded as free and equal, *could* have agreed to if they were in a position to consent within the general will. The contract is an idea of reason with practical effect in that it can guide legislators with a test for rightfulness...Like both Rawls and Kant, I also defend the idea of reasonableness and public reason. Reasonableness and public reason depend upon the demand of the 'as if' itself. Judges and legislators are called upon to proceed through the 'as if' because this is the test for the rightfulness of the law consistent with the evaluation of each one of us as a free and equal person.[158] (Italics are in the original.)

In a footnote, Cornell[159] points out that she is using as a device the hypothetical position of persons sitting round a table deciding what laws to agree upon. I will discuss in more detail below the way in which her position differs from that of Rawls. The image of what it means (or could mean) to be a person is therefore central to her work.

So far, it appears that Cornell's legal test merely replaces the 'reasonable man test' with the 'free and equal persons test'. However, these operate very differently, as can be illustrated by the problem of sexual harassment, mentioned above. The equality/difference problem, when transposed into sexual harassment law, is concerned with the question of what the 'reasonable man' would view as acceptable behaviour. Cornell offers a different approach in which women are not viewed as seeking protection as 'victims' but as claiming their worthiness as persons.[160] She therefore derives this position from her original philosophical analysis to argue that it is important to recognise,

> the way in which the devaluation of one's sex curtails *freedom* by imposing standards of behaviour which fails to accord with equal personhood...Thus, to protect the space for free play of one's sexual imaginary demands the recognition of the primary good of self-respect for each one of us as sexuate beings. Again, when women demand the space to be sexual in their own way and still be accorded respect for their worthiness as persons, they are demanding the equal chance to seek sexual happiness, not protection.[161] (Italics are in the original.)

---

158 Cornell (1995) pp. 12-13. I will explain Cornell's position in more detail below.
159 Cornell (1995) p. 242, fn.16.
160 Cornell (1995) p. 172.
161 Cornell (1995) p. 172.

She argues that the replacement of the 'reasonable man' test with a 'reasonable woman' standard is inadequate because it continues to divide women into those who take sexual harassment cases and those who 'keep a stiff upper lip' about male behaviour. Cornell's aim is to shift the court's attention from whether or not the woman was reasonable in claiming sexual harassment to an examination of the workplace by focusing upon 'whether or not the workplace itself enforced sexual shame so as to effectively undermine the social basis of self-respect'.[162]

I have much sympathy with the aims of Cornell's project and think that there is merit in any pragmatic use of law.[163] However, Cornell's work moves beyond a pragmatic position to embrace the view that we really are constituted as subjects with rights. She argues,

> Perhaps in the end I am Hegelian enough to think that we are actually constituted in modernity as subjects of right and so, in a sense, we cannot step outside this sphere of law.[164]

Similarly, in *Just Cause: Freedom, Identity and Rights*, she acknowledges her debt to Hegel,

> Of course, the idea that the concept of right is constitutive of the person takes us back to Hegel.[165]

She assumes that human sociability, and the recognition that we give each other, must now be attributed to (or, at least, channelled through) the law. This is far more important to Cornell's analysis of contemporary legal debates than is her employment of Lacan – a fact that the common description of Cornell as producing 'psychoanalytic feminism'[166] fails to register. In particular, Cornell views herself as having produced a solution to the equality/difference debate.[167] I will concentrate upon this debate and the way in which Cornell's approach provides an interesting response to the Person's Case.

---

162 Cornell (1995) p. 206.
163 I have argued that there are pragmatic problems with this approach to a legal test. Not only can its subtly be easily misinterpreted by judges but it ignores the practical considerations, such as the length of proceedings, the endless documentation and cross examination, that make applicants feel like victims, even whilst they simply claim 'personhood'. J. Richardson, 'A Burglar in the House of Philosophy: Theodor Adorno, Drucilla Cornell and Hate Speech', *Feminist Legal Studies*, Vol. 1, No. 1, 1999, pp. 3-31. I want to leave this objection aside to exploring the broader implications of Cornell's view of personhood.
164 Florence (1997) p. 15.
165 Cornell (2000a) p. 19.
166 This common description is understandable given her reference to Lacan and Irigaray in her work. See, for example, N. Naffine and R.J. Owens, 'Sexing Law' in Naffine and Owens (1997) p. 6.
167 D. Cornell (2000a) p. 17.

As discussed above, women were initially deemed not to be classifiable as 'persons'. This was changed as a result of the Person's Case,[168] thereby paving the way for allowing women to have some of the same rights as men. This scenario raises the well-worn equality/difference debate discussed above, as to whether women should be classified, in law, as 'just like men' in order to obtain the same rights as men or whether particular rights should pertain to women, *as women*.[169]

Cornell's conception of what it means to be a person responds to this debate. She argues that women should be viewed as subject to legal rights *as persons* (not as women). So, rights are to be viewed as attaching to the idea of being a person. This raises the equality/difference problem in the following terms: does Cornell's use of the neutral term 'person' simply involve subsuming women into a universal that is really envisaged as male, leading to the treatment of women as 'like men'? Cornell's answer hinges upon her unusual definition of the term 'person'. This can be illustrated by the way she talks about 'the project of becoming a person':

> What we think of as 'individuality' and 'the person' are not assumed as a given but respected as part of a project, one that must be open to each one of us on an equivalent basis.[170]

She does not envisage that we change individually, through an act of will, but that there is a collective transformation, an experimentation with different ways of living, that is to be facilitated by the law. In order that we should have any hope of being successful in this 'project of becoming a person' or 'going beyond the limit',[171] Cornell cites three conditions that should be protected by law:

---

168 *Edwards v Attorney General of Canada* (1930) A.C. 124.
169 This is Irigaray's position in L. Irigaray, *I Love to You: Sketch of a Possible Felicity in History* (London: Routledge, 1996); L. Irigaray, 'Why Define Sexuate Rights' in Irigaray (1993b) pp. 81-92. For Cornell's concerns about Irigaray's later work see, P. Cheah and E. Grosz, 'The Future of Sexual Difference: An Interview with Judith Butler and Drucilla Cornell', *Diacritics*, Vol. 28, No. 1, 1998, p. 21. Cornell describes her development of the 'imaginary domain' as a reaction to Butler's argument that to symbolise the imaginary as feminine entails a conservative move. See Butler (1997). Butler does not engage with Irigaray in Butler (1997) but Cornell refers to Butler's general arguments and a personal discussion with Butler in 1995 which 'pushed her quite hard on the ontologization inherent in Irigaray', P. Cheah and E. Grosz (1998) p. 21. I will trace the position Cornell develops in response more slowly, below.
170 Cornell (1995) p. 4.
171 For a discussion of the personal transformation involved in personhood, see Cornell (1995) pp. 4-5. For a discussion of the difference between 'parameters and limits' see Cornell (2000a) pp. 140-141. Inheritance of culture, language and country sets parameters but cannot impose limits 'that so rigidly define us that we cannot develop a personal response to the particularity of the situation'. Cornell (2000a) p. 140.

1) bodily integrity; 2) access to symbolic forms sufficient to achieve linguistic skills permitting the differentiation of oneself from others and; 3) the protection of the imaginary domain.[172]

As I discuss elsewhere,[173] Cornell's concern that we should be able to 'differentiate ourselves from others' is intimately linked with Cornell's 'project of becoming a person'. Differentiation from others is to be safeguarded by allowing access to symbolic forms and linguistic skills – an ability to define oneself rather than to view oneself as, for example, only a wife/partner/mother etc. with respect to others. This could be contrasted with a position in which 'differentiation from others' involves being able to throw them out of your house. Her emphasis upon symbolic form and imagination is in keeping with Cornell's whole system. Her model prioritises the imagination. It is this collective imaginary (both conscious and unconscious) that she refers to by the term 'imaginary domain'. Cornell proposes that the protection of the 'imaginary domain' should operate as a very broad legal principle. As discussed above, a woman who is subject to sexual harassment is to make a legal claim that the harassment interferes with her self-image and hence her project of becoming a person. Whenever a legal decision is made then the question addressed by the judges should be 'would free and equal persons agree to this?' Given the choice, persons would not agree to a legal decision that would undermine their imaginary domain which would include an image of themselves.

Cornell's emphasis upon the imaginary, as the domain of ideas that effect our lives, shifts attention away from the importance of mundane, repeated physical tasks and habits; the daily negotiation of power difference in bodily practices and ambiguity as to what constitutes abuse. To draw out this point, it is possible to compare Cornell's view of the imaginary with an alternative view of imagination proposed by Gatens.[174] As mentioned in Chapter 2, Gatens illustrates her conceptualisation of the imagination by focusing upon judges. She argues that it is difficult for the mainly male, white, upper middle-class judiciary to imagine themselves in the position of women. Her view of imagination, derived from her reading of Spinoza, is that it emerges from bodily experience. This makes Gatens much more pessimistic about the ability of the judiciary to make the 'mental leap' outside their own bodily experience that is required of them by Cornell. She does not engage with Cornell but warns against reliance upon racism and sexism training-days for a judiciary whose experience of women, for example, is in the context of mainly subservient roles. In other words, she denies that they are able to make the public use of reason required of them by Cornell.[175]

172 Cornell (1995) p. 4.
173 Richardson (2000).
174 M. Gatens, 'Power, Ethics and Sexual Imaginaries' in Gatens (1996) pp. 125-145.
175 This is akin to Foucault's 'anxiety about judging' that it always involves the idea that the judge is removed from the circumstances. M. Foucault, 'On Popular Justice: A Conversation with Maoists' in M. Foucault, *Selected Interviews and Other Writings 1972-1977*, C. Gordon, ed. (Sussex: Harvester Press, 1980) p. 30.

Selves, Persons, Individuals

Cornell would argue that defeatism is unnecessary, that Gatens simply produces an argument for a change in the selection of judiciary rather than an abandonment of Cornell's legal test. However, I use the example merely to illustrate a conceptual point about Cornell's vision of the imagination, which appears 'top-down' – removed from bodily experience. Cornell makes an analogous 'top-down' move in relation to the role of law. Law is positioned as acting down upon the person, facilitating his/her 'project of becoming a person' – just as social change is understood to occur as a result of changes in the imagination. For Cornell, there is a realm that works from above to alter something else.

There is also a closer link between these 'realms' of the 'imaginary domain' and of law than this analogy would suggest. The law is called upon to protect our collective imagination ('the imaginary domain') and yet the law is actually a creation of the imaginary domain itself. In other words, Cornell's argument that we are subjects with rights relies upon the argument that, in modernity, we see ourselves in this way. She is an astute political campaigner, and not naïve about the conservatism of actual court decisions, but understandably wants to make women's rights permanent. She wants us to think of a time when the fight for women's rights has been won and, for example, women in every country have gained the right to abortion. This determined optimism does, I think, lead her to take too seriously law's claim to dictate reality. She wants to give us scope to define ourselves anew rather than offering a definition of what it is to be a person, so that her model emphasises transcendence of our current position and the possibility of collective change. However, the one thing that is already defined is that being a person means being subject to law. This not only undercuts her emphasis upon our ability to define ourselves, it makes law integral to our self-definition from the start.

Cornell's position is complex with regard to the relationship between theory and practice. The element of her work that clearly lies within a liberal framework appears to be in tension with her practical work as a radical socialist feminist activist. I have argued that what lies behind this tension is a commitment to radical politics that views her theoretical position as a practical engagement with liberals.[176] She looks at her contemporaries, particularly Dworkin and Rawls and argues that if their arguments are accepted then her more radical arguments necessarily follow. It is therefore tempting to try to account for her more radical activism by viewing her theoretical work as strategic. However, she is clearly convinced by her position – it is not adopted simply for pragmatic purposes. This paradox can be accounted for by considering her Hegelian position. Just as Adorno was concerned to analyse the work of his contemporaries as an indication of 'where we are now', so Cornell deals practically with US liberals. It is not merely a strategy, but neither is it the last word that can be said about her theoretical

---

176 Richardson (2000).

position. This would account for her eclectic use of contemporary theorists – which would otherwise be accounted for only by her concern not to be viewed as the disciple of a particular man.[177]

The problem then becomes: if her stress is upon practical reason, does her suggestion work? Below, I want to argue that her engagement with the US liberals, in particular Rawls and Dworkin, could undermine the more radical aims of her project. Central to this problem is her innovative use of Rawls to produce the legal test: would free and equal persons agree to this legislation/judgment? I will briefly outline the way in which she reworks Rawls and then discuss the extent to which Cornell's test leaves her open to an unwanted libertarian response. This is used to illustrate how Cornell's reworking of Rawls leads her into a dilemma regarding the extent to which she can leave open the meaning of what it is to be a person, within her legal test itself.

Rawls and the Imaginary Domain

Cornell points out,

> Although I am relying on Kant's postulation of an original contract as an idea of reason, my formulation is not strictly 'contractarian', if one means, by contractarian, the use of a contract theory in a liberal way as a 'moral or justice proof procedure'. I am explicitly using the idea of the original contract as a heuristic device.[178]

This can be illustrated by considering Kant's comments about the original contract, which he also employs as a heuristic device:

> The act by which a people forms itself into a state is the *original contract*. Properly speaking, the original contract is only the idea of this act, in terms of which alone we can think of the legitimacy of a state.[179] (Italics are in the original.)

Cornell's work also derives from Kant's position that to be a person is linked with the moral imperative: to treat oneself and others *as if* one were free.

In *A Theory of Justice*,[180] Rawls also draws from Kant to set up a thought experiment. He asks the question that Cornell wants to keep in play: 'what would free and equal persons agree to?'. Rawls uses this thought experiment to derive fixed answers as to how society should be organised based upon what 'heads of household' would agree to if they did not know what position they would hold in society, i.e. if they were under a 'veil of ignorance'. This is to avoid, for example,

---

177 Florence (1997) p. 24.
178 Cornell (1995) p. 242.
179 I. Kant, *The Metaphysics of Morals*, trans. M.J. Gregor, (Cambridge: Cambridge University Press, 1996) pp. 92-93.
180 J. Rawls, *A Theory of Justice* (Oxford: Oxford University Press, 1972); see also J. Rawls, *Justice as Fairness: A Restatement* (Mass.: Harvard University Press, 2001).

those who knew they would be rich arguing against redistribution of wealth. He argues that persons under the veil of ignorance would produce a 'general conception of justice' with the central idea that,

> all social primary goods – liberty and opportunity, income and wealth, and the bases
> of self-respect – are to be distributed equally unless an unequal distribution of any or
> all of these goods is to the advantage of the least favoured.[181]

These are ordered in terms of priority, such that the protection of civil liberties cannot be undermined for other reasons, such as redistribution of wealth. In this way Rawls gives content to what 'free and equal persons' would decide under the veil of ignorance.

Political philosopher, Susan Moller Okin points out that Rawls initially envisaged the (male) 'heads of household' as meeting under the veil of ignorance,[182] a move which unwittingly undercuts his aim to exclude bias in his thought experiment. Okin[183] argues that if 'free and equal persons' risked entering into society positioned as women then a more radical reinterpretation is required than is given in Rawls' analysis. Nobody who risked being treated as a woman would leave unchallenged the unequal division of labour within the family, for example. Further, Okin[184] illustrates that Rawls ignores injustice within the family and even relies upon the assumption that the family is a just institution when he discusses the development of a sense of justice in Part Three of *A Theory of Justice.*[185]

In contrast, Cornell, with her different conception of personhood from Rawls and from Okin, wants to avoid deriving fixed arguments as to what would be agreed by free and equal persons. She wants to keep this question in play as a legal test, to be considered whenever a legal decision is to be reached.

Thought Experiment: Nozick's Application of Cornell's Legal Test

At this point, I will refer to Nozick's libertarian work to draw out one of my concerns with Cornell's legal test and to further examine her conception of personhood. I will defer detailed discussion of 'self-ownership' to Chapter 6. Cornell argues that whenever a piece of legislation is to be passed, and whenever judges have to make a legal decision, as a guide they should ask themselves: would free and equal persons agree to this? This does not assume that persons start from a

---

181 Rawls (1972) p. 303.
182 Rawls (1972) p. 128 and p. 146 cited S.M. Okin, *Justice, Gender and the Family* (New York: Basic Books, 1989) p. 196. See also Okin (1989) pp. 89-109; Rawls' response to Okin is in Rawls (2001) pp. 162-168.
183 Okin (1989) pp. 89-109.
184 Okin (1989) pp. 97-101.
185 In drawing up principles of moral psychology he states 'First Law: given that family institutions are just…' Rawls (1972) p. 490.

position of equality and freedom and Cornell is clear that they do not. However, it is intended to be a radical reworking of Rawls' work because it keeps in play and repeats the question of freedom and equality. The test 'would free and equal persons agree to this legislation or this legal judgment?' does not dictate what would be decided, neither does it produce one answer that is to be fixed for all time. This is because Cornell wants the person, and not the state, to define what it means to be a person. She is concerned that everyone is given an equivalent chance to develop their 'project of becoming a person'.[186]

This can be compared with Nozick's conception of what it is to be a person in what is for him an ideal, the 'minimal state':

> The minimal state treats us as inviolate individuals, who may not be used in certain ways by others as means or tools or instruments or resources; it treats us as persons having individual rights with the dignity this constitutes. Treating us with respect by representing our rights, it allows us, individually or with whom we choose, to choose our life and to realize our ends and *our conception of ourselves*, insofar as we can, aided by the voluntary co-operation of other individuals possessing the same dignity.[187] (Italics are added.)

Although Cornell's conclusions are very different from those of Nozick, and he is not a writer with whom she has engaged, there is a similarity between his reference to our 'conception of ourselves' and Cornell's emphasis upon the imaginary domain. Both are linked with personhood which is to be protected, with rights against competing claims. In Cornell's work, it must be remembered that the idea of the imaginary domain is intimately linked with her legal test: free and equal persons would not agree to any decision that would harm their image of themselves. For example, Cornell employs her test to argue that the right not to be sexually harassed and the right to have an abortion are fundamental legal rights, which are necessary if women are to be treated as free and equal persons.[188] To fail to allow these rights would damage the woman's imaginary domain, her self-image, and therefore it would damage her project of becoming a person. As Cornell's test is actually intended to be used by judges and legislators, this is an assumption that must be made when deciding what free and equal persons would agree to.

I want to think about the possible response of Nozick to Cornell's work in order to draw out Cornell's view of personhood. As he has not engaged with her I will base my arguments upon his clearly stated position in *Anarchy, State and Utopia*.[189] Imagine Nozick as a legislator faced with a decision to increase taxation to pay for the justice system to enforce the legal rights that Cornell proposes, such as the tort of sexual harassment, employee rights, Spanish language rights. These are torts, i.e. they give persons rights against others, but they are to be enforced by the state,

---

186 Cornell (2000a) p. 18.
187 Nozick (1974) pp. 333-334.
188 This is restated in Cornell (2000a) p. 3; Cornell (1995) pp. 31-91 .
189 Nozick (1974).

which must be paid for from taxation. Nozick, as legislator, is asked to employ Cornell's test: 'would free and equal persons agree to this?'. For Nozick, to be treated as if you were free is to be treated as if you own all rights over yourself that would be owned by a chattel-slave owner in a slave society. As owners of their labour, free persons have the right to keep anything they earn by the use of their labour. To be taxed above the level required to produce a minimal state[190] is therefore the equivalent of coerced labour, for Nozick. Nozick would argue that free persons should not be forced to pay taxes. Nozick can easily respond to Cornell's test because his position is based upon his own very different understanding of how 'free persons' would want to be treated by the state.

The 'equality' clause in the question is only slightly less straightforward because Nozick views free persons as 'equal'. Nozick's arguments for self-ownership do not result in a society in which there is equality of income and this is not part of his 'ideal'. However, Cornell's test does not address this point. It simply asks the judges and the legislature to speculate upon what free and equal persons would do and to legislate or judge accordingly. Nozick could argue that just as free persons would not be forced to pay taxes above those required for a minimal state, so equal persons – not subject to command by a superior body, neither the state nor a feudal master – would also have the right to keep the product of their labour. It is consistent with Nozick's position to assume that he would construe 'equality' in the context of Cornell's test, as entailing the rights of workers in a capitalist society as contrasted with those of a feudal serf, for example. By appealing to the idea of self-ownership and freedom, Nozick could argue that he was viewing persons as both free and as equal and that this fulfilled Cornell's test. Therefore as legislator he could argue that, applying Cornell's test, 'free and equal persons' would not agree to an increase in taxation to finance anything beyond a minimal state.

This argument could be viewed as unfair to Cornell because it tears away this legal test from her explanation of the development of personhood. I have artificially broken down Cornell's arguments in order to examine them. At this stage it is clear that Cornell cannot answer Nozick's hypothetical argument by limiting herself to the question 'would free and equal persons agree to this?' because both Cornell and Nozick have in play different views of freedom and equality. I will deal with a number of her potential responses, below.

Cornell's test is set up to compare different competing claims of persons in court and arguments to the legislature. Arguments about the framework of taxation laws, as opposed to their application, would have to take place in front of the legislature. As I have argued, there is nothing in Cornell's test that would prevent Nozick from arguing that free and equal persons would not agree to the taxation required to finance her proposed changes in tort law. To oppose this argument, Cornell could resort to the 'Rawlsian' move of expanding her definition of what free and equal persons would want. As outlined above, Rawls expands upon this to produce arguments that are not perfectionist, i.e. they do not dictate what it is to

---

190 For a summary of his position see Nozick (1974) pp. 52-53.

live a good life. However, he provides an answer to the question of what free and equal persons would agree to in a manner that Cornell expressly avoids. I will return to this point in the next section. Alternatively, Cornell could say that it would be Nozick's right to make this argument to his fellow legislators, but that others, with opposing views of what is necessary for their project of being a person, could offer alternative arguments. She could support those arguments on other grounds, but my point is that these could not be derived from her test alone.

The move of speculating what 'free and equal persons' would agree to – which Cornell wants to keep open – is very similar to speculations about life in the state of nature, to be discussed in Chapters 5 and 6.[191] In both cases, there is a thought experiment, an appeal to a different sphere, that supposedly empties the empirical world of some of its content. Later, I will discuss how Macpherson[192] and Pateman[193] both show how Hobbes imports an image of how persons behaved in his own culture into his state of nature. Similarly, Cornell[194] and Okin[195] have demonstrated how Rawls imports stereotyped images of the relationship between the sexes into his discussion of the 'heads of household' making decisions under his veil of ignorance. I want to extend this argument and think about this problem in the context of Cornell's own work.

Whenever theorists produce rules discovered under a veil of ignorance – by speculating, or asking what 'free and equal persons would agree to', or 'how persons would behave in a state of nature' – they have to import some existing views of persons. Failure to do so simply deprives their thought experiment of content. Cornell is conscious of this criticism, especially as she applies the point so effectively against Rawls. She argues that her test keeps open the question of what it is to be a person (and the possibility of change) because the answer is not to be settled for all time, instead the test is to be repeated as a legal test. In other words, she is not dictating what image of a person would be produced – by deciding what would be said under the veil of ignorance (or, by analogy, in the state of nature). However, her test is set up to be applied by the judges and legislature, who would import their own version of what free and equal persons would want, using her test. Whilst Cornell does refuse to imply, in a Rawlsian fashion, a fixed answer to the question of what free and equal persons would agree to, it may be that Cornell does this by the back door.

I want to argue that Cornell does import her image of what it is to be a person. She does this in two ways: firstly, she chooses examples to cash out how the test should be used; and secondly, and more broadly, to make her test work she needs to argue for a particular view of the process of 'individuation' (or how one becomes a

---

191 Cornell describes herself as using the idea of an original contract as a 'heuristic device'. Cornell (1995) p. 242.
192 C.B. Macpherson, *The Political Theory of Possessive Individualism: Hobbes to Locke* (Oxford: Oxford University Press, 1962).
193 Pateman (1988).
194 Cornell (1995) pp. 12-20.
195 Okin (1989) pp. 89-109.

person). Cornell has a choice: either she can resist filling in the gaps and importing her views of what free and equal persons would agree to; or she can provide examples of how it should work. If she chooses the former then she must put up with the fact that others such as Nozick can cash out her test to produce results that, as a socialist feminist, she could not endorse. This is inevitable because left without examples the test is so broad. Elsewhere,[196] I have argued that the judges, who have proved themselves as extremely accomplished at interpreting existing case law in ways that give expression to their own views,[197] would not have their discretion limited by such a broad test. The other alternative (of importing her view of free and equal persons into the test) would involve Cornell making the move that she criticises in Rawls.

Before looking at this in more detail, I want to examine why she may be concerned to avoid this second move by recalling the feminist concerns that are addressed by Cornell's arguments. Cornell's approach – of arguing that women should demand to be treated as free and equal persons by the operation of law – avoids the constraint imposed upon feminist thinking in the face of poststructuralist concerns about the category 'women', as discussed in Chapter 1. Cornell faces the problem that simply viewing women as persons has resulted in the treatment of women as if they were men, viewing male bodies and lifestyles as the norm against which women are compared. This is the case, for example, in the operation of the English *Sex Discrimination Act 1975*, which makes it unlawful to treat a woman 'less favourably than a man'. Cornell's answer to this problem is that the definition of what it is to be a 'person' is not to be viewed as paradigmatically male in her test because the definition of person is to be kept open by the repeated use of her test. It is therefore central to Cornell's argument that she does not fill in the meaning of what it is to be a person. It should also be noted that the way in which her test is proposed, as a practical legal principle, means that it is not to be filled in by persons themselves but by the legislature and by the judiciary, acting on their behalf. Hence my practical concerns about such a broad test.

Cornell, Autonomy and Self-Ownership

In this section, I will expand upon Cornell's image of persons, compared to that of Nozick. Recall that, in order that we should have any hope of being successful in this 'project of becoming a person', Cornell cites three conditions that should be protected by law:

> 1) bodily integrity; 2) access to symbolic forms sufficient to achieve linguistic skills permitting the differentiation of oneself from others and; 3) the protection of the imaginary domain.[198]

---

196 Richardson (1999) pp. 3-31.
197 J.A.G. Griffiths, *The Politics of the Judiciary*, 5th edition (London: Fontana, 1997).
198 Cornell (1995) p. 4.

The differentiation of oneself from others indicates Cornell's vision of 'autonomy'. She does not like the term, preferring to talk of 'individuation' rather than 'autonomy' and 'individual'. She wants the law to protect the process of individuation, by protecting persons' rights by the use of her test. Nozick, in contrast, starts with rights-bearing individuals, not a process of individuation; an entirely different move. Nozick is mentioned in a footnote, in which Cornell is critical of libertarian theories which,

> rest on an atomistic view of the self that is incompatible with an adequate account of how selves come to be persons with their individual identities.[199]

Nozick argues that self-ownership is necessary if persons are to be treated as autonomous. Nozick's persons are already 'individuals' from birth and the question is therefore addressed as to what duties they owe each other. In contrast, Cornell argues for greater legal safeguards than a minimal state could offer so that the law can protect the process of individuation (by which she means the attainment of personhood).[200] She describes this in terms of the law allowing persons space in which to develop. She does not want the law to encourage a particular conception of the good but to defend a person's project of individuation.

Cornell's position is closer to that of the analytic Marxist Gerald Cohen than to Nozick. As part of a number of arguments aimed at undermining the attractiveness of Nozick's argument based upon the assumption of self-ownership, Cohen[201] attacks Nozick's link between self-ownership and autonomy. Cohen defines self-ownership as the premise that we should be treated as if we had the rights of chattel-slave owners over ourselves.[202] Cohen's argument is that Nozick's principles of self-ownership produce a society in which fewer persons have actual autonomy than in other potential societies. For example, the losers in such a society – based upon the unrestrained capitalism that Nozick derives from self-ownership – would have to work for others in unregulated conditions, which Cohen argues, undercuts common ideas of what autonomy involves.[203]

---

199 D. Cornell (2000a) p. 167 fn.11. For an analysis of the meaning of 'atomistic' Cornell cites with approval C. Taylor, 'Atomism' in *Philosophy and the Human Sciences: Philosophical Papers 2* (Cambridge: Cambridge University Press, 1985) pp. 187-210. Taylor attributes 'atomism' to both Hobbes, in Taylor (1985) p. 187 and Nozick, in Taylor (1985) p. 188, amongst others, describing them as sharing 'a vision of society as in some sense constituted by individuals for the fulfilment of ends which were primarily individual' Taylor (1985) p. 187.
200 See Cornell (1995) pp. 4-5.
201 Cohen (1995).
202 Cohen (1995) p. 68.
203 Cohen (1995) pp. 236-238. I return to Cohen's arguments against self-ownership in Chapter 6.

Cornell could adopt a similar argument to that of Cohen, in a manner that is generally consistent with her position, by arguing that her test must be understood to contain her conception of individuation. This works because the society produced according to Nozick's rights of self-ownership would be a society in which Cornell's process of individuation ('the project of becoming a person') would be compromised.

Cohen, like Nozick, is fundamentally concerned with class and with the question of distribution of resources, whereas Cornell is concerned with broader questions of personhood and 'individuation', and focuses upon race and 'sexuate rights' – a term she employs to indicate that she is unwilling to sacrifice issues of sexuality and queer politics to issues of sex/gender. However, Cornell would agree that it is a prerequisite to the process of individuation that persons have access to the minimum material conditions of life for everyone to get off the ground their 'project of becoming a person'. These are not the conditions pertaining in the society that Nozick defends. So, Cornell could argue that her test does not stand alone; that when she states that the law must protect the imaginary domain she implies into her legal test her own understanding of personhood.

To summarise, Cornell could argue that her test 'would free and equal persons agree to this legislation/judgment?' must be read as giving expression to these conditions. This would mean that Nozick (as legislator in my thought experiment) could not read her test 'would free and equal persons agree to this?' by employing his view of what is meant be a 'free and equal person'. Cornell could then maintain that when her test is read so as to give effect to her view of personhood the legislature could assume that 'free and equal persons' would approve taxation statutes to enact and enforce the torts she proposes.

Further, Cornell's test is proposed with the intention that it can be used to consider competing rights between individuals. She could envisage that the 'free and equal persons' whom the legislature should consider would be those in poverty, rather than persons generally. It could be argued that these persons would not agree to living in a capitalist society (or, at the very least would not agree to a society without a welfare state) because such a society would jeopardise their project of becoming a person. The fact that there is no clear answer illustrates the problem of having to fill in Cornell's test, discussed above. Cornell could also argue that any free and equal persons, including those not in poverty, would agree to taxation for welfare. Living in a society that would be produced by Nozick's libertarian capitalism could be viewed as a situation which would jeopardise anyone's project of becoming a person, irrespective of poverty, because of the selfish values that are inculcated, for example.[204]

---

204 For a discussion of the relationship between such 'personal' values and political theory, see G.A. Cohen, *If You're an Egalitarian, How Come You're So Rich?* (Harvard: Harvard University Press, 2001).

Can Cornell make this move and still claim that she is not defining the content of what it is to be a person, thereby getting round the dilemma I proposed above? In other words, could she argue that her process of individuation is distinct from giving content to personhood? It is my view that the same dilemma does apply. This can be seen by considering which version of a society she would want the legislature to consider. This has to be filled in at some point. Either it is filled in by Cornell, which she explicitly wants to avoid, or it is filled in by the legislature/judge who may be open to a number of arguments as to what free and equal persons would agree to.

Comparison with Themes from Chapter 2

Both Nozick and Cornell are concerned with 'our conception of ourselves'. For Cornell our 'imaginary domain' should be protected by law. I want to give a more detailed account of Cornell's image of what it is to be a person, and the process of individuation, by comparing this with the general points about the self discussed in Chapter 2. In Chapter 2, I drew out the following common properties from contemporary views of the self, as an ontological concept (as contrasted with a person as a legal concept, as a self that is subject to law) by Oyama, Clark and Battersby:

1. there is an emphasis upon the embedded, embodied nature of cognition/self;

2. this results in an image of cognition/self that tends to focus upon their emergent properties;

3. linked with this, they are concerned with thinking of cognition/the self as dynamic rather than fixed;

4. there is an attack upon the subject/object divide (in Clark's work this is cognition/environment split) as traditionally conceived and a move to characterise the emergent process as one which involves rethinking this divide;

5. there is a shift away from the importance of centralised control.

How does Cornell's image of personhood and 'individuation' differ from this broad approach? Considering point 1, she has an image of personhood that is embodied and sexed. Sexuality is central to the project of becoming a person. She argues that,

> Since, psychoanalytically, the imaginary is inseparable from one's sexual imago, it demands that no one be forced to have another's imaginary imposed upon him or herself in such a way as to rob him or her of respect for his or her sexuate being.

Thus, what John Rawls has argued is a primary good, namely self-respect, is integrated into the very idea of the imaginary domain itself.[205]

This allows her to talk about the need for 'sexuate rights' as necessary for the laws' protection of this project, an argument that she supports without the need to depend upon psychoanalysis. It can be derived from the view that sexual identity is important to our image of who we are in our culture. There are potential arguments about the extent to which her image of a person is embedded. It is not 'embedded' in the same way as discussed in Chapter 2 because Cornell emphasises the imaginary domain and attempts to think 'as if from outer space'[206] in order to produce social change, and this methodology differs from the stress placed upon the emergence of change by changes in bodily habit, discussed in Chapter 2. However, Cornell's view of personhood is culturally embedded. This can be illustrated by the way in which she compares her work, derived from Hegel, to that of libertarians, discussed above. In her chapter 'Worker's Rights and the Defense of Just-Cause Statutes'[207] Cornell distinguishes her position from those influenced by Hobbes, and from theorists who start with the individual rather than a process of individuation of oneself from others. I will return to the work of Hobbes and self-ownership in Chapters 5 and 6.

Turning to point 2, Cornell's view of personhood as a project certainly implies the idea of the emergence of a person. Further,

A person is not something 'there' on this understanding, but a possibility, an aspiration which, because it is that, can never be fulfilled once and for all. The person is, in other words, implicated in an endless process of working through personae. On this definition, the person is neither identical with the self or the traditional philosophical subject.[208]

Point 3 is linked with this. For Cornell, the 'person' is not fixed. She envisages a process of transformation that is never complete.

Turning to point 4, Cornell starts with an image of individuals who are not separate from each other but then have to work at this separation between self and other. This split from the other is viewed in Lacanian terms, with an emphasis upon the symbolic. The law is called upon to protect,

---

205 Cornell (1995) p. 8.
206 Florence (1997) p. 15.
207 Cornell (2000a) pp. 83-117. A just-cause statute demands that employers apply justice to their reasons for a worker's dismissal and can be called upon to explain them. In England the common law of employment at will, which Cornell attacks, has been superseded by legislation granting workers rights against 'unfair dismissal'. This applies a reasonableness test. Similarly, Cornell advocates a 'rational cause' rather than a 'just cause' to avoid speculations about justice, Cornell (2000a) p. 84.
208 Cornell (1995) p. 5.

access to symbolic forms sufficient to achieve linguistic skills permitting the differentiation of oneself from others.[209]

The question about the relationship between subject and object in Cornell's work is derived from Hegel. In her later work, her emphasis is upon intersubjectivity which is to include women – rather than the relationship between subject and object.[210] This point can be illustrated by considering her analysis of the labour contract. She contrasts her theory, derived from Hegel, with accounts derived from Hobbes which she views as a deep influence upon the 'libertarian perspective adopted by the law and economics literature'.[211] What is at stake is not the question of regulation of the employment relationship but,

> what view of regulation truly promotes individual freedom...for Hegel state regulation is done in the name of the ideal reciprocal symmetry.[212]

This ties in with her discussion of the subject,

> For Hegel, reconciliation with the community in modernity is always mediated by the subject who comes to understand her community as a response to her own demand.[213]

Turning to point 5, recall that the law is called upon to protect access to symbolic forms in order to achieve linguistic skills which permit the differentiation of oneself from others.[214] From this it can be seen that Cornell does have an emphasis upon 'centralised control' of a person's actions, rather than the focus upon bodily habits or problem solving that characterised the approach of Clark, Battersby and Oyama outlined in Chapter 2. What is most important for Cornell is the ideal; she defends the notion that we can change our lives as a result of imagination. Adopting the approach from Chapter 2, I would argue that this is too 'top-down' and that it is also necessary to start from an analysis of what we do in our daily lives rather than what we imagine ourselves to be. However, I do not want to overstate the distinction between these approaches. For example, none of the approaches in Chapter 2 deny the importance of ideas and their material effects and Cornell would not deny the importance of daily activity. The difference lies in their emphasis.

This point is linked with the argument, discussed in Chapter 1, about the relationship between theory and political practice. Foucault and Deleuze[215] argue that it is possible to envisage a situation in which it is necessary to act, such that

---

209 Cornell (1995) p. 4.
210 Cornell (2000a) p. 85.
211 Cornell (2000a) p. 97.
212 Cornell (2000a) p. 97.
213 Cornell (2000a) p. 96.
214 Cornell (1995) p. 4.
215 Foucault and Deleuze (1980) pp. 205-217.

practice forms a link between different theoretical positions, and conversely that theory can provide a move between different practices. Similarly, it is possible to think about the relationship between feminist theory and practice in terms that can be both 'top-down' – in that ideas promote different practices (as emphasised by Cornell) – and 'bottom-up', so that different bodily practices open up different theoretical positions.

Chapter 4

Tort and the Technology of Risk

I want to turn from Cornell's arguments for the reform of tort law, based upon her original reworking of personhood, to consider the operation of tort law in current legal practice. This involves examining a different relationship between the person and law but my aim continues to be to highlight the ambiguity of women's current position with regard to personhood in order to rethink its meaning. To do so I will employ François Ewald's work on insurance. Insurance plays a central role in legal practice – a point that is lost if the focus is upon perfecting legal tests for liability derived from political philosophy, such as that proposed by Cornell.[216] Insurance is now compulsory in all areas in which there is a risk of being sued in tort, for example when persons act as employers, producers of products, professionals, road-traffic users or home owners. It is the insurance system that allows the operation of tort as a system of loss distribution.

Ewald[217] expressly draws upon Foucault's analysis of 'governmentality' from Foucault's late lectures, to be discussed below. In doing so Ewald brings together two areas of social theory that have become popular areas of research in recent years: risk analysis, as illustrated by Beck's *Risk Society*[218] and the 'governmentality' literature influenced by Foucault.[219] Analysing techniques of government that employ a 'scientific approach' to risk analysis, Ewald considers the way in which insurance companies have altered the operation of this area of law in France. I want to illustrate how this work is useful for understanding the English

---

216 See J. Richardson, 'Feminist Perspectives on the Law of Tort and the Technology of Risk', *Economy and Society*, forthcoming, in which I situate the common law within the literature on risk and uncertainty. Here, the focus is upon selfhood and personhood.

217 F. Ewald, 'Norms, Discipline and the Law' in R. Post, ed., *Law and the Order of Culture* (California: University of California Press, 1991b) pp. 138-161; F. Ewald 'Insurance and Risk' in G. Burchell, C. Gordon and P. Miller, eds., *The Foucault Effect: Studies in Governmentality* (Chicago: University of Chicago Press, 1991) pp. 197-210; F. Ewald 'The Return of Descartes's Malicious Demon: An Outline of a Philosophy of Precaution' in T. Baker and J. Simon, *Embracing Risk: The Changing Culture of Insurance and Responsibility* (Chicago: University of Chicago Press, 2002) pp. 273-301.

218 U. Beck, *Risk Society: Towards a New Modernity* (London: Sage, 1992).

219 Particularly influential are: M. Foucault, 'Governmentality' in J.D. Faubion, ed., *Michel Foucault: Power, The Essential Works 3* (London: Penguin Press, 2001a) pp. 208-209; M. Foucault, 'Omnes et Singulatim: Towards a Criticism of Political Reason' in S. McMurrin, ed., *The Tanner Lectures on Human Values, Vol. II*, Salt Lake City: University of Utah Press, 1991a) pp. 225-254. For early collections of governmentality papers: A. Barry, T. Osbourne, and N. Rose, eds., *Foucault and Political Reason: Liberalism, Neo-Liberalism and Rationalities of Government* (London: UCL Press, 1996); Burchell et al (1991).

common law tradition as compared with the French codified tradition with which Ewald is concerned. Secondly, I will argue that a feminist analysis opens up points that are ignored by Ewald: an examination of the risks associated with traditional women's lifestyles, such as the risk of loss of income upon divorce, risk of rape and of unwanted birth. These are considered in order to bring out the different ways in which women's position strains the usual images of personhood. This includes both the image of the 'self-owning individual' who is envisaged as owning and insuring his/her abilities as if they were commodities (which is discussed in more detail in Chapters 5 and 6) and alternative views of the self that draw upon Foucault's late work on governmentality.

In the next chapter I will look in detail at the work of Thomas Hobbes. The role of insurance can be considered by comparing the insurance contracts discussed in this chapter and Hobbes' hypothetical 'social contract'. As I will illustrate, by the twentieth century insurance became viewed as a safeguard against future harm by providing a mechanism for the distribution of loss. Similarly, the aim of the hypothetical social contract was to safeguard a 'commodious life'[220] by technical means. As Dean has commented,

> The political imaginary is of a contractual form of justice established no longer of a natural order of rights but by the conventions of society, and of an ideal of a society in which each member's burdens and shares are fixed by social contract which is no longer a political myth but something made real by technical means...The socialisation of risk does not seek to undermine capitalist inequality. Precisely the opposite: it is a means of treating the effects of that inequality.[221]

Similarly, Ewald[222] discusses the way that the use of insurance in France at the end of the nineteenth century lead to a change in political beliefs: it was no longer necessary to try to legitimise society by appealing to arguments such as those of Hobbes' social contract. If everyone was already a party to insurance contracts – whereby they would pay to be supported in times of need – then they would already be 'locked into' society. This concern with legitimation, which Ewald describes but does not share, starts with a view of individualism that is the focus of later chapters. If insurance provides the dream of a 'contractual form of justice',[223] based upon the hope that risks could be shared on the basis of need then it has obviously not been implemented; neither has it been an ambition that has been extended to women's traditional risks. I will start by detailing Ewald's arguments in the context of the English common law then move to a consideration of feminist issues that arise from

220 T. Hobbes, *Leviathan*, E. Curley, ed. (Cambridge: Hackett Publishing Ltd. 1994b) Ch. XIII, s. 14, p. 78.
221 M. Dean, *Governmentality: Power and Rule in Modern Society* (London: Sage, 1999). p. 186.
222 Ewald (1991a) pp. 209-210.
223 Dean (1999) p. 186.

this model. Finally, I will return to Cornell's work to consider it in the context of Ewald's historical analysis.

Governmentality and the Common Law

Ewald's method of thinking about insurance and the way in which 'European societies come to analyse themselves and their problems in terms of the generalized technology of risk'[224] explicitly draws from the late 'governmentality' work of Foucault. Foucault's conception of governmentality is linked with his conception of selfhood as illustrated by the following quotation:

> I am saying that 'governmentality' implies the relationship of the self to itself, and I intend the concept of 'governmentality' to cover the whole range of practices that constitute, define, organize and instrumentalize the strategies that individuals in their freedom can use in dealing with one another.[225]

'Governmentality' is therefore viewed as a series of practices that are involved in governing oneself, the household or the state. To unpack this, I will sketch Foucault's historical approach.

Foucault[226] discusses a transition that takes place in the relationship between the human body and sovereignty. Prior to the seventeenth century, the display of the King's body was a symbol of power. Foucault then points to a change in which the bodies of the subjects replaced the King's body as the focus of attention. He describes the development, in the seventeenth and eighteenth centuries, of the 'technology of labour' or 'disciplinary power' in which the maximum work was extracted from the workers' bodies. This technology was (and is) concerned with the spacial distribution of bodies, linked with surveillance and with repetitive bodily movements, such as soldier's drill or worker's adaptation to machines. He describes the emergence, in the eighteenth century, of a different technique of power, which modifies – rather than simply replaces – this technology of labour. This newer technology of power is described as the 'biopolitics of race'. This is addressed – not at individual bodies – but at populations: bodies as a 'global mass' and involves the management of birth, death, illness, production of food and the means of life. This administration of life involves inspection of details and the measurement of individuals against a norm, both the medical and educational examination being examples of these. In his essay on Governmentality, Foucault[227]

---

224 F. Ewald 'Insurance and Risk' in Burchell et al (1991) p. 210.
225 M. Foucault, 'The Ethics of the Concern for the Self as a Practice of Freedom' in M. Foucault, *The Essential Works: 1954-1984 Vol. 1, Ethics, Subjectivity and Truth* P. Rabinow, ed. (New York: The New Press, 1997c) p. 300.
226 M. Foucault, *History of Sexuality Volume One: An Introduction* (London: Penguin, 1981a) pp. 135-159.
227 Foucault (2001a).

illustrates how government became viewed as the management – or guidance of the conduct of – the relationship between persons and things: wealth, resources and territory but also accidents and misfortunes.

As I will illustrate below, Ewald's analysis of insurance takes up this work by viewing insurance as a technique for the governance of life. Unlike the common law tort system, the French civil code introduced a 'no fault' compensation system. This means that someone who suffers an injury as a result of a faulty medical operation, workplace or road traffic accident, for example, will be compensated through state insurance irrespective of whether or not another party was at fault. The compensation awarded is based upon the extent of the injury. It is Foucault's argument that the development of such 'no fault' compensation in France allowed civil law to be considered in terms of the distribution of the risk of injury. He argued that this move (in civil law) facilitated a similar shift in perspective with regard to crime, such that criminals became viewed as a locus of risk:

> By eliminating the element of fault within the system of liability, the civil legislators introduced into law the notion of causal probability and of risk, and they brought forward the idea of a sanction whose function would be to defend, to protect, to exert pressure on inevitable risks…Just as one can determine civil liability without establishing fault – but solely by estimating the risk created and against which it is necessary to build up a defense (although it can never be eliminated) – in the same way, one can render an individual responsible under the law without having to determine whether he was acting freely and, therefore, whether there was fault, but rather, by linking the act committed to the risk of criminality his very personality constitutes.[228]

Given that the English common law still relies upon proof of individual fault, it does not appear initially to fit within this analysis. However, I want to argue that this approach does, in fact, shed light upon different aspects of the common law tort system. This can be illustrated by Lord Denning's argument about the aims of tort law in the case of *Nettleship v Weston* (a tort case in which a driving instructor claimed in negligence against his pupil for the injuries he sustained when she crashed) that,

> Thus we are, in this branch of the law, moving away from the concept: 'No liability without fault.' We are beginning to apply the test: 'On whom should the risk fall?' Morally the learner driver is not at fault; but legally she is liable to be because she is insured and the risk should fall on her.[229]

Denning is unusual in that judges tend to avoid acknowledging that law takes account of the role of insurance. There is some evidence that this is a factor in their

---

228 M. Foucault, 'About the Concept of the "Dangerous Individual"' in J.D. Faubion, ed., *Michel Foucault: Power, The Essential Works 3* (London: Penguin Press, 2001b) p. 197.
229 *Nettleship v Weston* (1971) 2 QB 691, 700.

decisions.[230] Tort text books[231] deal with the aims of tort law by contrasting nineteenth century judicial attitudes which were based upon the idea that individuals should only be responsible for injuries caused by their own fault (a 'fault-based' approach), with twentieth century attitudes towards the use of insurance in order to spread risk (the 'solidarity' approach). This fits within Ewald's[232] analysis of risk paradigms – albeit that in France the solidarity approach is taken to its logical conclusion in the employment of no fault compensation:

> The nineteenth century saw the dominance of a paradigm of responsibility. In the twentieth century this was fundamentally transformed: the prevailing paradigm was one of solidarity...The paradigm of responsibility posits a certain economy of rights and duties in which the part played by moral obligations towards oneself and others is far greater than that of legal obligations...By contrast, the paradigm of solidarity, which is associated with the welfare state, considerably extends the role of legal obligations.[233]

In England, this move to solidarity has, in some cases, occurred by the back door, as for example in *Nettleship v Weston*. This case, like all negligence cases, was argued in terms of legal fault but Lord Denning's decision was clearly based upon the idea of loss distribution: the view that the insured party was able to pay and therefore should be held liable for the injury in law.

In order to consider the extent to which the common law can be viewed as a hybrid of what Ewald refers to as the 'juridical theory of responsibility' and insurance, I want to outline the way in which Ewald distinguishes between these and to consider the position of the common law in each case. As Ewald puts it,

> Insurance and law are two practices of responsibility which operate quite heterogeneous categories, regimes, economics; as such they are mutually exclusive in their claims to totality.[234]

In other words, there is a conflict between the nineteenth century civil system in which judges make decisions based upon fault (which still applies in the common law today – in theory if not always in practice) and the idea of insurance against losses. Insurance directly challenges the practice of law because 'insurance and the law of responsibility are two techniques which bear on the same object'.[235] This 'direct challenge' can be illustrated by comparing the impact of insurance with that

---

230 See for example H. Genn, *Hard Bargaining: Out of Court Settlement in Personal Injury Claims* (Oxford: Oxford University Press, 1987).
231 See, for example, M. Lunney and K. Oliphant, *Tort Law: Text and Materials* (Oxford: Oxford University Press, 2000) pp. 18-28.
232 Ewald (2002).
233 Ewald (2002) p. 273. He points to a more recent paradigm of prevention.
234 Ewald (1991a) p. 201.
235 Ewald (1991a) p. 201.

of the discipline of sociology.[236] Sociology undermines the idea of individual responsibility when, for example, Durkheim shows that the rate of suicide is consistent in a particular culture because it prompts an analysis of social factors rather than individual ones. Nevertheless, it does not 'directly challenge' tort law that focuses upon individual fault because its conclusions can be ignored in the daily practice of the courts. The operation of insurance, however, can actually replace the law of tort as a method of compensation for injuries. Where this has occurred, as in France, the use of insurance brings with it a different way of viewing injuries.

Whilst the common law appears to be part of the old system that is fault-based, it is my argument that the position is more complex. The common law is more of a fudge because it is pervaded by ideas of loss distribution and the techniques of insurance, whilst it still appears to remain unchanged from its nineteenth century concern with fault. This can be illustrated by Denning's quotation cited above when he decided a case on the grounds that: 'Morally the learner driver is not at fault; but legally she is liable to be because she is insured and the risk should fall on her.'[237]

In order to unravel the position of the common law of obligations (and the implications for thinking about personhood) I will go through Ewald's analysis in detail. In 'Insurance and Risk' Ewald[238] distinguishes between the impact of law and that of insurance by analysing risk in terms of three characteristics: that it is calculable, collective and it is a 'capital'. I will deal with each in turn. Firstly, he contrasts the approach of insurance with that of law based upon responsibility by arguing that, from the view of law, accidents could be avoided whereas anyone who works within the insurance industry calculates risks by working out the consistent figures of, for example, workplace injuries each year. This is akin to the argument about suicide that I have just discussed. From the point of view of judges, the individual defendant should have avoided the accident but from the point of view of insurers a certain number of accidents occur each year. I agree that these are different positions. However, the stress upon individual fault, discussed by current English common law judges, ignores the fact that the system depends upon the operation of insurance. In most cases the defendant, such as an employer, will have compulsory insurance and the case will either be settled by their insurers or conducted by their insurer's lawyers. The technology of risk is central to the process of tort.

The second of Ewald's points is particularly interesting with regard to the question of personhood and individualisation, to be discussed further at the end of this chapter. Ewald argues that,

> Insurance provides a form of association which combines a maximum of socialisation with a maximum of individuation. It allows people to enjoy the advantages of association while still leaving them free to exist as individuals. It

---

236 Ewald (1991a) p. 201.
237 *Nettleship v Weston* (1971) 2 QB 691, 700.
238 Ewald (1991a).

seems to reconcile those two antagonists, society-socialization and individual liberty.[239]

In other words, by insuring against an accident it is possible to share in loss distribution, using a technology that depends upon a calculation involving a population. It would be impossible to calculate the risk of a one-off incident because risk, by definition, is in the form of a calculation that a given number within a given population will suffer a certain fate. Nevertheless, as Ewald[240] puts it, insurers leave you alone. They are not like families, trade unions or other forms of mutual association that had/have a moral or educative function. Hence, they combine the social element of risk calculation and loss distribution with one of individualisation.

The common law, as critical lawyers[241] have been fast to point out, continues to individualise; to view accidents through the lens of the individuals concerned rather than within a broader social context. The only 'interference' from insurers comes in the form of attempts to amend high risk behaviour on behalf of potential defendants, such as employers, and carries with it the sanction of refusing to insure. Employees are encouraged to join trade unions as a form of insurance against legal actions. However, these are not likely to moralise as their role has shifted from collective action to providing such individual support for legal claims.[242]

Thirdly, Ewald describes risk as capital. This appears an odd term because it is not being used in the Marxist sense of being part of a process involving the exploitation of labour power. He argues that what is insured is not the injury itself but 'a capital against whose loss the insurer offers a guarantee'[243] and describes how insurance developed from insurance of shipping through to the development of life insurance, viewed as insuring 'human capital', and the linked view that one's ability to work can be insured:

> One can always argue that life and health are things beyond price. But the practice of life, health and accident insurance constantly attests that everything can have a price, that all of us have a price and that this price is not the same for all.[244]

In the section on wrongful births I will discuss the way that the position of women who have unwanted children as a result of negligent sterilisation represents the limit of this view.

---

239 Ewald (1991a) p. 204.
240 Ewald (1991a) p. 203.
241 For example, Conaghan and Mansell (1999).
242 S. Deakin, 'The Many Futures of the Contract of Employment' in J. Conaghan, R.M. Fischel and K. Klare, *Labour Law in an Era of Globalisation: Transformative Practices and Possibilities* (Oxford: Oxford University Press, 2002) pp. 177-196.
243 Ewald (1991a) p. 204.
244 Ewald (1991a) p. 204.

Ewald compares legal damages with insurance compensation by claiming that legal damages aim to compensate for the injury in full whereas insurance is set by a tariff. When Ewald discusses how strange it is to attempt to fix the cost of an injury he does not detail the way in which the law of tort calculates compensation (because his concern is with the French system, which is based upon insurance). However, to support my point that the common law, whilst appearing fault-based, is riddled with the technology of risk, I want to illustrate how damages are calculated.

Issues such as the risk of an early death are dealt with by using insurer's mortality tables. They allow lawyers to quantify the likelihood of death for different ages and sexes, thereby quantifying the loss of expectation of life. With the increase in medical techniques, such as genetic analysis, this sort of calculation will become more sophisticated. The fact that the calculation can be very technical does not, of course, mean that the initial figure can actually represent lost years of life. The aim is to make sure that injuries are graded in terms of compensation.

Whereas issues such as loss of years of life and loss of earnings are subject to calculation, different heads of damage are simply allocated a 'price' and lawyers negotiate by looking at previous cases. So, for example heads of damage such as 'pain and suffering' or 'loss of amenity' will be compared between similar cases. Unlike Ewald, I do not think that this approach is much different in principle from the imposition of insurance tariffs. It differs only in that it is more uncertain and hence time consuming and costly in terms of negotiation. The nuances and hence inefficiency involved in calculation of damages may make this a dated historical compromise.[245]

Dealing with uncertainty and calculations of risk is central to the civil litigation process when determining the question of liability as well as that of damages. The legal test of negligence incorporates risk (and uncertainty) within the reasonable person test, discussed in the last chapter. For example, the reasonable person as employer must calculate (or estimate) the risk of injury to employees, the severity of potential harm, the sensitivity of any employees and weigh these against the cost of taking action to minimise the source of danger.[246]

---

245 The Chief Medical Officer has made recommendations on clinical negligence cases and the introduction of no fault compensation, see P. Walsh, 'Editorial', *Clinical Risk*, Vol. 9, No. 2, 2003, p. 66. It is my argument that the current English system fits within this model but in a way that is inefficient within the parameters of the system itself. For discussion of these comments: B. Mahendra, 'Revisiting No Fault Compensation', *New Law Journal*, Vol. 151, No. 6987, 2001, p. 837; for the argument for no-fault compensation: U. Essen, 'Tort compensation for victims of Medical Accidents', *New Law Journal*, June 2001, pp. 846-854.

246 A comparable approach to risk occurs within contract law in which the question of who bears the burden of the risk of any particular harm is negotiated as part of the contract. For this reason, O'Malley, a legal theorist interested in risk analysis, has argued that the development of contract law provides a 'blueprint for government through uncertainty'. P. O'Malley, 'Uncertain Subjects: Risks, Liberalism and Contract', *Economy and Society*, Vol. 29, No. 4, 2000. See also Richardson (forthcoming).

In the context of Foucauldian influenced work it is important to note that this 'reasonable person' is not necessarily the 'average person', derived from statistical analysis. Judges decide what is reasonable behaviour (such as to satisfy the reasonable person test) and this may well differ from what the statistically average person would do. Both the reasonable person/man and the average man are fictions that are used in these different methods of judging individuals. In 'Norms, Discipline and the Law' Ewald[247] describes how Quetelet, with his theory of the average man,

> proposes a means of specifying individuals with reference to their position within a group, rather than by paying attention to their essence, their nature or their ideal state of being. The theory of the average man, then, is an instrument that makes it possible to understand a population with respect only to itself, and without recourse to some external defining factor.[248]

This allows Ewald to argue that the insurer's risk (as an objective principle of calculation and distribution) corresponds with the idea of the 'average man' in Quetelet's work. Unlike the reference to the 'reasonable man' in law, risk analysis makes no claims about morality but allows,

> the group to make social judgements with respect to itself in a way that always reflects the current state of society.[249]

This leads to Ewald's argument that insurance then offers a new rule of justice that no longer refers back to nature but to the existence of the group. A more precise description would be that the insurance rules are determined by insurance companies regulated by law. These rules are not random but are calculated according to the probabilities of risk. His point is that insurance replaces fault-based 'justice' with a 'justice' based upon the distribution of loss. Importantly, this distribution is based upon rules that depend upon a 'science of risk' and not upon charity. By the end of the nineteenth century such calculation of risk becomes integral to the way in which industrialised society views itself.

In Ewald's analysis of insurance as capital, he argues that, before social insurance covered workplace accidents in France, the possibility of workers taking litigation against their employers for compensation allowed them to take part in a struggle for individual dignity. The courts could publicly state that the employer was wrong. I think this is unhelpful. To view the common law in these terms would be a mistake because it ignores the extent to which insurance alters the operation of the common law. Employee claimants soon discover that they are not fighting their employers but their employers' insurers, whose specialist lawyers will make a commercial decision about compromising a case. It is clear that compulsory

---

247 Ewald (1991b) p. 146.
248 Ewald (1991b) p. 146.
249 Ewald (1991b) p. 146.

insurance in most areas of personal injury litigation means that the defendant rarely has control of the case. This will result in a settlement without trial in approximately 98% of cases.[250] These settlements may also contain confidentiality agreements as part of the compromise (which is why the figure is approximate). There is also concern that in serious cases the claimant[251] should enjoy the money before dying, a factor which allows insurance companies to settle such cases more cheaply.

Following from his description of these three aspects of risk, Ewald makes an important distinction between fault-based law and insurance and their link with liberalism:

> Liberal thought held that the attribution by nature of goods and ills is, of itself, just...It followed from this approach that judicial decisions on accident compensation had to be linked to investigation of the cause of the injury: it had to be ascertained whether a damage was due to natural causes, or to some person who should bear the cost. The problem was one of putting things back in order. Insurance proposes quite a different idea of justice: the idea of cause is replaced by the idea of distributive sharing of a collective, to which each member's contribution can be fixed by a rule.[252]

The common law fudges this distinction. Judges appear to continue fault-based liability by asking whether the defendant's action fell below the standard of the reasonable person, for example. However, the system would not work without compulsory insurance and so the vast majority of cases settle by negotiation with the insurer's lawyers. In addition, judges – at different times – look to see which party is insured and so should carry the burden, as Denning's quotation makes plain. The insurance industry takes into account the 'fixed rate' set by the courts instead of by the legislature as a tariff.

In Ewald's quotation above, he claims that judges in fault-based litigation ask the question: was the damage due to natural causes or was it someone's fault? In the 'wrongful birth' cases, discussed below, women are in the curious position of suffering damage that becomes classified as both 'natural' *and* as 'someone's fault'. Similarly, the ability to give birth, in some instances, disturbs the idea that all abilities can be classed as 'human capital' or commodities owned by the woman.

---

250 This is the estimated figure in F. Furedi, *Courting Mistrust: the Hidden Growth of a Culture of Litigation in Britain* (London: Centre for Policy Studies, 1999) p. 5. See also, Genn (1987).

251 For ease of reference, I have employed the nomenclature of the Civil Procedure Rules whether or not the case in question was subject to these rules at the time. I have therefore consistently referred to 'claimant' rather than 'plaintiff'.

252 Ewald (1991a) p. 206.

Women's Risks

I want to highlight different ways in which women's traditional risks fail to fit within the usual risk 'paradigms' (as neither fault-based compensation nor loss-based distribution) in order to think about the difficulties that the courts now have with their image of women. The most obvious way in which women continue to be excluded from insurance is by virtue of making up a disproportionate number of low paid workers. Ewald quotes Proudhon's argument that insurance is based upon the ability to insure rather than upon need, and so 'insurance proves itself a new privilege for the rich and a cruel irony for the poor'.[253] As women earn less than men this point applies to them. However, the problems of women's risks runs deeper than this.

In his historical analysis, Ewald ignores the position of housewives. It is clear that women are only parties to workers' insurance contracts as employees. Women's position within the home can be safeguarded with life insurance (against the death of her husband or partner) and mortgage indemnity insurance, but there is no insurance against a housewife's loss of income upon divorce. In 1942 Beveridge proposed that the benefits associated with unemployment should be extended to cover those women who had been separated from their (male) breadwinner. His anxiety was that housewives who were not 'at fault' may lose their livelihood and be ineligible for maintenance. He recognised the different positions of husband and wife in the following way:

> If [the needs caused by divorce, legal separation, desertion and voluntary separation] are regarded from the point of view of the husband, they may not appear to be insurable risks; a man cannot insure against events which occur only through his fault or with his consent, and if they occur through the fault or with the consent of the wife she should not have a claim to benefit. But from the point of view of the woman, loss of her maintenance as housewife without her consent and not through her fault is one of the risks of marriage against which she should be insured; she should not depend upon assistance.[254]

Beveridge's proposal to extend benefits into this new area of risk and to view housewives as a new category of persons who could be insured were rejected. In 1974 the Finer Committee[255] proposed a 'guaranteed maintenance allowance' as a means of ensuring a regular source of income for women and children upon divorce or separation. Again, this was rejected by the government of the day, leaving traditional housewives to claim maintenance through the courts with welfare benefits as an interim measure.

---

253 Ewald (1991a) p. 206.
254 W. Beveridge, *Social Insurance and Allied Services* (Cmnd. 6404) (London: HMSO, 1942) para. 347.
255 M. Finer, *Report of the Committee on One Parent Families* (Cmnd. 5629) (London: HMSO, 1974)

It does not require any of the sophisticated analyses of the emergence of self and other though relationality, discussed in Chapter 2, to recognise the difficulty of trying to establish fault in marriage. The writers of one of the main family law textbooks[256] (rightly) note the practical difficulty of attributing blame and also the difficulty in reconciling ideals of collective security and individual fault. Curiously, they then make the following comment about wives:

> In a welfare state, the moral virtue of contributing to a scheme which will provide relief against, for example, sickness and unemployment – both your own and your neighbours' – is, one hopes, self-evident. Contributing to a scheme which provides relief for the wives in other people's broken marriages, however, is not so easy to justify.[257]

If a woman has given up work to bring up a family and is without means because of separation or divorce then why is her loss of livelihood not viewed as akin to unemployment? The appeal to public sentiment, in the above quotation, is an appeal to the public/private divide in which women's work within the home is unacknowledged and viewed as natural. Despite the increase in women engaged in paid work, the feminisation of poverty upon divorce still makes this an important contemporary issue. The question of insurance for the risk of child birth, to be discussed in the next section, further illustrates the continuing view of women's traditional work of child care as 'natural'.

The insurance industry has recently moved into other areas, as illustrated by the offer of insurance to women in South Africa against the possibility of being raped and contracting HIV. The insurance offers them tests and treatment that are not available within their impoverished health service. Although I am concerned with the operation of the common law of obligations, this example is relevant because it illustrates a similar technique for the management of risk. From the view of technologies of risk, we represent different risks to each other. The criminal represents a risk as does a doctor or any person who may negligently cause injury. The same techniques of risk analysis can quantify them. It may be that I would be more upset by the same injury knowing that the person who inflicted it did so on purpose, because this could undermine, for example, my view of the world. However, for the calculation of risk, this can be viewed as 'trauma', as an additional part of the injury. This does nothing to undermine the possibility of the calculation of risk itself. As I have discussed, Foucault points out that we construct ourselves as subjects with the state as protector against sources of risk, including each other.[258] Whilst he discusses the construction of the criminal as a source of

---

256 B. Hoggett, D. Pearl, E. Cooke, P. Bates, *The Family, Law and Society: Cases and Materials*, 4th edition, (London: Butterworths, 1996) p. 104.
257 Hoggett et al (1996) p. 104.
258 Foucault (1976).

risk, the same reasoning applies to the law of obligations, with the assessment of systems – such as safety in factories, the operation of NHS, education – through audits that can alter the nature of the activity.[259]

From a feminist perspective the horror evoked by the example of South African women is important. It brings home the daily fear of these women for whom a more long term solution is obviously vital, but it also disrupts the usual image of insurance. This disruptive quality becomes obvious when women's position – outside the 'norm' – is examined. In England, rape is a crime and also a tort so that it is possible to sue for an injunction and damages. The Criminal Injuries Compensation Board Scheme allows the victim of any violent crime to obtain automatic compensation from the state. This is based upon a tariff system.[260] Victims can have awards rejected or reduced because their 'lifestyle' is deemed to put them at risk.[261] So, for example, the fact that a woman was a prostitute would be an objection to a rape claim. In this instance, the woman is outside the protection or 'social contract' provided by insurance. I now want to turn to a further set of cases in which risks associated with women's tradition lifestyle have been considered in detail by the courts.

Wrongful Birth Cases

In the last twenty years the so-called 'wrongful birth' cases have developed in tort law. In these cases, parents have taken negligence claims usually against a health authority or trust, on the basis that a faulty sterilisation operation, or incorrect advice, had lead to the birth of an unwanted child. The defendant health authority would be covered by insurance policies for negligence in these cases.

---

259 For a discussion of the 'audit explosion' see, for example, N. Rose, *Powers of Freedom: Reframing Political Thought* (Cambridge: Cambridge University Press, 1999b) pp. 153-155; M. Power, *The Audit Society: Rituals of Verification* (Oxford: Oxford University Press, 1997).

260 An earlier controversial case was that involving Meah in which he was awarded £45,000 compensation in a civil court for a road traffic accident which caused brain damage and allegedly caused him to engage in sexually aggressive behaviour. (*Meah v Creamer* (1985) 1 All ER 367). This award can be compared with the compensation of two of Meah's victims who sued him for sexual assault (award: £6,750) and rape (award: £10,250) *W v Meah, D v Meah* (1986) 1 All ER 935. These cases held that rape was to be classified as a personal injury. They were distinguished in *Griffiths v Williams* (1995) (unreported) *The Times*, 24 November. It was held that views of rape had changed and that £50,000 award was not too high. Under the current tariff system of the CICA in which 'repeated non-consensual vaginal and/or anal intercourse over a period exceeding 3 years' has a tariff of £17,500.

261 *Criminal Injuries Compensation Scheme 1996 para. 13-16*; enabling Act: *Criminal Injuries Compensation Act 1995*.

I am interested in the 'wrongful birth' cases because of the reasons why the House of Lords has moved away from standard principles of tort law. Central to this is the fact that women's position brings out a tension that already exists in the courts' view of personhood. This tension is implicit in the image of the person who insures his or her abilities as if they were commodities. This is exacerbated by considering the position of women because historically women have not been linked with this image of the possessive individual, who owns her abilities and must be compensated for work performed. To explain this further I will look a case in more detail below.

The main case in the area is the House of Lords decision in *McFarlane v Tayside Health Board (1999)*,[262] the only case of this type to come before the Lords. They decided that, provided a child is born healthy, awarding compensation for the costs of bringing up a child would not be 'fair, just and reasonable'.[263] However, the pain and suffering and inconvenience associated with the pregnancy and birth plus loss of earnings and any medical expenses associated with the pregnancy were awarded (with Lord Millett dissenting). This overturned a Court of Appeal decision[264] from 1985 in which damages had been granted based upon the upkeep of the child. It also overturned the lower court's judgment, illustrating the ambiguity felt about the issue by the judges.

The two main reasons for the decision are as follows: firstly, that the birth of a healthy baby was a 'blessing, not a detriment'.[265] I have argued that there is something very curious about the idea that a defendant can claim that a fault on their part was actually a blessing upon the claimant.[266] This was the position of Lord McCluskey in the Second Division of the Inner House of Court of Sessions. When he considered the case before the appeal to the House of Lords he pointed out that such an argument is not part of the usual procedure in tort, stating that:

> I know of no principle of Scots law that entitles the wrongdoer to say to the victim of his wrongdoing that they must look to their prospective and impalpable gains in the roundabouts to balance what they actually lose on the swings.[267]

Emily Jackson[268] has pointed out that marriage is usually viewed by the courts as a good thing and yet a solicitor who negligently failed to obtain a divorce for a client would be liable in negligence. However, the damages in such a case would not be

---

262 *McFarlane v Tayside Health Authority* (1999) 3 WLR 1301; (2000) 2 AC 59.
263 *McFarlane v Tayside Health Board* (2000) 2 AC 59 *per* Lord Steyn p. 82.
264 *Emeh v Kensington and Chelsea and Westminster Area Health Authority* (1985) QB 1012.
265 *McFarlane v Tayside Health Board* (2000) 2 AC 59 *per* Lord Millett at p. 114.
266 Richardson (forthcoming).
267 *McFarlane v Tayside Health Board* (1998) SLT 307 2 Div. pp. 316-317. The same law applies in both England and Scotland on this point of law.
268 E. Jackson, *Regulating Reproduction: Law, Technology and Autonomy* (Oxford: Hart Publishing, 2001) p. 36.

as great as the award of the cost of child care, a concern that also motivated the Lords, to be discussed below.

Secondly, there was an appeal to 'distributive justice'.[269] Lord Steyn expressed a concern with the distribution of resources in a community. He contrasted this with 'corrective justice', which aims to compensate for harm to the individual by restoring her, as much as is possible, to the position she would have been in had the negligence not occurred. In other words, he employed the term 'distributive justice' to mean that the money would be better left with the Heath Board rather than awarded to the claimants. Lord Steyn admitted that on the basis of corrective justice the claim should succeed but he argued that this should not be the case because of,

> an inarticulate premise as to what is morally acceptable and what is not... Instinctively the traveller on the Underground would consider that the law of tort has no business to provide legal remedies consequent upon the birth of a healthy child, which all of us regard as a valuable and good thing.[270]

The arguments that birth is 'a blessing' and the question of 'distributive justice' have only been applied when the child has been born healthy. Compensation for the extra costs of raising a child with a disability was awarded in *Parkinson v St. James and Seacroft Hospital.*[271] Similarly, such compensation was awarded in the case of a visually impaired mother and healthy child in *Rees v Darlington Memorial Hospital NHS Trust.*[272] The view was that the extra costs associated with the disability of either child or mother should be awarded because this would be viewed as just, fair and reasonable.

This decision and the concerns of the Lords highlight the historically ambiguous position of women with regard to individualism and legal personhood. One of the basic assumptions in tort law is that we are envisaged as individuals who are owners of our own abilities, such as our ability to work and our bodies. If anyone negligently injures us or prevents us from being able to earn a living we can claim damages because we own parts of our bodies and life chances in a way that is analogous to the way in which we own property. As I will discuss in more detail in the next chapter, this has not always been the position of women. With the increase of paid labour outside the home from around 1840s, men were viewed as owners of their abilities that are sold in the labour market. Wage labour became the usual way for men to make a living. However, women's work within the home became seen in more sentimental terms. This lies at the root of the Lords' reluctance to compensate for the upbringing of a child. Lord Millett, in particular, dissented from the

---

269 *McFarlane v Tayside Health Board* (2000) 2 AC 59 per Lord Steyn at p. 82.
270 *McFarlane v Tayside Health Board* (2000) 2 AC 59 per Lord Steyn at p. 82. The 'reasonable man' has been updated from the 'man on the Clapham omnibus' to the gender neutral 'traveller on the Underground'.
271 *Parkinson v St. James and Seacroft Hospital* (2002) QB 266.
272 *Rees v Darlington Memorial Hospital NHS Trust* (2002) 2 All ER 177.

judgment in that he would only award limited damages for the loss of the ability to decide the size of their family. He argued against awarding compensation for the pain and suffering and other costs associated with the pregnancy by rejecting a comparison between pregnancy and sickness on the grounds that pregnancy is a 'natural' event. In doing so, he accepted one of the arguments of the Defendant: that there could be no cause of action because pregnancy and child care were 'natural'.[273]

Women's position in this case does not fit within the liberal dichotomy described by Ewald and discussed in the last section, which is derived from the fact that: 'Liberal thought held that the attribution by nature of goods and ills is, of itself, just.'[274] Therefore, the judges in fault-based law had to distinguish between an 'ill' that was someone's fault and hence that should be remedied and an 'ill' that was 'natural' and should therefore be left as a burden for the individual who suffered it. Here, the pregnancy, despite arising as a result of negligent sterilisation, is also viewed as 'natural' so as to defeat the claim.

Whilst unwanted pregnancy and rape are not comparable experiences, it is worth noting that sex is viewed (and constructed) as 'natural' but that women's consent, if not desire, is now viewed as important. However, the issue of women's consent and the way in which women were viewed as able to enter into marriage contracts, which then prevented them from refusing to have sex with their husbands, has been subject to feminist critique, discussed earlier. The act of categorising pregnancy as 'natural' must be understood in this context. It has the effect of allowing the Lords to argue that child birth should be viewed as 'a blessing and a joy', something the woman may not have initially wanted (a point that is difficult to dispute in these cases of failed sterilisation) but that would bring her pleasure. This allows the Lords to refuse to compensate for the expenses and work involved in childcare. It is simply not viewed as work but as 'natural'.[275]

One of the Lords' worries was the problem of putting a value on human life and hence commodifying it, i.e. treating it as a thing that was made for exchange in a market. There are different 'commodities' involved in this argument. Firstly, there was the concern that the child may be viewed as a commodity. Alternatively, the woman's 'work' in physically carrying and giving birth could be viewed as a thing that she owns – and that has a market value as in the case of surrogacy contracts. In the case of surrogacy contracts attempts are made to try to avoid the image of the child as commodity by arguing that it is the woman's work that is being paid for.[276] In the context of the wrongful birth cases, it is important to note that the traditional

---

273 The other judges were able to view pregnancy as involving pain and suffering in a way that is reminiscent of the comparison between pregnancy and sickness in early sex discrimination cases, which are no longer good law. See *Haynes v Malleable Working Men's Club* (1985) ICR, 705, EAT.

274 Ewald (1991) p. 206.

275 For a discussion of the way in which the 'natural' and 'biological' is being rethought by Oyama see Chapter 2.

276 See Pateman (1988) pp. 209-214.

work of women in the home which included the provision of housework, companionship and sex has been given a price by the courts. Prior to 1982,[277] there was a head of damages in negligence that allowed men to be compensated for the 'loss of consortium of a wife'. In 1952, the Lords refused to extend this common law claim to a wife whose husband had become impotent as a result of the defendant's negligence. Lord Goddard made his view of the historical position of wives clear when, in turning down the wife's claim, he stated that,

> The action which the law gives to the husband for loss of consortium is founded on the proprietary right which from ancient times it was considered the husband had in his wife. It was in fact based on the same grounds as gave a master a right to sue for an injury to his servant if the latter was thereby unable to perform his duties. It was an action of trespass for an invasion of the property right which, arising from the status of villeinage or serfdom, the master had over his servant.[278]

Whilst this envisaged the courts putting a price upon women's traditional work, it did not allow women to insure for their loss of these abilities as if they were commodities. Women were not viewed as the owners of these abilities – which historically, under the doctrine of coverture, belonged to their husbands.

When a sterilisation operation has taken place privately it can give rise to a claim in contract as well as tort law. Contract law always raises the issue of consent because it is predicated upon the idea that individuals should be bound by what they agree to do. Whereas the aim of tort law is to try to put the claimant in the position she would have been in had the tort not occurred, the aim of contract law is to put the parties in the position they would have been in had the contract been performed properly. It would therefore be expected that, if a doctor agrees to perform a sterilisation operation, she or he will be bound by this agreement. However, in *Eyre v Measday*[279] the claimant sued in contract when a faulty sterilisation operation resulted in her pregnancy. The Court of Appeal decided that the doctor was not liable. They were not willing to hold that there was a warranty that the operation would be successful, despite the fact that the doctor told the claimant that the operation was permanent and that she would not be able to have children. There was no warning of any risk that the operation might not have been successful. The doctor was the only party who was able to insure in this case and was also in a better position to assess the risk of the sterilisation being faulty. The doctor was to blame for both the operation and the failure to warn (or check for) potential fault and could therefore be viewed as liable under the 'fault paradigm'.

---

277 The right to damages for loss of consortium was abolished by the *Administration of Justice Act 1982*.

278 *Best v Samuel Fox and Co. Ltd.* (1952) AC 716, *per* Lord Goddard at pp. 731-732. Pateman's discussion of the way in which women's position in the home should be viewed in terms of a 'sexual contract' rather than as a feudal relationship is considered in the next chapter.

279 *Eyre v Measday* (1986) 1 All ER 488.

Alternatively, if the aim of tort law is taken to be that of loss distribution, then it should have been relevant that the doctor was the only party in the case who was able to insure and hence had 'deeper pockets'. The problem appears to be that the judges have difficulty viewing negligently induced birth as an 'injury' even though it has a major impact upon the woman's life.

The wrongful birth cases can be viewed within the terms of the equality/difference debate, which was introduced in Chapter 1. On the equality side of the debate it appears strange that the usual rules of tort (and contract) should be ignored when women's traditional role of child rearing is discussed. As Lord Steyn[280] admitted, if the usual rules of tort law were applied then the claimant should have been awarded the full compensation for the costs of child rearing. If women, and women's traditional work of child rearing, are to be 'added into' tort law on the same basis as men then their claim should not be denied. There is a case for arguing that the resources would be better spent on the sick but why should there be reference to 'distributive justice' to defeat this claim but not other cases in tort law in which there have been large awards?

However, I think that there is more to be said on this issue and it is useful to think about what I have described as the 'difference' argument. From this perspective, birth should not simply be subsumed within personal injury, although it obviously involves pain and suffering. Similarly, child-care is not simply 'work'. This is the argument that was used by feminists when employer's treatment of pregnant women was compared with their treatment of sick men in the early operation of the *Sex Discrimination Act 1975*.[281] A difference approach would be sympathetic to the difficulty that the Lords had in viewing women as atomistic individuals, who are owners of their capacities, rather than part of society. Such a view of humanity derives from Thomas Hobbes' description in *Leviathan*, to be discussed in the next chapter. This approach would entail the abandonment of 'corrective justice' (with its focus upon individual harm) in favour of an emphasis upon 'distributive justice'. However, I have argued that, if this logic is to be pursued then the Lords' concern with 'distributive justice' cannot be limited to areas that are traditionally linked with women's unpaid work in the home.[282] It would be unnecessary to assume that, by acknowledging the uniqueness of pregnancy, it should follow that a different system of tort, or ideals of justice, should apply to women or areas of work traditionally linked with women.

For the Lords' emphasis upon 'distributive justice' to be consistent would require legislation to radically alter the civil justice system in accordance with need. In the narrower confines of the case itself this would involve thinking about the actual parents' needs. The Lords have been willing to consider the particular circumstances of the case when either the child or the mother has a disability. To be consistent with Lord Steyn's reference to 'distributive justice' this would have to be

280 *McFarlane v Tayside Health Board* (2000) 2 AC 59 *per* Lord Steyn at p. 82.
281 *Haynes v Malleable Working Men's Club* (1985) ICR, 705, EAT.
282 Richardson (forthcoming).

extended to a consideration of the parents' income and the resources necessary to bring up a child. A more equitable way of doing this, which would take into account the claims upon the health service, would be through social insurance rather than the tort system.[283] This is preferable because, under the usual principles of tort law, the courts calculate compensation based upon the amount the parents would be likely to spend on the child. So, for example, there would be arguments that if they would normally send a child to a private school this should be included in the award. This would mean that the amount of compensation would increase with the wealth of the parents and not with their needs.

My aim here is not to detail the many good arguments against current tort law as a system of loss distribution but to illustrate the ambivalent position of women with regard to risk and to the image of the person who insures. In specific areas of law it may be that women's traditional position, which resists commodification, could potentially be used constructively to argue for a more equitable distribution of resources. However, given the ease with which the public/private divide is employed in this area this may be over optimistic.

Women and Technologies of Power

So far, I have considered the operation of tort law in terms of women's failure to fit within the model of the self-owning individual, which I will discuss in detail in the next two chapters. However, the governmentality literature draws from Foucault's work and hence is not merely critical of the self-owning individual but works with (and is critical of) different images of the self.

In Foucault's analysis of the genealogy of the self, as outlined above, he points to different techniques by which the bodies of workers in factories, for example, were trained to maximise production (the disciplinary processes) and then traced the impact of biopolitics aimed at the level of the population. When Foucault describes different technologies of power, he does so using examples that often fit men's lives, such as the soldier's drill and workers' discipline. The empirical question arises as to whether similar technologies applied (and continue to apply) in the case of women. Alternatively, it may be that entirely different practices of power apply to women.

One example of the disciplining of the body can be considered by comparing the way in which girls in the 1950s were taught deportment compared with boys who were taught to march in step. In this case similar technologies of discipline

---

283 For more detailed arguments on this point see P.S. Atiyah, *Accidents, Compensation and the Law* (London: Weidenfeld and Nicolson, 1970); J. Conaghan and W. Mansell, 'From the Permissive to the Dismissive Society: Patrick Atiyah's Accidents, Compensation and the Market', *Journal of Law and Society*, Vol. 25, 1998, pp. 284-293; J.P. Cane, *Atiyah's Accidents, Compensation and the Law* (London: Butterworths, 1999); D. Harris, D. Campbell and R. Halson, *Remedies in Tort and Contract* (London: Butterworths, 2002) pp. 405-461.

apply but with a different end result. The resultant abilities of these men and women then differed. In 'Throwing like a Girl', Iris Marion Young[284] illustrates how women who have been trained in this way are constrained and come to underestimate the power of their bodies. Similarly, Bartky[285] details the way in which women wax 'unwanted' hair and suffer a number of painful and expensive beauty treatments. This self-disciplining of the body was not linked directly with bodies as a productive force in a factory but as consumers and as sex objects – a position that is no longer simply the preserve of women.

To apply Foucault's work in this way involves looking at women's lives and asking whether his analysis of different techniques of power can inform ways of thinking about women and selfhood. In particular, I am interested in the way in which Foucault's governmentality work informs the technology of risk and its relationship to the operation of tort law. In order to explore the usefulness of Foucault's analysis, I would like to draw links between this description of the disciplining of the body and the view of the self that I discuss in Chapter 2. Clark and Foucault's approaches (from completely different areas of philosophy) compliment each other. Foucault's description of 'disciplining the body' supplements Clark's description by providing a detailed analysis of techniques of bodily learning, which form part of the wider environment, and the ways in which these are intimately linked to networks of power. Clark's approach recognises the complexity of the learning process and the interactivity of the relationship between bodies and the environment, in contrast with readings of early Foucault that focus upon a more top-down approach in which the self appears to be constructed through discourse. Bodies are not viewed as passive matter that are imprinted from outside. They have a role in the complex process of learning.

I want to illustrate this relationship between the work of Clark and Foucault in more detail by expanding upon Clark's argument. Clark[286] starts at a basic level by describing the way in which we learn to walk, attacking the image that there is a centralised blueprint that simply produces a result in a top down way. Instead he points to recent studies that indicate that such learning may be better understood in terms of multiple local factors that include: bodily growth, environmental factors, brain maturation and learning. This means that different children will make different mistakes but will then compensate for them. The fact that our ability to walk depends upon a number of factors means that we can adapt to changes in the environment. Clark describes this 'delicate balance between individual variation and developmentally robust achievement'[287] in terms of 'soft assembly'[288] as

284 I.M. Young, *Throwing like a Girl* (Indiana: Indiana University Press, 1990).

285 S.L. Bartky, 'Foucault, Femininity and the Modernization of Patriarchal Power' in I. Diamond and L. Quinby, eds., *Feminism and Foucault: Reflections on Resistance* (Boston: Northeastern University Press, 1988) pp. 61-88.

286 Clark (1999) p. 40.

287 Clark (1999) p. 42.

288 Clark (1999) p. 42.

compared to the 'hard assembly' of a robot arm that has centralised control and one mechanism. This is because the local environment itself plays a strong role in selecting behaviours.

One further illustration underscores his point. He describes empirical research into how young children learn how to reach for objects. One child in the study started by flapping his arms and so in order to reach an object his task was to contract his muscles once he was near the target. This allowed him to dampen down the flapping and reach it. Another child produced low hand speeds and low torque. Her job was therefore to produce enough lift to enable the object to be reached. Other children produced various different approaches. Clark argues that the central nervous system (CNS) appears to be treating the overall system like a set of springs and masses:

> The job of the CNS, over developmental time is *not* to bring the body increasingly 'into line' so that it can carry out detailed internally represented commands directly specifying, e.g. arm trajectories. Rather, the job is to learn to modulate parameters (such as stiffness) which will then interact with intrinsic bodily and environmental constraints so as to yield desired outcomes. In sum, the task is to learn how to soft-assemble adaptive behaviours in ways that respond to local context and exploit intrinsic dynamics.[289]

There is no overall plan or blueprint. The environment is part of the process that allows for local adjustments.

There is common ground between the targets that Foucault and Clark attack, within their differing fields. Foucault argues that,

> I wonder whether, before one poses the question of ideology, it wouldn't be more materialist to study first the question of the body and the effects of power on it. Because what troubles me with these analyses which prioritise ideology is that there is always presupposed a human subject on the lines of the model of classical philosophy, endowed with a consciousness which power is then thought to seize on.[290]

He is attacking the autonomous self-legislating Kantian self that was never meant to include women. When he argues that power does not seize upon this abstract entity he makes a similar move to Clark when Clark argues that we do not learn facts in a vacuum. Our cognition is situated in the world to such an extent that it is a part of it. The philosophers that I draw from in Chapter 2 do not argue for the 'dissolution of the self'. In different ways they propose a rethinking of the self that is not predicated upon the male as norm (Battersby) nor upon a crude distinction between 'nature' and 'culture' (Oyama) nor upon models of cognition that ignore the environment (Clark). The importance for these writers of refusing a separation

---

289 Clark (1999) p. 45.
290 M. Foucault, *Power/Knowledge: Selected Interviews and Other Writings 1972-1977*, Gordon, C., ed. (Sussex: Harvester Press, 1980a) p. 48.

between mind and body resonates with Foucault's 'history of ideas that cannot be separated from the physical material practices of which they are (always already) realized'.[291] This is illustrated by the argument that the history of the theories of psychiatry, medicine and criminology cannot be separated from their practical and institutional forms: the mental hospital, hospital and prison. When Foucault discusses the Enlightenment ideals of freedom, right and law he refuses to view them as disembodied – just as Clark refuses a vision of cognition that is 'all in the head' and not intimately part of an environment that requires fast and messy solutions to problems.

Turning from the disciplining of individual bodies to issues of biopolitics of populations, women's bodies are central to the concerns about birth. There has been much work about the self-regulation of pregnant women. This fits within Foucault's governmentality work because women have a choice as to how to deal with risk. It is important for Foucault that the subject of governmentality is free to act otherwise. If women were forced to behave in a certain way then the discussion would cease to be about techniques of government and instead would be about violence. Risk analysis provides a way in which these choices are framed. For example, Lupton[292] in 'Risk and the Ontology of Pregnant Embodiment' describes the way that concerns about the risks associated with pregnancy have resulted in self-regulation. Similarly, in 'Recent Developments in the Government of Pregnancy' Lorna Weir[293] discusses the way in which risk in pregnancy is managed in terms of 'clinical risk technique'.

Cornell and Ewald

Whereas Cornell is concerned with the process of 'individuation' in which each person takes his/herself as a project – along with his/her equivalent rights to this project that are to be protected by law – Ewald discusses the way in which the operation of law and social administration produce 'individuation'. This is achieved by such techniques as statistical and risk analysis which is understood as an example of governmentality, the conduct of conduct, as described by Foucault.[294]

I have used Ewald's analysis to show how contemporary English tort law employs the techniques of risk analysis and also fits within the broader concept of governmentality. By employing this framework, it can be shown that the English law could fulfil the same function and develop in ways that are more efficient, by

---

291 W. Montag, 'The Soul is the Prison of the Body: Althusser and Foucault, 1970-1975', *Yale French Studies*, Vol. 88, 1995, p. 73.

292 D. Lupton, 'Risk and the Ontology of Pregnant Embodiment' in D. Lupton, *Risk and Sociocultural Theory: New Directions and Perspectives* (Cambridge: Cambridge University Press, 1999) pp. 59-85.

293 L. Weir, 'Recent Developments in the Government of Pregnancy', *Economy and Society*, Vol. 25, No. 3, 1996, pp. 372-392.

294 See, for example, Foucault (1991a) pp. 87-104.

moving to the use of no fault compensation. This operation of law would undercut the use of Cornell's legal test in such cases because it would no longer be necessary to go to court to prove fault. It may be necessary to argue over the amount of damages but it is unlikely that Cornell's test was meant merely to ask: would free and equal persons agree to this amount of compensation? Tariffs are likely to be set to avoid litigation. Presumably, Cornell would be happy with this method of loss distribution, given her position on welfare generally. She could argue that her test would apply in other areas.

Can Ewald account for Cornell's description of a project of becoming a person? There is an initial similarity. It could be argued that Cornell's image of 'the project of becoming a person' sits too comfortably with the image of oneself as an enterprise which Ewald discusses within his work on 'insurance as a moral technology':

> To calculate a risk is to master time, to discipline the future. To conduct one's life in the manner of an enterprise indeed begins in the eighteenth century to be a definition of a morality whose cardinal virtue is providence.[295]

Similarly, Rose discusses the contemporary development of risk technology in the following terms that again resonate with Cornell's 'project of becoming a person':

> One is always in continuous training, lifelong learning, perpetual assessment, continuous incitement to buy, to improve oneself, constant monitoring of health and never-ending risk management. Control is not centralized but dispersed; it flows through a network of open circuits that are rhizomatic and not hierarchical.[296]

In earlier work, Rose[297] links this to a shift in the regulation of risk from the 'social' arena – by social security, mutual societies – to the domain of individual choice in the market place. This is an image which also pervades state provision in which the recipient is viewed as a client,

> The enhancement of the powers of the client as consumer – consumer of health services, of education, of training, of transport – specifies the subjects of rule in a new way: as active individuals seeking to 'enterprise themselves', to maximize their quality of life through acts of choice, according their life a meaning and value to the extent that it can be rationalized as the outcome of choices made, or choices to be made...*Political reason must now justify and organize itself by arguing over the arrangements that are adequate to the existence of persons as, in their essence, creatures of freedom, liberty and autonomy.*[298] (Italics are added.)

---

295 Ewald (1991a) p. 207.
296 Rose (1999b) p. 234.
297 N. Rose. 'Governing Advanced Liberal Democracies' in Barry et al (1996) p. 57.
298 Rose (1996a) p. 57.

Cornell can argue that her view of individuation does not define personhood but leaves it open for each person to say what it is for her or him to be a person. However, her view of the emergence of personhood itself – that it is worked upon as a project – represents a way of life that those writing in the area of 'governmentality', such as Rose and Ewald, aim to explain and historically situate. The practical question becomes whether Cornell's work is cleverly pitched to extract concessions for women within this contemporary neo-liberal framework or whether it fits too comfortably within it. How radical is Cornell's image of 'the project of becoming a person', that will be understood by the courts as a project between competing 'possessive individuals', owners of their bodies and abilities – save possibly in the area of women's traditional work?

Cornell's view of personhood does not simply include 'the emergence of individuals' but of different ways of living. She can argue that, just because many will today view their project of becoming a person in terms of possessive individualism (which, I think, is now intimately linked to the deployment of the techniques of risk) does not mean that this is all that 'persons' can become. This is something that she keeps open – not simply for individuals – but in terms of cultural change in the meaning of 'persons' in future generations, hence the utopian theme in her work. This is why her view of personhood cannot be subsumed into the view of the person as enterprise.

I do not believe that Cornell's entire framework can be aligned with this approach, although this is one way in which potential legislatures/judges are likely to view Cornell's legal test. Ewald links the employment of the technique of risk to instrumental reasoning. Above, I have said that this evokes the figure of the 'possessive individual'. Cornell expressly distinguishes her position on what it is to be a person, from that of libertarians, whose image of what it is to be a person, she argues, derives from Hobbes, and which she describes as 'atomistic individualism'.[299]

To recap my argument, the contemporary view of the 'reasonable man' of tort law is one who employs risk analysis as a tool in the operation of instrumental reason; who owns his body and its abilities and is traditionally male. Until relatively recently, women have not been viewed in this way. The traditional housewife has not been viewed as owning her labour power, which is characterised by being sold for a wage, because she received housekeeping money from her husband. The risks of the traditional housewife have not been viewed as insurable. In keeping with this approach, the courts have been unwilling to compensate women if they have given birth to a healthy child because of negligent sterilisation, for example. There is some evidence that the courts are also changing their approach in this area, to the limited extent that compensation is awarded for the pain and suffering of pregnancy[300] and of the upkeep of children with disabilities in

---

299 Cornell (2000) p. 167 fn.11.
300 *McFarlane v Tayside Health Authority* (1999) 3 WLR 1301.

the 'wrongful birth' cases.[301] To extend this technique of calculative reason to women would be in keeping with the move to include women as possessive individuals, as owners of their bodies and abilities, linked to their increasing participation in paid work and the breakdown of the traditional housewife/breadwinner model. However, there are problems with this view of selves as possessive individuals. In the next two chapters I want to consider the relationship between women and 'possessive individualism' when I move from considering the law of tort to that of contract.

301 *Greenfield v Irwin (A firm)* (2001) WLR 1279; *Rand v East Dorset* HA (2000) 56 BMLJ 39.

Chapter 5

The Sexual Contract

I will now turn from tort law to the area of contract law in order to further explore the anomalous position of women with regard to selfhood, personhood and individualism. Contract law focuses attention upon the question of consent and, historically, upon an image of persons with an autonomous will.[302] The basis of contract law is that it regulates obligations that are entered into by 'agreement', in contrast with tort law in which the obligations, for example, the duty to behave with reasonable care so as not to harm anyone foreseeably affected by our actions, are imposed by the courts. There has been much feminist analysis of the way in which women's consent has been treated in the operation of law, for example, in the areas of rape[303] and consent to medical consent.[304] Just as Marx[305] points out that workers were not really free to choose whether or not to work, so women could be viewed as historically pressured into the traditional marriage contract. The relationship between the employment contract and the marriage contract and their relationship to personhood is the focus of this chapter. I will then use this analysis to look at 'possessive individualism' in more detail in the next chapter.

In this chapter, I move from a discussion of Ewald's analysis of insurance, and its application to tort law, to Carole Pateman's reading of Hobbes' version of social contract theory and its relationship to other contracts. This involves moving from an analysis of actual insurance contracts and the way in which they can be viewed as 'social' in that these contracts hold out the possibility of redistributing risk. Even if this hope of a 'contractual justice' has not been fulfilled, these insurance contracts are just as concerned with the questions of safeguarding the means to live a 'commodious life'[306] as Hobbes' social contract to be discussed below.

One central argument made by both socialists and feminists has been that employment contracts and marriage contracts have little in common with the paradigm of a contract as an exchange between two equal 'individuals', that is so dominant within political and legal theory. As I will discuss below, Carole Pateman explores the way that an exchange between two persons – in which one must exchange something, such as his/her ability to work, which cannot be separated from his/her body – is characterised by his/her subordination. She draws out the relationship between subordination (and hence the possibility of exploitation) under the marriage contract and compares it to subordination under the employment

---

302 See P.S. Atiyah, *The Rise and Fall of the Freedom of Contract* (Oxford: Oxford University Press, 2000). For an alternative view of the self see Chapter 2.

303 See for example Smart (1989) pp. 26-49.

304 See for example, O'Donovan (1997) pp. 47-64.

305 K. Marx, *Capital: A Critique of Political Economy, Volume One* (London: Penguin, 1976) Ch. 6, p. 280.

306 Hobbes (1994b) Ch. XIII, s. 14, p. 78.

contract, discussing the ways in which they differed but were interrelated. I will argue that aspects of her rethinking of this relationship between marriage contracts and employment contracts are still useful even though, as she acknowledges in an article written in 1996,

> The patriarchal structures with which I was concerned have been considerably weakened, and the heyday of the worker/breadwinner was from 1840-1970.[307]

Nevertheless, I agree with her later comments that,

> Women and men alike are now being drawn into a global division of labour, and assessments of which women may gain or lose, and whether new forms of subordination are developing, are, necessarily, enormously complex and difficult when the restructuring is gathering pace. I believe my arguments in *The Sexual Contract* can throw light on the course of some recent developments, but to examine the issues would require another, very different, book.[308]

At a time when the UK government has stated that it aims to try to facilitate a 'new relationship' between work and family life',[309] thereby taking the radical step of recognising the unspoken relationship between work both within the home and outside the home,[310] it is worth returning to Pateman's historical analysis to understand the paradoxical position of women with regard to personhood and individualism. Pateman argues that it was contract – the legal device – that played an important role in women's subordination because it was the existence of contract that produced both married women and workers, as parties to the marriage and employment contracts. As she puts it,

> Contract does not merely 'legitimise' or 'facilitate' certain relationships. Relations that constitute central institutions in modern civil society, notably marriage and employment, are *created* through contract. 'Husband' and 'wife' or 'employer' and 'worker' come into being through the mechanism of contract.[311] (Italics are in the original.)

I want to examine her theoretical arguments in detail and to look at their implications for the contemporary English law of obligations and for the

---

307 C. Pateman, 'A Comment on Johnson's Does Capitalism Really Need Patriarchy?', *Women's International Forum*, Vol. 19, No. 3, 1996a, p. 204.

308 Pateman (1996a) p. 205.

309 http://www.dti.gov.uk/er/fairness/fore.htm.

310 For a discussion of this point and assessment of the legislation and initiatives see, J. Conaghan, 'Women, Work and Family: A British Revolution?' in J. Conaghan, R.M. Fischel and K. Klare, *Labour Law in an Era of Globalisation: Transformative Practices and Possibilities* (Oxford: Oxford University Press, 2002).

311 C. Pateman, 'Contract and Ideology: A Reply to Coole', *Politics*, Vol. 10, No. 1, 1990, p. 30.

paradoxical position of women. Hutchings[312] has argued that Pateman's position has strength despite holding onto the concept of the 'sovereign individual'. Here, the 'sovereign individual' is used as a 'composite term' which includes the 'possessive individual':

> I am using the term to cover what is variously referred to in the literature as the possessive, the autonomous, the abstract, the disembodied or the unitary subject of traditional/liberal/modernist political and moral theory, or sometimes as the Cartesian, the Hobbesian or the Kantian subject/agent/individual.[313]

I will discuss some feminist responses to Pateman's *The Sexual Contract* in this chapter but will defer a more thorough analysis of the 'possessive individual' until the next chapter.

Hobbes' Story

Pateman describes Hobbes as 'the most brilliant and bold of the contract theorists.'[314] I want to concentrate upon Hobbes because, for Pateman, he is instrumental in replacing 'classical patriarchy' with 'modern patriarchy', a shift which is at the core of Pateman's thesis to be discussed in detail below. In addition, Hobbes is one of the few Western philosophers to identify the subordination of women as a political matter, as a matter of convention, rather than as a natural condition. Hobbes' analysis was soon superseded by that of Locke who reverted to the view of women's position as naturally subordinate. As Pateman puts it,

> Hobbes was too revealing about civil society. The political character of conjugal right was expertly concealed in Locke's separation of what he called 'paternal' power from political power and, ever since, most political theorists, whatever their views about other forms of subordination, have accepted that the powers of husbands derive from nature and, hence, are not political.[315]

> Feminist scholars have undertaken some very revealing and exciting work on the classic texts of political theory, but little attention has been paid to Hobbes, whose writings are of fundamental importance for an understanding of patriarchy as masculine right.[316]

---

312 K. Hutchings, 'The Death of the Sovereign Individual' in M. Griffiths and M. Whitford, *Women Review Philosophy* (Nottingham: Nottingham University Press, 1996) pp. 1-25.
313 Hutchings (1996) p. 2.
314 C. Pateman, '"God Hath Ordained to Man a Helper": Hobbes, Patriarchy and Conjugal Rights' in M.L. Shanley and C. Pateman, *Feminist Interpretations and Political Theory* (Cambridge: Polity, 1991) p. 59.
315 Pateman (1991) p. 69.
316 Pateman (1991) p. 54.

The narrative of the social contract initially told by Hobbes warned of the potential dangers which could occur if the English civil war resulted in a breakdown of law. It was based upon some supposed 'facts' about human nature, which was conceived of as selfish, competitive, acquisitive and rational. Individuals' selfishness makes life in the state of nature, in which there are no laws, 'solitary, poor, nasty, brutish and short'.[317] However, individuals' ability to reason allows them to recognise that it is in their long-term interests to escape the state of nature by means of the social contract. Their agreement to give up their freedom to the sovereign then allows the sovereign to enforce the law, which includes the enforcement of contracts. Importantly for Pateman's rereading of the social contract, this includes the sovereign's enforcement of marriage contracts.

In Hobbes' state of nature, there could be no marriage contract and hence it would only be the mother who could (possibly) say who had fathered her child.[318] In the state of nature, Hobbes argues, it would be up to the mother to either let the child die or look after it. If she protected it then she would be the head of the family. As the following quotation makes clear, her child's obedience would be obtained by consent and in exchange for protection, not owed to parents *per se*. In *Leviathan*, Hobbes states that dominion can be acquired in two ways:

[4] Dominion is acquired two ways: by generation or conquest. The right of dominion by generation is that which the parent hath over his children, and is called PATERNAL. And is not so derived from generation as if therefore the parent had dominion over the child because he begat him, but from the child's consent, either express or by other sufficient arguments declared. For as to generation, God hath ordained to man a helper, and there be always two that are equally parents; the dominion therefore over the child should belong equally to both, and he be equally subject to both, which is impossible; for no man can obey two masters. And whereas some have attributed the dominion to the man only, as being of the more excellent sex, they misreckon in it. For there is not always that difference in strength or prudence between the man and the woman as that the right can be determined without war. In commonwealths this controversy is decided by the civil law, and for the most part (but not always) the sentence is in favour of the father, because for the most part the commonwealths have been erected by the fathers and not by the mothers of families...

[5] If there be no contract, the dominion is with the mother. For in the condition of mere nature, where there are no matrimonial laws, it cannot be known who is the father unless it be declared by the mother...[319]

---

317 T. Hobbes, *Leviathan*, ed. C.B. Macpherson (London: Penguin books, 1968) Ch. XIII, p. 186.

318 Hobbes (1994b) Ch. XX, p. 129. 'It cannot be known who is the father unless it be declared by the mother.'

319 Hobbes (1994b) Ch. XX, pp. 128-129.

Hobbes is therefore unique amongst the social contract theorists, in starting with an image of the state of nature in which women are viewed as being equal with men. This is because each individual is equally able to kill the other:

> For as to the strength of body, the weakest has strength enough to kill the strongest, either by secret machination, or by confederacy with others that are in the same danger with himself.[320]

There is often an ambiguity as to when the use of the term 'men' is actually meant to include women within political theory. This is not easily resolved by 'adding in' women, because this ambiguity itself performs a role in that it allows women to appear as individuals who can take part in the social contract at certain times and not at others. Pateman describes the way in which women are held to be 'individuals' as part of the social contract and yet are outside it – as objects of the sexual contract. As outlined above, Hobbes is less guilty than the later social contract theorists because his rigorous application of individualism to both men and women leads him to view women as equal to men in the state of nature. This leads Pateman to ask why they would give up this state to enter into a civil society in which they were subordinate to men.

By a careful reading of the social contract theorists, Pateman argues that within these texts is hidden a 'sexual contract'. This claim involves a complex analysis of the way in which she views change in, but also a continuation of, patriarchy. Pateman describes this in terms of the overthrow of 'classical patriarchy' – which was based upon a model of sovereign power as analogous to the 'natural' power of the father within the household[321] – with modern patriarchal power which is based upon the sexual contract.

Pateman[322] points to inconsistencies in Hobbes' story that result from his view that everyone is equal in the state of nature. Why should they have agreed to give up their freedom and equality to enter into a society governed by laws which did not treat them as equal? At the level of story-telling, this question raises the paradoxical issue of women's consent.[323] Under the doctrine of coverture, women were viewed as being persons who could consent to the marriage contract, which then took away their legal personhood and their ability to make further contracts.

Pateman[324] details possible amendments to the social contract narrative to try to remove this inconsistency within Hobbes' story. So, she discusses the likelihood that women could all have been 'captured' within the state of nature because they

---

320 Hobbes (1994b) Ch. XIII, p. 74.
321 For a detailed historical analysis of different theories of classical patriarchalism see, G.J. Schochet, *Patriarchalism in Political Thought* (Bristol: Basil Blackwell, 1975). Also, J.P. Sommerville, ed., *Filmer: Patriarchia and Other Writings* (Cambridge: Cambridge University Press, 1991).
322 Pateman (1991) pp. 53-73.
323 See, for example, Pateman (1980) pp. 71-89.
324 Pateman (1988) pp. 43-50.

would have been weakened by bringing up children.[325] She does raise the question of how this could apply to all women, not all of whom would choose to have children, especially if this increased their risk of capture. She also discusses the possibility that women would agree to enter into civil society on lesser terms than men in order to gain the benefits of civil society. However, without assuming that women are unequal within the state of nature it is difficult to see why such an agreement should take place.

In Hobbes' state of nature there could be no contract – as none can be enforced – and therefore no marriage contract. Within Hobbes' story, one of the reasons for entering into civil society by means of the social contract, is to empower the sovereign to enforce contracts between his or her subjects. The social contract in Pateman's retelling of the story involves a deal that is struck between males to have a sovereign who will guarantee the marriage contract. Hence, their access to women's bodies and labour will be enforced.

Her rereading of the transition from the state of nature to civil society borrows from Freud as well as from Hobbes. In Freud's[326] myth of the primal horde the patriarchal father is able to have sex with all women in the group and the overthrow of the father involves a shift from the rule of the father to the rule of the brothers, who then have sexual access to women. In Pateman's reworking of the move from classical patriarchy to the 'fraternal contract' the state guarantees husbands' conjugal rights. The marriage contract, enforced by the state, is therefore central to her story:

> [the sexual contract] both establishes orderly access to women and a division of labour in which women are subordinate to men.[327]

The first question to be considered is the actual status (and meaning) of the social/sexual contract itself. Pateman makes clear that, like Hobbes, she does not really believe that there was such a contract. Pateman is examining the stories that were, and are, told to explain and justify the existence of law. It is important to consider the way in which such stories are understood by Pateman to avoid being absorbed into a discussion that takes the social contract too seriously as a historical fact. Pateman says that,

---

325 Hobbes does say that a woman can decide whether or not to raise a child and if she does then the child is deemed to contract with her to obey her as its head of household. Hobbes assumes that once a contract is made it should not be breached, even if it was made under duress. However, he introduced limitations upon sovereign power such that the point of moving from the state of nature was to preserve life. If the sovereign threatens your life, you have the right to disobey.

326 S. Freud, *Totem and Taboo: Some Points of Agreement between the Mental Lives of Savages and Neurotics* (London: Routledge and Kegan Paul Ltd., 1950) pp. 141-146.

327 Pateman (1988) p. 119.

The political fiction of the original contract tells not only of a beginning, an act of political generation, but also of an end, the defeat of (the classical form of) patriarchy. Moreover, the story is not merely about ends and beginnings, but is used by political theorists and, in more popular versions, by politicians, to represent social and political institutions to contemporary citizens and to represent citizens to themselves. *Through the mirror of the social contract, citizens can see themselves as members of a society constituted by free relations.*[328] (Italics are added.)

This is evocative of the image of the mirror that Irigaray uses, in *Speculum*,[329] to draw attention to women's ambivalent position within male-centred political theory. Both argue that it is the failure of women to fit within the political system that allows it to operate. Both explore symbolic systems or narratives in which women are not themselves subjects but are necessary to reflect men, to allow men to attain subjecthood. Irigaray's[330] miming of Marx, for example, evokes the way in which women can be viewed as objects of exchange and has the effect of positioning men as subjects amongst each other. Pateman, in a different register, produces a similar analysis.[331] Pateman is at pains to stress that she is simply discussing the stories that have been told to explain or justify the origins of the state.

In certain respects, Pateman's stated aim is similar to that of Adriana Cavarero[332] (whose work owes an explicit debt to Irigaray): to appropriate male stories and to unravel them by illustrating how weak they are when the anomalous position of women is considered. Cavarero's is also a constructive project in that there is a move to rework the patterns themselves; to produce different images of women. Although Pateman is dealing with stories, *The Sexual Contract* is different, not only in its refusal of the narrative style, but also in the centrality that is given to this particular story.[333] It involves a close reading of the texts of, amongst others, Hobbes, Locke, Rousseau and Hegel to argue that the 'sexual contract' operates as an unstated assumption within these texts themselves. This story is said to be important because of its use within contemporary political rhetoric.[334] By drawing this analogy between Pateman and both Irigaray and Cavarero, I am interested in what is opened up by this analysis in terms of the image of the female subject.

---

328 Pateman (1988) p. 221.

329 Irigaray (1985).

330 L. Irigaray, 'Commodities among Themselves', in L. Irigaray, *This Sex which is not One* (New York: Cornell University Press, 1985c) pp. 192-197; L. Irigaray, 'Women on the Market' in L. Irigaray, *This Sex which is not One* (New York: Cornell University Press, 1985a) pp. 170-191.

331 See also Wittig's reading of the social contract which focuses upon enforced heterosexuality, M. Wittig, 'On the Social Contract' in *The Straight Mind and Other Essays* (London: Harvester Wheatsheaf, 1992) pp. 33-45.

332 See, for example, Cavarero (1995) p. 8.

333 Cavarero has also written about Hobbes in 'Pace e libert nel pensiero politico di Thomas Hobbes', *Per la filosofia*, Vol. 9, 1987, pp. 73-79, and Locke in *La teoria politica di John Locke* (Padova: Ed. Universitarie, 1984).

334 Pateman (1988) p. 221.

Pateman uses the social contract theorists' own words and method against them, to disrupt their work by focusing upon the anomalous position of women within it. This method has been subject to criticism, in that she appears to take the narrative of the social contract too seriously. In a generally sympathetic review, Hutchings argues that,

> It is in her readings of the actual omissions, ambivalence and sometimes explicit misogyny in these texts that Pateman is at her most convincing. However, her use of hypothesis to fill the gaps in the social contract story, her claims about links between that story and historical realities and the inconsistencies in her arguments are more difficult to defend.[335]

I think that Pateman's work is important and has contemporary relevance as a critique of contract. As Hutchings[336] acknowledges, the way in which Pateman employs the technique of 'retelling stories' should not detract from her demonstration that women have an ambivalent status with regard to individualism. Whilst I agree, I think that the importance of Pateman's work, linked with this analysis of possessive individualism, is her attack upon the daily *subordination* that takes place in different, but historically complimentary ways, within marriage and employment. This background is useful in order to think about the ways in which contract continues to be employed today.

Defending Pateman

There have been a number of criticisms[337] of Pateman that focus upon her reworking of Hobbes' story to argue that Hobbes did not envisage women's capture and subordination in the state of nature. In his recent translation of *Leviathan*, Curly,[338] for example, argues that women's subordination in the state of nature does not fit with Hobbes' acceptance of women as sovereigns. He cites Hobbes' discussion of ecclesiastical powers[339] in which Hobbes states that a female sovereign can appoint someone to speak on her behalf as head of the Church, because – even though women are forbidden to speak in church – she can appoint someone by her authority: 'For authority does not take account of masculine and feminine.'[340] Similarly, Van Mill[341] argues that men would not risk putting themselves in danger in order to subjugate anyone in the state of nature.

---

335 Hutchings (1996) p. 18.
336 Hutchings (1996) p. 18.
337 For example, Curley's footnote in Hobbes (1994b) Ch. XIII, p. 78; D. Van Mill, *Liberty, Rationality and Agency in Hobbes' Leviathan* (New York: State University of New York, 2001) pp. 198-200.
338 Hobbes (1994b) p. 78.
339 Hobbes (1994b) Ch. XLII, p. 372.
340 Hobbes (1994b) Ch. XLII, p. 372.
341 Van Mill (2001) pp. 198-200.

I have two responses to this line of criticism of Pateman's reading of *Leviathan*. Firstly, I think that the abstract discussion of the state of nature needs to be inverted to explain what is at stake in this story, to be discussed below. More importantly, as mentioned above, criticisms aimed at Pateman's rewriting of the sexual contract miss their mark because Pateman's work does not rely upon the credibility of this particular aspect of her reworking of a fictional narrative. Her speculation about the implied capture of women within Hobbes' state of nature can be viewed simply as a device to illustrate her attacks upon contractarian belief.[342]

My first point involves inverting the temporality of Hobbes' story. Hobbes' description of the social contract was a cautionary tale to show what would happen if the English Civil War resulted in a breakdown of the rule of law. It was not an historical analysis, not something that had already happened, but a state of affairs that could pertain at some future point. From this perspective, the cautionary tale can be applied to women. When the temporality of this is reversed, it could be argued that this is a warning to women that rebellion could produce a breakdown in law and that they would fair worse in the state of nature than in civil society. However, this assumption is based upon Hobbes' image of the universality of possessive individualism, that can itself be challenged by considering the historical position of women, a point to which I will return in the next chapter.

The second point is related to the first. As I will discuss in detail in the next chapter, Pateman's work is an exposition of the way in which any contract for the 'exchange' of a human ability that is not separable from the worker's body, produces daily subordination through the use of a fiction that there is a free exchange. This derives from, but also amends, Marx's[343] analysis of the exchange of labour power for a wage and the exploitation that results when both are treated as commodities. Pateman draws together an analysis of marriage contracts as well as employment contracts, prostitution contracts[344] and surrogacy contracts to show how these operate in practice. Her stress is upon daily subordination. This does not rely upon a rereading of Hobbes such that women are to be viewed as prisoners within a hypothetical state of nature. Pateman's move allows her to emphasise the political nature of the marriage contract itself and to trace its development alongside the employment contract. As she recognises, the marriage contract is no longer central to the lives of women. Later in this chapter I will go on to develop her analysis of the marriage contract and employment contract, discussing the use

---

342 This is supported by the focus of Pateman's most recent work in which she drops the discussion of the 'sexual contract' but continues to analyse the subordination that occurs through thinking of 'property in the person' or 'self-ownership' as implying that one's labour power can be alienated. C. Pateman, 'Self-Ownership and Property in the Person: Democratization and a Tale of Two Concepts', *The Journal of Political Philosophy*, Vol. 10, No. 1, 2002, pp. 20-53.

343 K. Marx, *Capital: A Critique of Political Economy, Volume One* (London: Lawrence and Wishart, 1954).

344 For Pateman's analysis of prostitution contracts see also C. Pateman, 'Defending Prostitution: Charges Against Ericsson', *Ethics*, Vol. 93, 1983, pp. 561-565.

of implied terms in contemporary English law. This raises the question of how to reconceptualise the position of women who are now constructed as 'dependant',[345] not upon men, but upon the state. Pateman also raises questions about the meaning of self-ownership, and the rights of dominion over others, that will be the subject of next chapter.

A further possible objection to Pateman's work should also be considered at this point. Foucault attacked the idea that 'political power obeys the model of a legal transaction involving a contractual type of exchange'.[346] Foucault's work serves as a warning against discussions of family, civil society and state as monolithic entities. He describes his analysis of power as the opposite of Hobbes' *Leviathan*:

> In other words, rather than ask ourselves how the sovereign appears to us in his lofty isolation, we should try to discover how it is that subjects are gradually, progressively, really and materially constituted through a multiplicity of organisms, forces, energies, materials, desires, thoughts, etc. We should try to grasp subjection in its material instance as a constitution of subjects. This would be the exact opposite to Hobbes' project in *Leviathan*, and of that, I believe of all jurists for whom the problem is the distillation of a single will – or rather, the constitution of a unitary, singular body animated by the spirit of sovereignty – from the particular wills of multiplicity of individuals.[347]

Whilst it may appear that this criticism must apply to Pateman: that she has failed to 'cut the head off the sovereign' and views sovereignty, or the law, as that which instantiates the sexual contract, I want to defend the usefulness of her analysis of contract law. She links her critique of the marriage contract with that of the employment contract and of the story of the social/sexual contract. It is possible to highlight central themes in Pateman's work on the marriage contract and employment contract in a manner that goes beyond an analysis of sovereignty. Although these contracts are enforced by law, her work can be viewed as focusing upon the daily lives of women who are subject to the marriage contract (and of workers subject to employment contracts). Whilst it is possible to agree with Foucault that the intricacies of such relationships cannot be caught by a simple analysis of the contract, a point which Pateman would acknowledge, Pateman is right to point out the role that contract plays in creating wives and employees.[348]

---

345 For an analysis of the politics of the term 'dependency' that is also applicable to English law, see, N. Fraser and L. Gordon, 'A Genealogy of 'Dependency': Tracing a Keyword of the U.S. Welfare State' in N. Fraser, *Justice Interruptus: Critical Reflections on the 'Postsocialist' Condition* (London: Routledge, 1997).

346 M. Foucault, 'Two Lectures' in Foucault (1980a) p. 88.

347 Foucault (1980a) p. 97.

348 Hindness argues that, within contemporary society, contract can be viewed as itself providing a technique of power, for example as a process that produces the 'job seeker' who views him/herself as an individual who is contracting with the state. This is a change from the role of contract within liberal theory and will be discussed in Chapter 6. B. Hindness, 'A Society Governed by Contract?' Davis et al (1997) pp. 14-26.

It is useful to consider what Pateman wants to achieve by telling the story of the sexual contract. She concludes by indicating that its retrieval does not provide a political programme but opens up a new perspective from which to assess political possibilities.[349] In this respect her aim is constructive. Just as Irigaray reworks masculinist stories to allow something different to emerge, so Pateman wishes to problematize,

> [N]ature, sex, masculinity and femininity, the private, marriage, and prostitution...work and citizenship.[350]

This link between the operation of marriage contracts, employment contracts and citizenship is also illustrated in her recent article 'Self-Ownership and Property in the Person: Democratization and a Tale of Two Concepts'.[351] Pateman is consistent with her earlier work when she argues that subordination within the workplace and the home prevents both men and women from developing the personal attributes necessary for 'active citizenship'.[352]

A further criticism is levelled at Pateman by Moira Gatens. Gatens[353] points out that, despite the useful detailed readings of the social contract theorists, Pateman's model is underpinned by a view of women as sexually vulnerable to men. For Pateman, the social contract is set up as allowing men 'sexual access to women'. Pateman works with an image of men's mastery over women. Similarly, Fraser[354] argues that this does not adequately describe the relationship between men and women. However, Pateman's image does include the possibility of change. Pateman concludes positively arguing that,

> Men have a vested interest in maintaining the silence about the law of male sex-right, but the opportunity exists for political argument and action to move outside the dichotomies of patriarchal civil society, and for the creation of free relations in which manhood is reflected back from autonomous femininity.[355]

Pateman does not flesh out her view of 'autonomous femininity' and does not rely upon her image of what it is to be a self to support her important political critique of contract or her attack upon possessive individualism. This critical aspect of her work is therefore consistent with the image of selfhood that was discussed in Chapter 2, even if this is not a view of self that she employs.

---

349 Pateman (1988) p. 233.
350 Pateman (1988) p. 233.
351 Pateman (2002) pp. 20-27.
352 Pateman (2002) p. 34.
353 M. Gatens, 'Contracting Sex: Essence, Genealogy and Desire' in Gatens (1996) pp. 76-91.
354 N. Fraser, 'Beyond the Master/Subject Model: On Carole Pateman's *The Sexual Contract*' in Fraser (1997) pp. 225-235.
355 Pateman (1988) p. 233.

Whilst Pateman does acknowledge the changing nature of the family,[356] it is Brown[357] who tries to further this analysis by shifting her focus to the dichotomies within liberalism itself, rather than the contract *per se*. Although she criticises Pateman, Brown's analysis is similar to Pateman's in a number of respects. To examine these, it is useful to move away from the social contract itself and to detail Pateman's analysis of two particular contracts: the marriage contract and the employment contract.

The Relationship between the Social Contract, Marriage Contracts and Employment Contracts

Before considering these contracts separately it is worth briefly discussing their relationship with the social contract. Gatens[358] argues that Pateman's analysis of the social contract sits uneasily with her consideration of the marriage and employment contracts. Again, I want to defend Pateman on this point. Whilst the social contract is employed by theorists as a heuristic devise, this theoretical move does stem from and, to some extent, perpetuates the same cultural beliefs as other uses of contract, i.e. it employs a contractual framework through which to consider social relations.

In the story of the social contract as told by Hobbes,[359] it is the social contract that allows other contracts to exist, by producing the conditions under which their enforcement can be guaranteed. However, it is possible to reverse this argument. What we understand by 'contract' is not fixed. It is being created by the way in which the term 'contract' is used, for example the way in which the law of contract is understood in the courts when dealing with specific types of contract, such as marriage contracts and employment contracts. This meaning of contract can then be read back into the story of the social contract.

Similarly, images of the story of the social contract can colour the meaning of 'contract'. The question of when (and whether) the weaker party can end a contract continues to be subject to argument in both the social contract theory and in the courts' analyses of employment contracts and marriage contracts. Hobbes argued that the sovereign should enforce contracts, including the social contract, even if those subject to it had been forced into agreement by the use or threat of violence. The only time a subject could reject the social contract would be if her/his life were to be threatened. This is a necessary exception for Hobbes, in order to be consistent with his argument that the subject's motivation for giving up his freedom is to

---

356 C. Pateman, 'Beyond the Sexual Contract?' in G. Dench, *Rewriting the Sexual Contract: Collected Views on Changing Relationships and Sexual Divisions of Labour* (London: Institute of Community Studies, 1997) pp. 1-9.

357 W. Brown, 'Liberalism's Family Values' in Brown (1995) pp. 135-165.

358 M. Gatens, 'Contracting Sex: Essence, Genealogy and Desire' in Gatens (1996) pp. 76-91.

359 As discussed above, Hobbes is important for Pateman because he is not typical of the social contract theorists who viewed women's subordination within the family as natural.

survive. This is central to Hobbes' image of 'human nature'. If the sovereign could kill one of his subjects then the subject would have been better off taking his or her chances in the state of nature. As I will discuss below, if an employer threatens an employee's life then this would certainly be viewed as a fundamental breach of contract. The employee would be able to treat the contract as already ended. Importantly, the same is not true within a marriage because court action is required before either party can end the contract.

Workers who suffer poor working conditions know that they have to endure them because the other options are worse and they are not persuaded that the use of contract spells equality. Similarly, married women may well not consider the contractual nature of marriage unless attempting to escape a violent man or divorcing. Nevertheless, this does not mean that to criticise contract is to criticise a fetish, as Brown argues against Pateman.[360] Further, the courts are willing to read an employment contract into a relationship which complies with the courts' tests as to whether the person working is an employee rather than an independent contractor.[361] Contractual terms are implied into the contract irrespective of the parties' intentions or whether they had complied with the law by signing a written contract of terms and conditions. The mechanism used within employment law is therefore to decide that there is a contract and then to imply terms into this contract.

Compare this legal mechanism to the law relating to women who are mothers and cohabiting, but are not subject to a marriage contract. In a traditional relationship, in which women work in the home and have not contributed money or monies worth to the purchase of the house, the unmarried woman is in a less secure position with regard to financial claims if the relationship ends. However, the law will imply obligations upon men with regard to the upkeep of children. This now operates through the Child Support Agency,[362] which imposes an obligation upon the father to support the child and operates in an analogous manner to the way in which employment tribunals impose obligations upon employers, discussed above. Whether the father's obligations to the child are viewed as an implied contract, entered into upon the birth, or through another mechanism, does not necessarily

---

360 W. Brown, 'Liberalism's Family Values' in Brown (1995) pp. 135-165.
361 This distinction stems from the Beveridge Report which replaced the nineteenth century terms of independent contractor, casual worker, servant, labourer and workmen. See Deakin (2002) p. 179.
362 This is not an endorsement of the Child Support Agency. See for example, M. Freeman, 'Divorce: Contemporary Problems and Future Prospects' in M. Freeman, *Divorce: Where Next?* (Aldershot: Dartmouth, 1996) pp. 1-8. Freeman argues that 'It is as unsurprising as it is unfortunate that the moral panic engendered around the CSA should concern its impact upon men...rather than on the plight of one-parent female-headed households or the feminisation of poverty' Freeman (1996) p. 2. The rejection of the Beveridge proposal to include housewives as a class to be insured against marital breakdown was discussed in the last chapter.

make much difference to the outcome. The position of gay couples has also moved from a position of not being recognised by the law, with those ensuing advantages and disadvantages, to one of increased regulation.[363]

Once the courts were willing to extend the use of implied terms in contracts, in order to protect the weaker party, the nineteenth century laissez faire image of two persons making an agreement was lost.[364] Through the use of protective statutes, the law will impose obligations upon the stronger party. This also impacts upon the weaker party in unpredictable ways 'on the ground'. For example, a father may view child support payments as an exchange that allows him to maintain contact with both the child and the mother. The discussion of contract is important because it still occurs, even though the relationship between status and contract is ambiguous. Pateman's strength is in drawing these two together. For the last two sections of this chapter I will consider Pateman's work in the context of contemporary English marriage contracts and employment contracts.

The Marriage Contract

Pateman gives an historical account of the legal ambiguity of women's position within the marriage contract, brought out by comparing it with the slave contract and the employment contract. She raises a number of legal issues that are not of contemporary relevance and yet provide an important background to cultural understandings, and contemporary legal deliberations, about marriage. She avoids the trap of treating law as an ideal form that needs to be consistent. It is often inconsistent because 'legal reasoning' tends to provide a *post hoc* justification for the decision reached.[365]

Both Nancy Fraser[366] and Wendy Brown[367] provide useful responses to Pateman's position, with regard to a contemporary understanding of the marriage contract, at a time when the nuclear family is breaking down. Fraser focuses upon one aspect of Pateman's work: her reading of the relationship between the parties to the contract. As mentioned above, she argues that Pateman views this relationship in terms of 'master/subject'[368] which does not adequately describe the marriage relationship.

---

363 See D. Bell and J. Binnie, 'Sexual Citizenship: Law, Theory and Politics' in J. Richardson and R. Sandland, *Feminist Perspectives on Law and Theory* (London: Cavendish, 2000) pp. 167-186.
364 For an extended discussion of this point see Atiyah (2000).
365 For support see, for example, Mossman (1991); Griffiths (1997).
366 N. Fraser, 'Beyond the Master/Subject Model: On Carole Pateman's *The Sexual Contract*' in Fraser (1997) pp. 225-235.
367 W. Brown, 'Liberalism's Family Values' in Brown (1995) pp. 135-165.
368 This is a difficult phrase for Fraser to use. Although this is not discussed, the reason that the common terms 'master/slave' or 'master/servant' – which is still a feature of employment law texts – is avoided clearly because Pateman draws out the difference between these situations. One of the strengths of Pateman's work is her historical analysis of the employment contract that derives from consideration of the position of wives – rather than vice versa.

Fraser holds onto the importance of considering women's position within society as a whole – in order to make the simple point that marriage involves more than male sex-right within the marriage itself. She draws upon the work of Okin[369] to produce an argument that appears relevant to the position of women in the UK as well as the US,

> If marriage still too often resembles a master/subject relation, this is due in large measure to its social embeddedness in relation to sex-segmented labor markets, gender-structured social-welfare policy regimes, and the gender division of unpaid labour...In general, then, although the legal reform of marriage remains significantly incomplete, the institution in the United States today is probably better understood as an unequal partnership in which 'voice' correlates inversely with opportunities for 'exit' than as a master/subject relation.[370]

She also argues that the relationship of 'master/subject' may provide an interpretative framework for some couples but not for others. I think this is right, but also that this does not generally undermine Pateman's analysis of the social contract theorists nor upon the different types of subordination historically attached to the marriage contract and employment contract.

In contrast, Brown's concerns do focus upon Pateman's project as a whole and attempt to supersede it. Brown[371] draws an analogy with the work of Weber to illustrate her argument that Pateman's position is historically correct but is *no longer* relevant. Weber, she argues, illustrated the way in which capitalism relied upon a Protestant work ethic and then pointed to the fact that a work ethic is no longer needed for the maintenance of capitalism. This Protestant work ethic is now only reproduced in certain aspects of the culture. Similarly, she argues that Pateman correctly outlines the historical role of contract in women's subordination, but that Pateman fails to see that contract is no longer necessary for its continuation. To continue to fight against contract, Brown argues, would be like attacking Protestantism in the hope of undermining capitalist exploitation.

This argument is more applicable to marriage contracts than to employment contracts. As discussed at the beginning of this chapter, Pateman has admitted that,

> The patriarchal structures with which I was concerned have been considerably weakened, and the heyday of the worker/breadwinner was from 1840-1970.[372]

Nevertheless, Pateman argues that the sexual contract still provides a useful tool for contemporary analysis. Brown goes on to develop her own position which draws upon Pateman. At a basic level, she argues that Pateman's attack on the marriage contract cannot account for the position of single women, with or without children. Women are

---

369 Okin (1989) cited N. Fraser, 'Beyond the Master/Subject Model: On Carole Pateman's *The Sexual Contract*' in Fraser (1997) p. 228.
370 N. Fraser, 'Beyond the Master/Subject Model: On Carole Pateman's *The Sexual Contract*' in Fraser (1997) p. 228.
371 W. Brown, 'Liberalism's Family Values' in Brown (1995) p. 135.
372 Pateman (1996) p. 204.

no longer forced into the marriage contract for survival or even for social recognition. Brown ignores legal change in the nature of marriage itself and seems to regard these as largely irrelevant. Here, it must be emphasised that Brown is writing in the context of US law and not English law. It is arguable that, in England, there has been a shift away from the last vestiges of the doctrine of coverture. The House of Lords decision in *R v R* (1991)[373] (that women could no longer be legally forced to have sex with their husbands) is a move towards the courts seeing marriage in terms of contract and away from status – although this is as yet not fully realised in England. For example, the bar on gay marriages means that the parties to the contract must be male and female, i.e. based upon status in this regard.

There is a split between the ways in which the English courts deal with marriage – and, where possible, incorporate the position of cohabitees within their remit – and popular views of marriage. A stark example of the way in which the courts reason when viewing marriage through the framework of contract is provided by the case of *R v R* (1991). In the High Court, at first instance, the discussion of rape within marriage in this case centred upon a consideration of implied terms within the marriage contract. This will be examined below but the contractual framework employed must be borne in mind whilst considering Brown's argument that contract is no longer an important factor in maintaining women's subordination.

As I will discuss below, there is an argument within employment law that the increase in the use of implied terms (in part through an increase in protective legislation in such areas as health and safety) has resulted in a shift away from the traditional image of contract.[374] As Pateman rightly points out, the problem with the marriage contract (and employment contracts) is that the contracting parties enter into relationships of subordination because the weaker party purports to contract something which cannot be separated from her/his body. Whether or not this body is female may well be relevant to the service that is to be provided and cannot be abstracted away from any analysis.

Brown's central argument is that,

> the legacy of gender subordination Pateman identifies as historically installed in the sexual-social contract is to be found not in contemporary contract relations but in the *terms* of liberal discourse that configure and organize liberal jurisprudence, public policy and popular consciousness.[375] (Emphasis is in the original.)

So, Brown, advocates a move away from the sexual contract and towards an analysis of the liberal discourse that is premised upon it. Given that Pateman's sexual contract takes the form of a reworking of a story, it is initially difficult to understand how Brown's move can be useful. Some of Brown's analysis in illustrating how 'liberal

---

373 *R v R* (1991) 4 All. ER 481.
374 A. Thompson, 'The Law of Contract' in I. Grigg-Spall and P. Ireland, eds., *The Critical Lawyers' Handbook* (London: Pluto, 1992) pp. 69-76.
375 W. Brown (1995) p. 138.

ontology is fundamentally and not continently gendered'[376] covers very similar ground to that of Pateman, particularly Pateman's earlier work on the problematic nature of women's consent.[377] However, Brown's work is helpful in broadening Pateman's analysis – in a manner similar to that of Fraser – to consider the breakdown of the family. This involves recognising that the marriage contract as such is not required for women's subordination. This does not undermine Pateman's argument so much as move forward to consider the position of women for whom the state is increasingly 'the man in their lives'.[378] As discussed above, the law in this area could be conceived as contractual because the courts are willing to impose some obligations upon unmarried fathers – just as they impose obligations upon employees without a written employment contract. This involves blurring a distinction between status and contract that is already present in both employment and marriage contracts, to be considered in more detail below.

In Brown's discussion of the way in which women's bodies are viewed as vulnerable to rape, she considers a link between the image of women as being unable to defend the boundaries of the state and as being unable to defend their own bodily boundaries. The role of the female body – and its supposed vulnerability to rape – is then considered within myths of origin of the state, including the story of the social/sexual contract. These myths of origin justify law as necessary to protect women from their so-called 'natural' vulnerability to rape. It is this unquestioned assumption that women are naturally susceptible to rape that Gatens[379] accuses Pateman of maintaining. By considering the social contract within the context of other myths of origin, Brown avoids emphasising 'contract' *per se*.[380] Women are positioned as being vulnerable to rape and the law is viewed as being their protector, a set-up which

---

376 W. Brown (1995) p. 150.

377 This links with criminal law and the many debates around the problem of the role of consent in rape law and its relationship to citizenship. See Pateman (1980) pp. 71-89. This point is also taken up by Ngaire Naffine in Naffine (1998); with regard to medical consent and subjectivity by Katherine O'Donovan in O'Donovan (1997) pp. 47-64. For Brown's discussion on consent see Brown (1995) pp. 162-4.

378 This is also the concern of Fraser who has analysed the political meaning of need and dependency. See, for example, N. Fraser, 'Women, Welfare and the Politics of Need Interpretation' and 'Struggle over Needs: Outline of a Socialist-Feminist Critical Theory of Late Capitalist Political Culture' in Fraser (1989) pp. 144-187; 'A Genealogy of 'Dependency': Tracing a Keyword of the U.S. Welfare State' in Fraser (1997). This is the area that is missing from historical (1840-1970) discussions of the marriage and employment contracts in *The Sexual Contract* but which is addressed in Pateman's later work. See C. Pateman, 'The Patriarchal Welfare State' in J.B. Landes, ed., *Feminism: the Public and Private* (Oxford: Oxford University Press, 1998) pp. 241-274.

379 M. Gatens, 'Contracting Sex: Essence, Genealogy and Desire' in Gatens (1996) pp. 76-91.

380 Brown's discussion, which also includes a discussion of Freud, resonates with the move that Whitford makes in linking the social contract with the 'symbolic contract'. See also M. Whitford, 'Irigaray, Utopia and the Death Drive' in C. Burke, N. Schor and M. Whitford, eds., *Engaging with Irigaray* (New York: Columbia University Press, 1994) pp. 379-400.

Brown describes as a 'protection racket'.[381] This can be viewed as an *inversion* of what has actually happened. As Pateman illustrates, law did not protect women. It created a realm, the 'state' of marriage, in which women could be forced to have sex legitimately. To draw on Marcus,[382] these stories about law (and the legal proceeding themselves) perpetuate an image of woman's body as already raped and men as naturally potential rapists. This is to view these stories, not as perpetuating a false consciousness, but as an inverted description of the way in which social relations operated in a society at a particular time. To make this move does not entail an assumption that these social relations are fixed.

The case of *R v R* (1991) can be used as an illustration of the way in which marriage has been discussed in terms of contract. The precedent that a husband can legally force his wife to have sex dates from Sir Matthew Hale's *History of the Pleas of the Crown* (1736),[383]

> But the husband cannot be guilty of rape committed by himself upon his lawful wife, for by their mutual matrimonial consent and contract the wife hath given up herself in this kind unto her husband which she cannot retract.

This was applied in the ecclesiastical courts in *Popkin v Popkin* (1794) in which Lord Stowell said that,

> The husband has a right to the person of his wife but not if her health is endangered.[384]

This is a noteworthy use of the term 'person' given that women were not viewed as 'persons' until the courts declared that they had achieved personhood in the Persons Case.[385]

The discussion in *R v R* (1991) centres upon the legal framework of contractual implied terms. This is the same framework in which employment contracts are discussed and the use of the implied term within these contracts is strikingly similar. This mechanism has allowed the courts to alter contracts according to their own – usually conservative – beliefs.[386] A quotation from Owen J., the trial judge at first instance, illustrates how the framework of contract is used. In this case, Owen J. is

---

381 Brown (1995) p. 188.
382 S. Marcus, 'Fighting Bodies, Fighting Words: A Theory and Politics of Rape Prevention' in J. Butler and J.W. Scott, eds., *Feminists Theorize the Political* (London: Routledge, 1992) pp. 385-403.
383 M. Hale, *Hale's History of the Pleas of the Crown* (1736) Vol. 1, Ch. 58, p. 629 cited in *R v R* (1991) 4 All ER 481 at p. 604.
384 Cited *R v R* (1991) 4 All ER 481, at p. 604.
385 *Edwards v Attorney General of Canada* (1930) A.C. 124. This is discussed in Chapter 3.
386 For a detailed analysis see, for example, Griffiths (1997).

saddled with the contractual legal framework through which the law views marriage, but, in a climate influenced by feminism, he also seeks to mitigate against the misogyny of earlier decisions:

> What, in law, will suffice to revoke that consent which the wife gives to sexual intercourse upon marriage and which the law implies from the facts of the marriage?...It must be sufficient for there to be agreement between the parties. Of course, an agreement of the parties means what it says. It does not mean something which is done unilaterally...As it seems to me, from his action in telephoning her and saying that he intended to see about a divorce and thereby to accede to what she was doing, there is sufficient here to indicate that there was an implied agreement to a separation and to a withdrawal of that consent to sexual intercourse, which the law, I will assume and accept, implies.[387]

Whilst, for the majority of the population, contract may not provide a conceptual framework through which to consider rape, it does provide such a frame of reference for judges – even if it is only evoked to justify a decision that is made on the grounds of public policy. Here, the trial judge is discussing the implications of the husband's act of telephoning his wife to say that he intended to seek a divorce. Owen J., the trial judge, can be understood to be posing the following question: *was this telephone call sufficient to indicate an implied agreement to divorce which would be sufficient to revoke the wife's implied consent to sex within the marriage contract?*

Owen J. refers to the principle in contract that an agreement is not something that can be made unilaterally. This point can be examined using an example from employment law. If there is a fundamental breach of contract by one of the parties, the other party can assume that, because of this action in itself, s/he is no longer bound by the contract. So for example, if my employer hit me I could walk out and claim unfair dismissal. The violent action alone would be taken to mean that the employer no longer intended to maintain the employment contract and, therefore, that I was released immediately from my obligations under the contract. If I ignored this behaviour then I would be deemed to have *accepted* the employer's breach of contract and the contract would be deemed to continue. Married women are in a worse position than employees in this respect because there is no violent act, short of murder, that can automatically release them from the marriage contract. Ironically, in this sense, employment contracts are more 'private', as they can be ended without the intervention of the courts.

Further, the position of women within marriage can be compared to that of women who were sexually harassed at work, prior to the landmark case of *Porcelli v Strathclyde R.C.* (1984).[388] Before this decision, women had to show that an act of

---

387 *R v R* (1991) 1 All ER 747, at p. 754 discussed by the Lords in *R v R* (1991) 4 All ER 481, at p. 606.
388 *Porcelli v Strathclyde R.C.* (1984) ICR 177. This Scottish case is now part of English law. For a summary of current law on sexual harassment, see S. Johnson and M. Rubenstein, 'Sexual Harassment and the Law', *Equal Opportunities Review*, No. 102, February, 2002, pp. 16-17.

sexual harassment was linked to some other contractual disadvantage, for example, a demotion or dismissal, in order to claim damages for a breach of *Sex Discrimination Act 1975*. In *Porcelli*, the Court of Sessions decided that sexual harassment was to be treated as a detriment in its own right and so it was no longer necessary to show any further detriment. This can be compared with the situation pertaining under the marriage contract. In the case of *R v R* (1991), Owen J. did not assume that the rape alone, as an act in its own right, could demonstrate even a willingness to end the marriage contract. This had to be demonstrated by the telephone call in which divorce was discussed.

Implied terms have become important within the employment and matrimonial contracts because they regulate relationships of subordination. The demands of these relationships cannot be dictated in sufficient detail by the contract itself, and therefore the courts are willing to imply extra terms into the contract. Within the twentieth century this has also been a mechanism by which protective legislation has been implemented. The temporal sequence of these contracts needs to be thought through, to understand their effects, in order to consider whether Brown is right in her argument that contract is no longer important in women's subordination. Whereas an employment contract may be the subject of negotiation between employer and employee (or his/her trade union)[389] during the course of the relationship, the same framework of negotiation may not occur within marriage – although informal daily negotiation may well occur.[390] The courts are normally involved only after the relationship has broken down. Therefore, the implied term arises later. However, this provides a framework through which the relationship can be viewed by the parties and which can provide leverage when a relationship is breaking down. This is particularly the case when legal advice is sought within the duration of the relationship.[391]

Linked with this point, Elizabeth Kingdom[392] has argued in favour of the adoption of cohabitation contracts, for both married couples and cohabitees, allocating responsibility for domestic tasks. Whilst it is useful to focus upon such issues at the start of the relationship, Okin's arguments are relevant, here. Okin[393] points out that the family systematically produces vulnerability through women's disproportionate

---

389 There has been a shift in the role of trade unions away from that of collective negotiation to that of monitoring and enforcing individual members' legal claims. See Deakin (2002) pp. 193-194; H. Collins, K.D. Ewing and A. McColgan, *Labour Law: Tests and Materials* (Oxford: Hart Publishing, 2001) pp. 56-58.

390 See, for example, R. Lister and C. Callender, 'Income Distribution within Families and the Reform of Social Security', *Journal of Social Welfare and Family Law*, Vol. 21, No. 3, 1999, pp. 203-220.

391 In a Kafkaesque manner, myths abound as to what is law, especially amongst people who are afraid to seek legal advice. I had a client who thought that her children would be taken away if she instigated divorce. In these circumstances, the myths can be even more conservative than the law.

392 E. Kingdom, 'Cohabitation Contracts and the Democratization of Personal Relations', *Feminist Legal Studies*, Vol. 8, 2000, pp. 5-27.

393 Okin (1989) pp. 167-169.

contribution to child care. Here, the comparison between marriage (or cohabitation) contracts and employment contracts is helpful. Whilst negotiation in both situations may be useful, more radical change is required in order for this to become democratic – a point that Kingdom acknowledges.[394]

Returning to the case of *R v R* (1991), the case proceeded to the Court of Appeal and the House of Lords, both of which decided to take what the Court of Appeal called 'the radical solution':[395] that there was no longer to be a marital immunity to rape. This decision was described as the 'removal of a common law fiction which has become anachronistic and offensive'.[396] The Lords did not attack the use of a contractual framework through which to think about marriage. On the contrary, they employed a contractual framework but held that a particular contractual term (that a woman could be assumed to consent to sex with her husband) could no longer be implied into the marriage contract. This leaves open the possibility that further regulation of marriage contracts could occur through the courts' use of implied contractual terms.

Pateman's analysis of the marriage, civil slave and employment contracts draws out the complexities of trying to view long term relationships within this contractual frame.[397] Brown discusses this in terms of an ideological moment in which the exploitative nature of the relationship is obscured when contract is portrayed as a free exchange between equals – in keeping with Pateman's analysis and that of Marx. For Brown, there is also a discursive moment in which identities are created. My rereading of Pateman makes Brown's move unnecessary. Pateman herself argues that the contract produces wives and employees. It is possible to rework Pateman's analysis in a manner that plays down the moments when she assumes that women's vulnerability is fixed. I will deal with this further in the next chapter.

Brown attempts to supersede Pateman by focusing upon the way in which liberalism produces dichotomies: equality/difference, liberty/necessity, autonomy/dependence, rights/needs, individual/family, self-interest/selflessness, public/private, contract/consent.[398] This is a useful analysis, which draws out dichotomies which are already implicit in Pateman's own work. Brown is right to argue that there is a move away from the predominance of the marriage contract itself – if by this she means that marriage is no longer central within the subordination and exploitation of women compared with the time when marriage served as a legal disability. However, the case of *R v R* (1991) illustrates the way in which contract is still applied within the courts. In addition, there is still an appeal to contract, particularly in terms of the growing areas of surrogacy, reproductive technology and debates around cohabitation contracts as well as employment contracts.

---

394 Kingdom (2000) p. 23.
395 *R v R* (1991) 2 WLR 1065 and *R v R* (1991) 4 All ER 481.
396 *R v R* (1991) 2 WLR 1065 and *R v R* (1991) 4 All ER 481.
397 This has been recognised by contract lawyers as well as by employment lawyers (who are unable to avoid noticing this point). See I. MacNeil, *The New Social Contract* (Yale: Yale University Press, 1980).
398 W. Brown, 'Liberalism's Family Values' in Brown (1995) p. 152.

The Employment Contract

Against Brown, I will argue that contract is still prevalent within the way in which employees think about their position. Whereas Pateman's earlier work[399] considered the problem of 'political obligation' in terms of questions of obligations to obey the state, in *The Sexual Contract*[400] she is concerned with *civil* contractual obligations. In other words, Pateman is concerned with obligations between individuals and between individuals and companies.[401] Her Marxist argument regarding the employment contract resolves a problem that is still discussed within contemporary employment law text books and employment case law. It is worth considering this because it is relevant to the way in which a worker is viewed as having property in his person, to be discussed in more detail in the next chapter.

The problem for the courts is that it is difficult to draw up a distinction between employees and independent contractors if it is assumed that the employment contract is a contract for a particular piece of work. There are a number of tests employed in this area.[402] One way in which this problem is avoided is by dividing the employment contract into two stages: firstly, the exchange of work for wages; and, secondly, the creation of an expectation that the same exchange will occur again in future. This can be illustrated by the following quotation from Freeland, an employment lawyer:

> [T]he contract has a two-tiered structure. At the first level there is an exchange of work and remuneration. At the second level there is an exchange of mutual obligations for future performance. The second level – the promise to employ and be employed – provides the arrangement with its stability and with its continuity as a contract.[403]

This glories in the title of 'mutuality of obligations test' and has been used in cases[404] to consider the question of whether to classify a worker as an employee (with employment rights) or an independent contractor (with even fewer rights). This problem only arises for liberal employment lawyers because they view the employment contract as being an exchange of labour – rather than labour power (i.e. the capacity to labour) – for money. The difference is important because the exchange of labour for money would imply that all labour was paid for, i.e. that employees received the value of the goods they produced. As Marx[405] argued, if this were true then there would be no valorisation of capital as a result of the extraction of surplus

---

399 For example, C. Pateman, *The Problem of Political Obligation: A Critique of Liberal Theory* (Cambridge: Polity, 1985).

400 Pateman (1988).

401 Companies have legal personality.

402 S. Deakin and G.S. Morris, *Labour Law* (London: Butterworths, 2001) p. 148.

403 M. Freeland, *The Contract of Employment* (Oxford : Clarendon Press, 1976) p. 20.

404 *Hewlett Packard Ltd. v O'Murphy* No. EAT/612/01; (2001) WL 1135163; the argument has been used to exclude non-traditional workers (disproportionately affecting women) from employment rights, see *O'Kelly v Trust House Forte* (1984) QB 90.

405 Marx (1954) p. 172.

value. In other words, the worker would be paid for all of the working day and not simply a part of it.

Pateman also details the way in which the employment contract differs from the marriage contract. As Whitford[406] points out, Pateman covers similar ground to Irigaray, whilst concentrating upon an historical perspective. This part of *The Sexual Contract* does not fit exactly with Irigaray's rereading of Marx and yet raises similar issues relating to the relationship between women's subordination and capitalism. Both want to keep hold of important aspects of Marx's analysis whilst refusing to privilege the employment contract. Pateman points to four main ways in which the 'free' labour of employees differs from 'unfree' labour of married women (and slaves): workers are paid a wage rather than provided with 'protection'; the employment contract is limited in time whereas married women have an open-ended obligation with regard to housework; the worker is not deemed to contract out himself (or 'person' as Lord Stowell put it in *Popkin v Popkin (1794)*, discussed above) but his labour power – part of the property in the person; the worker stands on an equal footing with the employer as a 'juridically free and equal citizen'. With regard to this last point alone, regarding formal equality, married women have achieved the same status as men. The fact that married women were not viewed as having property in their person is another way of saying that only men were traditionally viewed as possessive individuals, or as having self-ownership, to be discussed in the next chapter.

The peculiarity of the employment contract can be brought out by Pateman's[407] comparison between three different versions of the relationship between workers and 'property in the person'. If it is assumed that one's ability to work can be treated as a commodity and can be alienated completely, this results in a slave contract. There are no limitations upon the work and this is associated with a difference in status between master and slave. The current situation is that the worker's labour power is sold in accordance with a contract on a more piecemeal basis and both employer and employee are viewed as juridically equal. This represents a middle path for Pateman. The third alternative is to deny that human abilities can be removed from the person. The employment contract really requires a worker to turn up and be told what to do. Pateman's third alternative is therefore to question why 'the renting of persons' is viewed as compatible with political equality. Her focus is therefore upon subordination and the interrelationship between marriage and employment contracts and the welfare state. As she puts it,

> But if democratisation is to take place, property in the person must be left behind with civil subordination. Two of the most important questions are whether the right of self-government should continue to be (partially) alienable, and whether the renting of persons should be deemed compatible with democratic citizenship.[408]

---

406 M. Whitford, *Luce Irigaray: Philosophy in the Feminine* (London: Routledge, 1991) pp. 169-191.
407 Pateman (2002) p. 31.
408 Pateman (2002) p. 52.

To illustrate the difference between employment and marriage contracts I will return to the question of the termination of the contract. To recap, whereas the domestic sphere – as compared to civil society and the state – was viewed as 'private', as soon as the question of termination of the contract arises the marriage contract can be viewed as more 'public' than the employment contract. It is necessary to be careful about the use of the terms: public/private. In law, to describe a case as involving 'public' law means that the state is involved. 'Private' law therefore covers any litigation between individuals and/or companies that, by definition, have legal personality. However, here I simply mean that employment contracts can be severed without court involvement whereas the termination of a marriage must be read out in open court, i.e. made public in the broader sense of the term. It is impossible to repudiate a marriage contract without the involvement of the courts. So, in the example mentioned above, if an employer hits an employee then this constitutes constructive dismissal and the employee can accept the breach of contract, and can leave and claim damages for unfair dismissal. However, wife beating will not be taken as repudiation of the marriage contract.

Further, it is relevant to consider why only damages are available in these circumstances within the employment scenario. Reinstatement is not awarded when the employment relationship is judged by the employment tribunal to have broken down. In this way, the courts discuss the employment relationship in the same terms as a divorce, in which irretrievable breakdown of the relationship must be demonstrated.[409] The personal nature of the employment contract is also viewed as important within other legal tests. For example, there is deemed (by the courts) to be an implied term of 'mutual trust and confidence' in all employment contracts. In considering this, the courts have, on occasions, applied a psychological test. It has been argued that the implied existence of the 'mutual trust and confidence' term means that not only must the employee have trust and confidence in her/his employer, s/he must also be able to believe reasonably that the employer has trust and confidence in her/him. For example, an employer requesting that an employee take a psychiatric examination was deemed to have breached this term because this behaviour 'objectively'[410] implies that the employer does not have trust and confidence in the employee.[411]

Brown's critique of Pateman must be considered in the context of the courts' wide ability to imply terms into employment contracts. In this case, the relationship is still viewed in terms of 'contract' but this contract is far from the paradigm image of an exchange between two equal individuals. The marriage contract has changed, dropping some of its 'brutal origins',[412] and at the same time is becoming less relevant, as it shifts, to some degree, away from status. Pateman's critique of contract illustrates

---

409 *Matrimonial Causes Act 1973 s1(1).*
410 In law, the term 'objective' is used to describe the courts' decisions.
411 *Bliss v South East Thames Regional Health Authority* (1985) IRLR 308.
412 J.S. Mill, 'The Subjection of Women' in *Essays on Sex Equality*, ed. A.S. Rossi (Chicago: University of Chicago Press, 1970) p. 130 cited Pateman (1988) p. 119.

why this is not a solution for feminists, however. Women would not be better off if they could 'freely' negotiate the marriage contract, as I will discuss below. The employment contract is becoming more akin to a device for dealing with a status relationship, through the use of implied terms and protective legislation.

Brown should not be so confident that 'contract' has lost its pulling power. In a book review of *The New Contractualism?*[413] to be discussed in the next chapter, Dickenson has argued that,

> What is wrong with the sexual contract, and its expression in marriage, is not that it is a contract but the fact it is sexual. Critics like Pateman ... tend to confuse the historical circumstances which prevailed at the time liberalism got under way – specifically the massively inegalitarian doctrine of coverture in marriage – with the essence of contract itself.[414]

Dickenson[415] argues that contractual relations can ensure mutual recognition and respect between equals. But where are these (non-sexual) egalitarian contracts that she takes as the standard of comparison here? In *The New Contractualism?* Marcia Neave[416] expresses her doubts that a move to allow couples to negotiate the marriage contract by way of pre-nuptial agreements would increase women's freedom and autonomy, detailing the factors – derived from women's customary unequal role with regard to child care – that make women less able to negotiate on equal terms with men.

When Dickenson argues for 'egalitarian' contracts, is she really thinking of employment contracts? I have illustrated the way in which courts have used the device of implied terms to construct (in different ways) both marriage contracts and employment contracts after the relationships have ended. These result in contracts that have little in common with the idea of simple exchange or even the voluntary assumption of responsibilities.[417] Perhaps consumer contracts – in which we should be free to buy genetically modified foods from international companies – provide Dickenson with her ideal of equal exchange? If the (non-sexual) egalitarian contract is not to be found in practice then perhaps it is an ideal. Another question arises: is the model of equal persons that these egalitarian contracts employ a useful feminist ideal? It may be that the best example that can be found of such an idealised form of exchange contract is the trading that occurs between equal sized companies. But does such an account take the position of women as typical or as aberration? I will continue to consider these questions in the next chapter on 'possessive individualism'.

---

413 Davis et al (1997) cited in Dickenson (1998) pp. 108-111.

414 Dickenson (1998) p. 110.

415 Dickenson (1997).

416 M. Neave, 'The Hands that Sign the Paper: Women and Domestic Contracts' in Davis et al, *The New Contractualism?* (Melbourne: MacMillan, 1997) pp. 71-86. She cites Pateman approvingly at pp. 77-78.

417 For a discussion of contract law which highlights this point, see A. Thompson, 'The Law of Contract' in I. Grigg-Spall, and P. Ireland, eds., *The Critical Lawyers' Handbook* (London: Pluto, 1992) pp. 69-76.

Chapter 6

Possessive Individualism

Possessive individualism encompasses both a view of the self and normative political claims, some of which were touched upon in the last chapter. It also represents a point of tension and an area of political struggle at this point in time. The tension and political opportunities for change occur as a result of the breakdown of the traditional breadwinner/housewife model. At issue is the question of the extent to which women are treated as having self-ownership or property in their person or whether other (better) models can be adopted.

The position of women is a blind spot in the concept of possessive individualism. As an ontological concept it can be shown that we do not 'spring up like mushrooms'.[418] We are not individuals from the start. In Chapter 2 I discussed contemporary theories from different areas of philosophy which detail the emergence of selves, processes that are not envisaged as complete after childhood. Whilst these start from a position in which women are the norm, they also give a much better account of what it is to be a self for men than does possessive individualism.

However, the concept of possessive individualism is also normative. It is possible for proponents of this view to argue that we *should* be treated as if we were owners of our own abilities in order to have autonomy or to be treated justly. This is Nozick's[419] argument when he evokes Kant to argue that self-ownership is necessary if we are to be treated as ends and not means.[420] In this chapter I want to deal with these arguments. Again, I believe that this framework depends upon a failure to consider the position of women. Both Pateman and Okin illustrate the incoherence that arises when women are treated as possessive individuals. This theoretical analysis is important at a time when, as illustrated by the wrongful birth cases in Chapter 4, there is some ambiguity amongst judges over whether the courts should view women as owners of their abilities. It is also a view of the self that is assumed by proponents of 'law and economics',[421] which is influential within legal theory.

---

418 T. Hobbes, *Man and Citizen* (De Homine *and* De Cive), ed. B. Gert (Indiapolis: Hackett Publishing Company, 1998) Ch. VIII, p. 205.

419 Nozick (1974) pp. 32-33.

420 The form of this argument has some parallels in Cornell's radical rereading of Kant: that any legislator/judge should address the question of whether we would agree to the legislation/judgment if we were to be treated as free and equal persons. This cashes out with very different political consequences. For a discussion of the relationship between Cornell and Nozick see Chapter 3.

421 For example, R.A. Posner, *Economic Analysis of Law* (Boston: Little Brown, 1992) cited and discussed in Radin (2001) pp. 3-8.

In order to look at the meaning of possessive individualism in more detail I will consider the work of Crawford Brough Macpherson, which Tully describes in the following terms:

> Initially a challenge to the perceived wisdom, it soon became the reigning orthodoxy and then it was subjected to intense and sustained criticism.[422]

I will then discuss self-ownership by looking at some of the arguments of analytical Marxist Gerald Cohen and consider the ways in which both Pateman and Okin demonstrate that any view based upon possessive individualism depends upon its exclusion of women for its coherence.

As discussed above, by ignoring the position of women, proponents of possessive individualism also ignore the development of selves. At the end of the chapter I look at Anna Yeatman's[423] reaction to Pateman and her arguments that men were trained to view themselves as possessive individuals. The current training of persons to view themselves as possessive individuals is then considered, along with the gendered implication of Hindness'[424] argument that contract is now employed as a technique of control within the welfare state.

Possessive Individualism/Self-Ownership/Property in the Person

The term 'possessive individualism' is associated with the work of Macpherson. Macpherson[425] draws upon Marx to argue that men were treated as possessive individuals in the work of Hobbes, amongst other philosophers,[426] because this

---

422 J. Tully, 'After the Macpherson Thesis' in J. Tully, *An Approach to Political Philosophy: Locke in Contexts* (Cambridge: Cambridge University Press, 1993) p. 71.

423 Yeatman (1997).

424 Hindness (1997).

425 Macpherson (1962).

426 He includes in his analysis the following: Hobbes, The Levellers, Harrington, Locke, Hume, Burke, Bentham and James Mill. The first four are analysed in Macpherson (1962); Hume is discussed in C.B. Macpherson, 'The Economic Penetration of Political Theory: Some Hypotheses', *Journal of History of Ideas*, Vol. 39, 1978, pp. 101-118; Burke is dealt with in C.B. Macpherson, *Burke* (Oxford: Oxford University Press, 1980) and the utilitarians are discussed briefly in C.B. Macpherson, *The Life and Times of Liberal Democracy* (Oxford: Oxford University Press, 1977). For critical summaries of this work see D. Miller, 'The Macpherson Version', *Political Studies*, Vol. XXX, No. 1, 1982, pp. 120-127; Tully (1993) pp. 71-95. The many criticisms of Macpherson's thesis centre around the historical analysis as to when possessive individualism occurred. As I am interested in contemporary analysis of women's ambivalent position with regard to possessive individualism, and since it is not denied that persons are treated as having property in the person, i.e. as possessive individuals, I am not detailing this historical debate.

describes the behaviour of men within the emerging market economy and liberal tradition. The paradox of women's position is ignored by Macpherson.

Pateman argues that Macpherson's phrase 'possessive individualism',

> brilliantly encapsulates the character of the attributes that are presented as belonging 'naturally' to individuals. When the attempt is made to see individuals in complete abstraction and isolation from each other, to see them as 'ineluctably *separate* units', they necessarily appear as 'naturally' free and equal with each other. They also appear to be possessors of property, including the property they own in their personal attributes and capacities.[427] (Emphasis is in the original.)

In *The Political Theory of Possessive Individualism: Hobbes to Locke*,[428] Macpherson attacks the roots of the liberal democratic state, which he finds in English seventeenth-century political thought. Whilst recognising that Hobbes' arguments in support of a monarch – whose power is restricted only by his subjects' need to resist anyone who threatens their survival – is hardly liberal, Macpherson argues that the individualism that influenced subsequent theory starts with Hobbes.[429] The difficulty with the original seventeenth-century individualism lay in its 'possessive quality':

> Its possessive quality is found in its conception of the individual as essentially the proprietor of his own person or capacities, owing nothing to society for them....The relation of ownership, having become for more and more men the critically important relation determining their actual freedom and actual prospect of realizing their full potentialities, was read back into the nature of the individual. The individual, it was thought, is free in as much as he is proprietor of his person and its capacities. The human essence is freedom from dependence on the will of others, and freedom is a function of possession. Society becomes a lot of free equal individuals related to each other as proprietors of their own capacities and of what they have acquired by their exercise.[430]

Macpherson's definition of 'possessive individualism' as the image of individuals who own their person or capacities, is very similar to that succinct definition of 'self-ownership' proffered by the contemporary analytic Marxist, Gerald Cohen:[431]

---

427 Pateman (1985b) p. 25. This is a discussion about Hobbes and I extend Pateman's analysis to include Nozick, below. Both Rawls and Cornell make a move that involves thinking about 'free and equal persons'. However, neither Cornell nor Rawls adheres to a view of possessive individualism or self-ownership as I will define it in this section, i.e. the view that one's labour (and the fruits of ones labour) should be viewed as one's own property. Both want a greater distribution of resources than can be derived from this position. For further discussion of this point see Chapter 3.
428 Macpherson (1962).
429 Macpherson (1962) pp. 1-2. This point is also made by Cornell, discussed in Chapter 3.
430 Macpherson (1962) p. 3.
431 Cohen (1995).

to own oneself is to enjoy with respect to oneself all those rights which a slave owner has over a complete chattel slave.[432]

'Possessive individualism' or 'self-ownership' both provide an image of individuals as free to sell their labour power as a commodity, a defining feature of a capitalist mode of production. Marx[433] points out that workers are 'free' in both senses of the term. They are 'free of' the means of production. In other words, they do not own the means of production, and so have to work for those who do own these. They are also 'free' because they are treated as owners of their own labour power and are therefore not compelled to work for one particular 'master'. A society in which workers are treated as possessive individuals is therefore defined not only against a slave society, but against a feudal society.

Possessive individualism – or self-ownership – appears to describe a relationship between a subject and an object that it owns. To clarify this point, it is worth considering the way in which this view of ownership has arisen. Macpherson[434] has traced the way that this view of property arose historically – illustrating the point that property ownership entails a regulation of relations between persons, not the relationship between a person and a thing. Cohen adds the following to his discussion of self-ownership:

> Note that what is owned, according to the thesis of self-ownership, is not a self, where 'self' is used to denote some particularly intimate, or essential, part of the person. The slaveowner's ownership is not restricted to the self, so construed, of the slave, and the moral self-owner is, similarly, possessed of himself entire, and not of his self alone. The term 'self' in the name of the thesis of self-ownership has a purely reflexive significance. It signifies that what owns and what is owned are one and the same, namely, the whole person. There is, consequently, no need to establish that my arm or my power to play basketball well is a proper part of my self, in order for me to claim sovereignty over it under the thesis of self-ownership.[435]

Although Macpherson discusses the possessive individual as 'owing nothing to society' this does not contradict Cohen's definition of 'self-ownership', which I am arguing is synonymous with it. Cohen's[436] analysis takes the form of an attack upon the concept of self-ownership generally and the implications of it that are drawn by

---

432 Cohen (1995) p. 214.

433 Marx (1976) Ch. 6, p. 280.

434 C.B. Macpherson, 'Liberal Democracy and Property' in Macpherson (1978b).

435 Cohen (1995) pp. 68-69. The definition becomes relevant to his arguments against Nozick – as illustrated by the reference to the basketball play, discussed as a thought experiment about Wilt Chamberlain by Nozick in Nozick (1974) pp. 161-163. It should be noted that my discussions of 'self' in earlier chapters do not refer to an intimate part of the person but to the whole of the 'person' as Cohen uses the term, here. I have reserved the term 'person' in relation to legal issues whereas self is used as an ontological concept.

436 Cohen (1995).

Nozick, in particular. As discussed in Chapters 3 and 4 (with respect to Cornell's legal test), Nozick argues that we should be treated as if we have those rights over ourselves that would belong to a chattel-slave owner in a slave society. Therefore, we should not have our labour appropriated by taxation, above that necessary to sustain a minimal state.

In attacking Nozick, Cohen claims that self-ownership (or possessive individualism, as I have discussed it) cannot be easily dismissed by Marxists because they make a similar move. When Marx claimed that the extraction of surplus value involved 'theft' from workers, the claim was based on the assumption that workers should own the fruits of their own labour, i.e. be treated as possessive individuals (or as having self-ownership). Nozick makes exactly the same move in attacking taxation on the grounds that possessive individuals should have the right to the fruits of their labour. Cohen illustrates that the premise of self-ownership can be dropped and that without it Marxism has the resources to argue against Nozick, by showing that the laissez-faire liberalism, that would result from a society based upon Nozick's possessive individualism, would reduce the autonomy[437] of the working class.

To illustrate his use of the term further, Cohen goes on to criticise James Tully for Tully's argument that in order to talk about self-ownership it would be necessary to separate selves from their abilities. Cohen adds,

> For the existence of 'selves' is not required by the thesis of self-ownership, and if ownership requires separability of what owns from what is owned, then self-ownership is impossible.[438]

It is this point and its implications that bring out what is central to Pateman's work. For Pateman, contracts in which one party agrees to use part of his/her body or an ability that cannot be separated from the body will necessarily involve *subordination*:

> The employer obtains right of command over the use of the bodies of workers in order, unilaterally, to have power over the process through which his commodities are produced.[439]

Pateman recognises, or course, that an ideal situation for both employer and husband is that the subordinate party regulates his or her self. Part of the work of both wives and employees is to try to predict the 'needs' of the husband or

---

437 Cohen defines 'autonomy' as having a range of choice. G.A. Cohen, 'Once more into the Breach of Self-Ownership: Reply Narveson and Brenkert', *The Journal of Ethics*, Vol. 2, 1998, pp. 86. Whether or not Nozick defines autonomy in this way does not affect Cohen's argument that self-ownership would reduce the range of choice of the working class in such a society. This is discussed in Cohen (1998) pp. 86-87.
438 Cohen (1995) p. 69.
439 Pateman (1988) p. 215.

demands of the employer. Pateman[440] prefers to use the term 'property in the person' derived from Locke[441] because she is concerned that recent debates in political theory around the more popular term 'self-ownership' tend to play down the 'ownership' aspect of the term. Like Cohen, she objects to the way in which 'self-ownership' is often employed as synonymous with 'autonomy'.

In order to think about Pateman's emphasis upon subordination it is useful to return to my discussion of agency in Chapter 2, which brings together the work of the philosopher of science, Oyama with Battersby's feminist metaphysics and Andy Clark on cognition. The relationship between employer and employee and husband and wife is negotiated. This process of negotiation can be envisaged in terms of the emergence of relationships in which the self is not passive but neither is she (or he) completely free. The image of a self that is most consistent with this is of one which emerges through relations with others, which is shaped and shapes her/his daily circumstances.[442]

'Kettle Logic'

In her critique of Pateman, Diana Coole[443] describes Pateman's arguments in *The Sexual Contract* as analogous to 'kettle logic'. According to Freud, 'kettle logic' involves the following arguments:

> I never borrowed your kettle.

> And it was in perfect condition when I returned it.

> Anyway, it was damaged when I got it.

She argues that it presents women with the same inconsistencies:

> Women have never been treated as possessive individuals.

> When they are it is a patriarchal trap.

---

440 Pateman (2002) p. 22.

441 'Every Man has a *Property* in his own *Person*. This no Body has any Right to but himself.' J. Locke, *Two Treatises of Government*, ed. P. Laslett, (Cambridge: Cambridge University Press, 1999) Book II, Ch. V, p. 287.

442 For details of the experience of this negotiation, which is obviously aided by those in a similar situation, see, for example, S.L. Bartky, 'Feeding Egos and Tending Wounds: Deference and Disaffection in Women's Emotional Labour' in *Femininity and Domination: Studies in the Phenomenology of Oppression* (London: Routledge, 1990) pp. 99-119; R. Pringle, *Secretaries Talk: Sexuality, Power and Work* (London: Verso Books, 1989). These make clear the extent to which isolated women are in a much weaker bargaining position.

443 D. Coole, 'Patriarchy and Contract', *Politics*, Vol. 10, No. 1, 1990, pp. 25-29.

Anyway, the whole concept is a fiction.[444]

Coole's accusation that Pateman is guilty of 'kettle logic' can only be addressed by considering women's ambiguous position with regard to both contracts and to possessive individualism. The logic of her objection raises the question of whether possessive individualism is necessarily assumed when a contractual framework is employed. To clarify this involves considering Pateman's analysis of contract in more detail. Pateman distinguishes between different types of contract. Firstly, it is possible to enter into contracts in which two things are swapped or in which parts of the human body which can be detached (such as sperm or kidneys) are exchanged. There may be concerns about the way in which parts of the body are treated as commodities sold by desperate persons in a black market[445] but this is not at issue in Pateman's analysis of the marriage and employment contracts. She is interested in contracts in which one's abilities are viewed as a commodity. To view oneself as owning one's abilities is central to the definition of a possessive individual, or 'self-ownership' or 'property in the person'.

The logic of Coole's criticism can be unpacked in the following way. If Pateman is arguing that all contracts for the use of a person's abilities are necessarily envisaged as occurring between possessive individuals then she must claim that either: the marriage contract is not really contractual or that women are 'added in' to this contract as possessive individuals. Pateman points to the way in which the marriage contract is an odd sort of contract because of the inconsistency of women's position. Historically, women could 'consent' to the marriage contract but then lost their right to enter into further contracts. Unlike workers, they were not viewed as owning their ability to work, hence the struggle between husbands and employers over women's labour, to be discussed below. Wives were viewed as agreeing to provide consortium, i.e. sex, companionship and housework, which was exchanged upon marriage. So, to the extent to which wives were said to own and exchange their ability to give consortium it could be argued that the should be viewed as possessive individuals and marriage can be viewed as a contract. However, this is not a satisfactory way of looking at the marriage contract because the definition of possessive individualism is that you are the owner of your abilities, such that you can sell them in a market place. The paradigm case of this is the employment contract in a capitalist society. Labour power is commodified in a manner that housework and sex within marriage were not. So, women fall outside 'possessive individualism' in the traditional marriage contract.

This then opens Pateman to the argument that the traditional marriage contract is more akin to a relationship based upon status, a throwback to feudalism. She resists this move because it fails to capture the historical uniqueness of the marriage contract and its intimate relationship with the employment contract between 1840-

---

444 D. Coole (1990) p. 25.
445 See, for example, Radin (2001); N. Scheper-Hughes, 'The Global Traffic in Human Organs', *Current Anthropology*, Vol. 41, No. 2, 2000, pp. 191-224.

1970. The traditional marriage contract is more akin to a civil slave contract because upon entry rights were lost, including the ability to be viewed as the owner of one's labour power. At stake in this historical analysis is the possible response of Pateman to contemporary arguments by feminists such as Dickenson[446] that women's position will be improved by the further use of contract.

Another way of thinking about this ambiguity produced by the position of women is to question whether it is possible to envisage a contract that does not assume that the parties are possessive individuals. The possessive individual is only a product of a capitalist society, by definition. Prior to the repeal of the Master and Servant Legislation in 1875, workers were not viewed as owners of their abilities which they could freely trade on the market.[447]

Coole's accusation of kettle logic also refers to the idea of possessive individualism as a legal fiction. Again, I think that Pateman's analysis, derived in part from Marx, is correct. We cannot separate our abilities from our bodies and exchange them for money. What this fiction amounts to is the subordination of one party. Pateman's critique of the fiction of possessive individualism therefore directs her to a radical attack, not only upon traditional marriage but upon contemporary employment practices. Both produce persons who are told by others what to do on a daily basis, which undermines the possibility of democracy.[448]

This provides Pateman with a potential response to Miller's[449] argument that Macpherson's emphasis upon the 'possessive individual' in readings of the social contract theorists emphasised the 'economic' at the expense of the 'political'. Miller argues that Macpherson's analysis of the social contract theorists was incorrect because the social contract theorists were concerned with questions of legitimation of the law rather than the alienation of labour power. This is a false distinction because the treatment of labour power as a commodity is not simply a matter of exploitation but of daily subordination. This is clearer in Pateman's writing than it is in that of Cohen, for example, because she is focused upon the relationship between employment contracts, marriage contracts and the arguments around the social contract. By considering the position of women the question of subordination rather than economic exploitation is foregrounded.

---

446 Dickenson (1997).

447 For a discussion of this see A. Edie, I. Grigg-Spall and P. Ireland, 'Labour Law: From Master and Servant to the Contract of Employment' in I. Grigg-Spall and P. Ireland, *The Critical Lawyers' Handbook* (London: Pluto, 1992) pp. 106-113. The *Employers and Workmen Act 1875* removed the magistrates' criminal jurisdiction for breach of employment contract.

448 Deakin points out that the employment contract sets limits upon the power of employers but that their prerogative, derived from the master and servant relationship, remained in the form of an implied duty to obey. The limits upon the employment contract have been imposed through protective legislation. Deakin (2002) p. 180.

449 Miller (1982).

Against Miller, the question of 'alienation of labour power', with its image of possessive individualism is a political question because it produces selves who are told what to do on a daily basis. At this point, it is possible to move beyond Pateman's conception of what Hutchings terms 'the sovereign individual'. Pateman's attention to daily relationships makes this aspect of her analysis compatible with an approach to the self that is more akin to those discussed in Chapter 2. It does not rely upon a view of women as natural victims. On the contrary, the aim of her political analysis is to attack and change women's position. The fact that she holds together the marriage contract, the employment contract and the social contract to raise questions about democracy strengthens her analysis.

Pateman/Marx: 'Old Issues Reconsidered'

In 'Does Capitalism Really Need Patriarchy?: Some Old Issues Reconsidered', Carol Johnson argues that Pateman's analysis of *The Sexual Contract* is an attempt to subsume an analysis of capitalism within patriarchy, which she defines as,

> a system of male domination that involves the subordination of women. Patriarchy takes different forms in different societies and different historical periods. It interacts with other forms of oppression, such as class, race and sexuality, in very complex ways.[450]

Johnson returns to a debate that took place in the 1970s and 1980s in which feminists discussed how to employ Marx's analysis of capitalism whilst rejecting crude reductions of women's oppression to issues of class.[451] This was superseded by the influence of poststructuralism and concerns about the sweeping use of term 'patriarchy' which is viewed as universalising the position of women, thereby ignoring differences between them such as race, sexuality, disability and class. In Chapter 1, I emphasised the need for historical and cultural sensitivity to such issues.

By drawing upon Barbara Taylor's[452] detailed analysis of the historical treatment of women, Johnson illustrates the conflicts over women's labour that took place between capitalists and husbands. For capitalists, women were a source of cheap labour that could potentially be used to undercut men's wages. This

---

450 C. Johnson, 'Does Capitalism really need Patriarchy?: Some Old Issues Reconsidered', *Women's Studies International Forum*, Vol. 19, No. 3, 1996, p. 201.

451 See, for example, H. Hartmann, 'The Unhappy Marriage of Marxism and Feminism: Towards a More Progressive Union' in L. Sargeant, ed., *Women and Revolution: A Discussion of the Unhappy Marriage of Marxism and Feminism* (London: Pluto Press, 1981).

452 B. Taylor, *Eve and the New Jerusalem: Socialism and Feminism in the Nineteenth Century* (London: Virago, 1983). See also Davidoff et al (1999).

conflicted with husbands' concern to control both women's unpaid labour within the home and labour outside the home. Johnson rightly argues that these conflicts drop out of any analysis that views patriarchy and capitalism as intertwined.

In her response, Pateman[453] agrees with the historical analysis provided by Johnson, that there have been conflicts between employers and husbands over women's labour. Pateman disagrees with Johnson's assertion that, in *The Sexual Contract*, she views capitalism as a type of patriarchy. Instead, she argues that her analysis of contract is compatible with Johnson's position. Her concentration on contract was intended to show the way in which patriarchy, from the seventeenth century, was contractual in form. It developed along with capitalism and helped to shape it:

> I emphasised that there were significant differences between the employment contract (capitalism) and the marriage contract (patriarchy). Husbands were not like capitalists, nor were wives like workers. The marriage and employment contracts both gave rise to different types of civil subordination, but the respective subordination of workers and wives took different forms. When I argued that the employment contract presupposed the marriage contract, or stressed the mutual interdependence of two contracts, I was not 'collapsing' one into the other. I was drawing out the logic of the relationship.[454]

As discussed above, I agree with Pateman's argument that the historical subordination of workers and of wives took a different form and grew up together. This history needs to be understood in order to comment upon the contemporary paradoxical position of women. For example, the debate about the granting of 'special rights' for women in order to promote equal opportunity constructs women as those in need of extra help whilst playing down the way in which men continue to have 'special rights' by virtue of women's disproportionate work within the home.[455] Here, the term 'special rights of men' is doing the same work as 'the sexual contract' in Pateman's earlier work in referring to the extent of women's unpaid work within the home.

Okin's Attack upon Possessive Individualism/Self-Ownership/Property in the Person

In a compelling argument, Susan Moller Okin[456] pushes a theoretical framework derived from possessive individualism to an absurd conclusion by considering the position of women. If Cohen can be viewed as akin to Macpherson, in that he engages with possessive individualism from a (useful) Marxist perspective but

---

453 Pateman (1996a) pp. 203-205.
454 Pateman (1996a) p. 203.
455 See for example, C. Pateman, *Democracy, Freedom and Special Rights* (Swansea: The University of Wales Swansea, 1985a).
456 Okin (1989) pp. 74-88.

tends to ignore the position of women, then Okin's approach can be aligned with that of Pateman. Whereas in *The Sexual Contract* Pateman gives a detailed reading of Hobbes, Locke, Rousseau and Hegel, Okin focuses upon the work of Nozick. Okin argues that if the position of women is considered then Nozick's image of society, derived from possessive individualism, would actually become a slave society with mothers as owners of their children! This is not a conclusion that he would endorse. Indeed, this conclusion renders his position incoherent because it is impossible to be both a slave and a possessive individual at the same time. Whilst Nozick[457] does not argue against the possibility of possessive individuals being able to enter into slave contracts, this transaction would assume that the slave started out as a possessive individual and sold the rights in his/her self. Okin shows that, if the position of women is taken into account, nobody would acquire such rights over themselves in the first place, unless given them by their mothers.

Okin's argument is based upon the breadth of Nozick's[458] definition of 'production', from which he derives his arguments for a minimal state. This is therefore central to his theoretical position. He argues that, if the means to produce goods are justly acquired, the producer should be entitled to the product, irrespective of the needs of others. Whilst altruism would be a good thing, it should not be compelled by the state because this would be tantamount to theft of the 'holdings' (goods) from the individual producer. As Nozick puts it,

> Whoever makes something, having bought or contracted for all other held resources used in the process (transferring some of his holdings for these co-operating factors) is entitled to it. The situation is *not* one of something's getting made, and there being an open question of who is to get it. Things come into the world already attached to people having entitlements over them.[459]

Okin shows how reproduction, the labour involved in pregnancy and in the traditional childcare performed by women, fits the criteria of *production* within Nozick's analysis. In Nozick's terms, women can be viewed as the producers of children. They acquire and use sperm as part of the production process. This sperm can usually be viewed as 'justly acquired' as a gift and hence the legal title of both the sperm and the product (the child) passes to the woman. Alternatively, sperm could now be purchased over the Internet. Nozick is happy with the idea that whatever a person is given or buys belongs to him/her, as does the product of the individual's labour upon these materials. He explicitly dismisses the idea that someone would need to have complete control over (and understand) the process of production of something in order to become its owner because this would preclude

---

457 Nozick (1974) p. 331. He explains that the idea of selling off rights in oneself could produce slavery, although the aim of the discussion is to consider a non-minimal state, Nozick (1974) p. 283.
458 Nozick (1974) p. 160.
459 Nozick (1974) p. 160; cited and discussed Okin (1989) p. 78.

the ownership of other 'products', such as trees.[460] Okin concludes that when the position of women is considered within Nozick's framework then women can be viewed as *owning* their children.

In a thought experiment, about the possibility of everyone holding shares in each others lives, Nozick briefly deals with the question of children being owned by their parents but does not reach a conclusion.[461] As Okin illustrates, Nozick's gender neutral language at this point allows him to ignore the position of women.[462] There is a contradiction between the fact that Nozick's framework leads to ownership of the child by the mother but depends upon the idea that individuals can be viewed as owning their capacities and the fruits of their labour. He also ignores the more consistent position of Hobbes on the question of whether possessive individualism necessarily leads to the conclusion that individuals should be viewed as owning their children. As discussed in the last chapter, for Hobbes, it is not the generation of children, but their protection, which allows one of the parents to have dominion over the child by virtue of an implied contract.[463] Hobbes, being more thorough in thinking through the implications of individualism, argues that children are to called 'free men' 'by the natural indulgence of the parents'.[464]

Although Okin does not mention Marx it is useful to think about her position as the corollary of Marx's analysis of reproduction. Her argument reverses the priority that Marx gives to *production* when he analyses the reproduction of children in terms of its work for capital, i.e. as reproducing the labour force as a commodity. He considers this by arguing that the cost of labour as a commodity *includes* the cost of its reproduction – a point taken up by Marxist feminists.[465] As Marx puts it,

> The labour-power withdrawn from the market by wear and tear and death, must be continually replaced by, at the very least a fresh supply of labour-power. Hence the sum of the means of subsistence necessary for the production of labour-power must include the means necessary for the labourer's substitutes, i.e. his children, in order that this race of peculiar commodity-owners may perpetuate its appearance on the market.[466]

---

460 Nozick (1974) p. 288.
461 Nozick (1974) p. 287.
462 Okin (1989) p. 80.
463 Hobbes (1994b) Ch. XX, pp. 128-129.
464 T. Hobbes, De Corpore Politico' in *The Elements of Law* (Oxford: Oxford University Press, 1994a) Ch. XXIII, p. 133.
465 For discussions of the domestic labour debate and Marxist feminist debates in the 1970s and early 1980s see, for example, J. Brenner and M. Ramas, 'Rethinking Women's Oppression' in J. Brenner, *Women and the Politics of Class* (New York: Monthly Review Press, 2000) pp. 11-58; L. Sergeant, ed., *Women and Revolution: A Discussion of the Unhappy Marriage of Marxism and Feminism* (London: Pluto Press, 1981).
466 Marx (1954) Ch. 6, p. 168.

In contrast, Okin[467] prioritises an analysis of *reproduction* to show that possessive individualism is incoherent once women's labour in reproducing children is included as production. Both are attacking a view of selves as 'peculiar commodity-owners' or possessive individualism.

Okin's illustration of the blindness of Nozick's theory to women leads to a discussion of the relationship between self and other. Whether the proponent is Hobbes or Nozick, the idea that the possessive individual owns himself and his labour and owes nothing to society for them becomes an acute source of tension when reproduction and education is considered, a point that I will discuss in detail in the next section.

The Education of 'Possessive Individuals'

One of the peculiarities of Hobbes' and Nozick's vision of selves as possessive individuals is the way in which they are not envisaged as children who gradually develop. Neither is there any sense that individualism, with its split between self and other, is a diminished view of selves at any age – as discussed in Chapter 2. Whilst Hobbes does discuss the role of the family as inculcating political values,[468] what is central in Hobbes' image of selves is that they are individuals from the start.

In Yeatman's[469] reading of Pateman's *The Sexual Contract*,[470] Yeatman points out that the sons of property-owning households, within the seventeenth century, were *trained* to view themselves as possessive individuals. One aspect of the sons' education involved training them to think of themselves as owners of their own abilities and as having been born with them. Part of the son's training would therefore involve teaching them to act as if they had not been received such lessons on how to behave.

Yeatman links her point that sons were educated to view themselves as possessive individuals with a discussion of Maine's[471] famous statement that modernity is characterised by a transition from status to contract. She points to the status element that takes place within a society governed by contract to emphasise that these sons had a *status* (linked with their treatment as possessive individuals)

---

467 Okin (1989) p. 80.
468 In teaching obedience to the family, the parent is teaching obedience to the state. Hobbes (1994b) Ch. XXX, p. 223. For a discussion of the education of children in both the state of nature and civil society see R.A. Chapman, '*Leviathan* Writ Small: Thomas Hobbes on the Family', *American Political Science Review*, Vol. 69, 1975, pp. 76-90. Reprinted in P. King, *Thomas Hobbes: Critical Assessments III* (London: Routledge, 1993) pp. 629-656. Chapman reads Hobbes as claiming that parents teach children to 'consent' to obey them.
469 Yeatman (1997) pp. 39-56.
470 Pateman (1988).
471 H. Maine, *Ancient Law* (London: J.M. Dent and Sons, 1917) p. 100.

that allowed them to enter into contracts – a position denied to married women. In this way, she shifts Hobbes' and Pateman's philosophical stories into a historical description of a way of life:

> Contract is the device which enables sons, once they are old and educated enough to assume the capacities of a rationally orientated individual will,…to set up their own households. It is clear from this that the education of the son is conceived precisely in terms of the cultivation of this individualised, rational will…By being constituted as wills of their own, the sons assume their own dominium. The individualisation of dominium is expressed in their status as wills of their own with independent householder status…Classical liberal contractualism, then, is predicated on the individualisation of patrimonial dominium. The structure of classical liberal thought follows from this.[472]

In a footnote,[473] she says that this approach 'jibes' (clashes) with Pateman's discussion of a fraternal contract. Yeatman is considering individual families in the seventeenth century, rather than the story of the sexual contract, to emphasise that the sons had to be trained to view themselves as a possessive individuals. She reads this back into Pateman's story to argue that Pateman ignores the fact that the sons in her tale of the fraternal contract and the overthrow the patriarch would also have to be trained to view themselves as possessive individuals. She attributes this in part to the role of the father – curiously not to the mother or servant.[474]

Yeatman's move of thinking about the historical ways in which sons were educated to view themselves as possessive individuals, and as propertied heads of household, is useful. It informs her consideration of the way in which training to view oneself as an individual takes place today. In particular, she is concerned with the way in which women are encouraged to take part in 'empowerment' training and their treatment in the context of the welfare state, a point to which I will return below. The relationship between being a possessive individual and being a head of household is also important. It is not mentioned in the definition of possessive individualism given by Macpherson, nor by Cohen's definition of self-ownership, because both ignore the position of women and deal only with employment. The reference to 'heads of household' as one of the features of possessive individualism fits within Pateman's discussion of the relationship between marriage contracts and employment contracts.

As discussed in the last chapter, I do not think that readings of Pateman which dwell upon her rhetorical rewriting of Hobbes in terms of the sexual contract hit their mark. This is because I downplay the extent to which Pateman relies upon Freud and also take Pateman at her word that she is merely retelling a story.[475] This reading is consistent with the way in which her work has developed since *The*

---

472 Yeatman (1997) p. 44.
473 Yeatman (1997) p. 56.
474 Yeatman (1997) p. 44.
475 Pateman (1988) p. 219.

Sexual Contract.[476] Yeatman's criticism leaves undisturbed what I value in Pateman's work: her analysis of the problems of possessive individualism and of contract. It is a little harsh to accuse Pateman of failing to question the way in which the sons in her story are trained to become possessive individuals when her analysis of contract is aimed at undermining this image of the self as a possessive individual – by showing the subordination that results from it. Nevertheless, Yeatman's switch to historically situating an aspect of the story provides what Hobbes fails to give: an analysis of the emergence of the self that views itself as a possessive individual as a result of emerging with and through his relations with others. Yeatman is able to do this by historically situating possessive individualism rather than viewing it as a universal statement about human nature. In making this move she has more in common with Pateman (and with Macpherson) than she acknowledges.

New Contractualism, Old Problems?

The image of a social contract, in different guises, has been a thread that has run through this book: Cornell's question of what free and equal persons would agree to, detailed in Chapter 3; Hobbes' social contract and the way in which this is rewritten by Pateman, discussed in Chapters 5 and 6. Ewald's analysis of loss distribution through the techniques of risk analysis and insurance contracts, discussed in Chapter 4, could even be viewed as 'social contracts', albeit of a different type. Whilst, like Hobbes' social contract they are concerned with security, they differ in that they are actual contracts employing a technique that potentially could be used for social distribution of loss. I will now look at another closely related 'social contract': the 'new contractualism' that has been discussed by a number of Australian theorists including Yeatman.[477]

Many women now rely upon the state rather than a man to provide income when they are performing the unpaid labour of child care and are hence constructed as 'naturally dependent'. Therefore, analyses of the operation of the welfare state represent a contemporary extension of Pateman's concerns in *The Sexual Contract*. Many Australian theorists, in particular, have analysed the way in which the relationship between the welfare recipient and the state has been construed as a 'social contract'. This needs to be considered in detail because it is unlike the standard story of the social contract and extends the meaning of the terms 'social contract' and 'possessive individual'.

The question of what it is to be a self, person or individual is deeply implicated in this 'social contract' between welfare recipients and the state. To predicate this upon an image of the 'possessive individual' appears to be a strange move as the possessive individual on welfare can only be described as *potentially* owning his or

---

476 See, for example, Pateman (2002).
477 Yeatman (1997).

her ability to work. I want to return to contemporary analyses in the area of governmentality, first discussed in Chapter 4, to trace the way in which the 'unemployed' are encouraged to view themselves as owners of their abilities. Given women's history of being excluded from possessive individualism – as not being owners of the abilities that could be sold in the market place – this can include strategies of 'empowerment' for those, predominantly women, who are recipients of welfare.

O'Malley,[478] draws upon governmentality analysis to argue that,

> 'Empowerment' thus appears as a strategy of neo-liberal governance, creating 'techniques of the self' which fold into the new subject such central characteristics of political rationality as the changed relations of expertise and the revised autonomy of the individual. Such enterprising individuals, in their turn, are enjoined to enter into – a form of new contractualism – in which the 'social contract' is displaced by a myriad of 'partnerships', 'charters', relationships of 'customer and provider' and 'involvements of stakeholders'. They are formed into imaginary voluntaristic and mutually beneficial agreements between whole new classes of equals: in which empowered subjects contract with each other and with a state that now presents itself as fragmented into a myriad of 'market actors'.[479]

There are a number of points within this quotation that I want to unpack below. O'Malley references the work of Rose[480] to explain which aspects of contemporary society he is referring to by the rubric of 'neo-liberal governance' and 'advanced liberalism'. O'Malley distinguishes contemporary liberalism from nineteenth-century liberalism by arguing that in the nineteenth century the 'market' and 'state' were viewed as separate realms. Contemporary 'neo-liberalism' is characterised by the way in which techniques employed in the market are adopted by the state, for example: the use of outsourcing, competitive tendering by state and non-state agencies, cost-benefit analysis, 'reinventing' bureaucrats in the image of entrepreneurs. These techniques are applied, not only in the market, but also within state government itself and in other contexts, such as within universities and the daily lives of individuals.

Similarly, Rose[481] details developments in the twentieth century in which the privacy of the employment contract was weakened as governments accepted that pay and conditions should be regulated for social peace. He describes how the family wage was viewed as a way that males were to be linked into the social order.[482] In these circumstances, the state took on the management of risk for (male) workers through social insurance, for example: unemployment benefit, accident insurance, health and safety legislation. As discussed in Chapter 4, Rose describes a

478 http://law-crime.rutgers.edu/omalley1.html.
479 http://law-crime.rutgers.edu/omalley6.html.
480 N. Rose, 'The Death of the Social? Re-figuring the Territory of Government', *Economy and Society*, Vol. 25, No. 3, 1996b, pp. 327-356.
481 Rose (1996b).
482 Rose (1996b) p. 338; See also Deakin (2002).

shift in the treatment of risk, away from the use of mutual or friendly societies and the state towards individual market choice, for those who can afford to purchase security. Whilst the state envisaged risk and welfare in terms of families, to women's detriment, now the ability to insure has been taken back into the market and has been aimed at both women and men – if they can pay for it. Given the pay differential between men and women, of course, fewer women are in a position to pay for such private insurance.

Employing the same broadly Foucauldian analysis, Hindness[483] produces an up to date supplement to Foucault's 'The Punitive Society',[484] by tracing the techniques by which the unemployed are encouraged to constitute themselves as self-governing individuals who can fit within society, by being viewed as 'customers/consumers' of welfare who must optimise their ability to join the marketplace. Whereas the social contract, in its different forms, has been used as an argument in support of the law, Hindness argues that contract is now a *technique* linked with self-government.

To explain this, I will highlight Hindness' (unattributed) link with Pateman. Like Pateman, Hindness links the social contract of liberal theory with marriage contracts and employment contracts. He argues that in all cases there is an agreement on behalf of those entering into the contract to regulate their own behaviour. In liberal theory, this has meant that the governed should behave *as if* there were a social contract. In marriage and employment this self-regulation extends beyond what could be written down. The extension of the use of 'contract' to the 'unemployed', which includes increasing numbers of women-headed families, is viewed by Hindness as a way in which both men and women come to view themselves as self-governing individuals.

The theme of contract and welfare is taken up by O'Malley.[485] He outlines the 'new contractualism' as characterised by the way in which government services in Australia, and in Britain and the US, are allocated in terms of a 'contract' between the welfare claimant and the state. Often this means that the services are supplied by private tender. He argues that this is merely a way of controlling the limited resources given, whilst appearing to empower individuals. This argument fits comfortably with Pateman's analysis of the marriage contracts that it often replaces. Again, the woman is a party to the contract and yet is in a weaker position with regard to the actual operation of the contract because she is construed as dependent if she performs unpaid childcare.

In addition, the way in which women are encouraged to see themselves is of interest in the development of the meaning of 'possessive individualism'. In the above quotation, O'Malley refers to the way in which the techniques of governmentality use the idea of empowered individuals. I want to expand upon this, focusing upon the position of women, to argue that this fits within a possible shift

---

483 Hindness (1997) pp. 14-26.
484 Foucault (1997b) pp. 23-37.
485 http://law-crime.rutgers.edu/omalley6.html.

towards the treatment of women as possessive individuals and within the increased commodification of the domestic sphere. This is in keeping with my case analysis relating to marriage that shows some move towards contract rather than status.[486]

There has been a study of the techniques of 'empowerment' which I also want to link with the development of possessive individualism. Cruikshank,[487] describes the 'self esteem movement' which was spear-headed by the 'California Task Force to Promote Self-Esteem and Personal and Social Responsibility' in 1983. This views the idea of working on oneself (Cornell's project of becoming a person?) as a social obligation rather than a matter of private satisfaction. By taking courses in self-esteem the unemployed are trained to view themselves as individuals as 'jobseekers',[488] who can take up the offers that are open to them by the market. Hindness points out that the idea of the social contract was 'individualistic' but not 'individualising', i.e. the emphasis was upon the 'free and equal individual' but no account was taken of the individual circumstances. In contrast, 'new contractualism' is tailored to individual circumstances and is therefore also individualising.

Similar points are made by both Mitchell Dean[489] in 'Governing the Unemployed Self in an Active Society' and by Yeatman[490] in 'Contract, Status and Personhood', drawing upon their experiences in Australia to make points that are more generally applicable. Yeatman argues that contract does not free the individual from society but 'reshapes the status of the person in society so as to become an individualised one'.[491] As discussed above, she compares the way in which propertied sons who were to be male heads of household were educated to view themselves as possessive individuals. This training has now been broadened to include women, but, importantly, without the assumption that these 'heads of household' will have access to traditional wives.

In Chapter 4, I claimed that the work on risk analysis shows that the 'self-owning' possessive individual is now encouraged to employ cost-benefit analysis to calculate risk and act in order to minimise harm. The worker who owns the rights over himself, his abilities and the fruits of his labour characterises Hobbes'

---

486 In Australia, this has also been linked with a move to change legislation so that couples can negotiate potential divorce settlements prior to the marriage. For a discussion of how women are potentially in a more vulnerable position if this further shift to contract occurs see Neave (1997) pp. 71-86, discussed in Chapter 5.

487 B. Cruikshank, 'Revolutions Within: Self-Government and Self-Esteem' in Barry et al (1996) pp. 231-251.

488 The term is employed in the UK in the *Jobseekers Act 1995* in which welfare benefits may be tied to the claimant's willingness to retrain. See also A New Contract for Welfare: Principles into Practice (Cmnd. 4101) (London: HMSO, 1998).

489 Dean (1995) pp. 559-583.

490 Yeatman (1997) pp. 39-56.

491 Yeatman (1997) p. 43.

'possessive individual'. In neo-liberalism, the instrumental reason that he (and, more recently, she) now employs includes an analysis of risk, with investment in pensions and insurance provided on the market.

Pateman's analysis of women's position in terms of contract, rather than as a feudal relic, can be brought to bear to think about 'new contractualism'. There has been a shift in liberal theory from the Hobbesian image of that we 'spring up like mushrooms'[492] as possessive individuals to an assumption that possessive individualism represents an ideal image of free and equal persons that we (men and women) can be encouraged to be, as consumers. This includes the consumption of the means of securing against risk, which has moved from mutual societies and the state to individual market choices at a time when women are potentially being 'added in' as possessive individuals. Whereas Yeatman (and other feminists such as Dickenson) view this as an important step because there are advantages to women in being treated as possessive individuals, the work of Pateman warns against such a sanguine approach to contractualism.

---

492 Hobbes (1998) p. 205.

Chapter 7

Conclusion

The question addressed by this book is: what is meant by the terms 'self', 'person' and 'individual'? The operation of the law of obligations has provided the context in which this question has been considered. I have argued that it is unnecessary to move from a 'modern' to a 'postmodern' view of the self, both of which are based upon the image of males as the paradigm case. It is possible to think about universals, the category of women, without such universals being 'global', i.e. relating to the species as a whole. Deconstruction is inadequate to this task, as is illustrated by Spivak's[493] concern that she could not be a pure deconstructionist and attack sexism. This is not a problem inherent to all philosophy, but with a type of philosophy that is currently popular within feminist legal theory. One of my aims has been to illustrate that there are better theoretical approaches that do not produce such dissonance.

In the introduction, I expressed my sympathy with the argument made by, for example, black women, lesbians, women with disabilities and working-class women that feminism considers women as a universal category in such a way that their voices are marginalised. This is a strong argument, particularly as the same move has been applied by feminists to mainstream political theories to show the effect of women's exclusion within traditional discussions of selves, individuals and persons, which take male bodies and lifestyles as the norm. However, the call for sensitivity to difference has become mixed up with the claim that it is impossible to consider what women have in common in our culture at this point in time. Conaghan[494] has warned against this fear of talking about women as a group, which has the potential to constrain feminist legal theory.

Rather than focusing upon poststructuralism, I have drawn from broader resources in philosophy to address this question of feminists' ability to talk about, and make claims on behalf of, women as a group. Linked with this question is what Scott[495] has described as the paradoxical position of women, which arises when men have positioned themselves as the finest example of the universal category of persons. In order to intervene politically, women have had to argue that they are like men, for example equally rational, and yet this neglects the fact that both theoretical frameworks as well as institutions have been constructed to fit with the traditional male lifestyles and bodies. In feminist legal theory this has been termed the equality/difference debate.

In Chapter 2, I addressed this problem by bringing together diverse areas of contemporary philosophy that offer a different way of thinking about the self, that does not assume the position of males as the norm against which women are

---

493 Spivak (1990) p. 12.
494 Conaghan (2000) p. 367.
495 Scott (1996).

measured. Oyama, writing within the philosophy of science, rethinks the complexity of the relationship between nature and culture, such that it is not 'construction' all the way down. This does not involve a denial of the fact that we need language in order to discuss what it is to be a self, or a woman, nor that the question of power is implicated in these claims. Oyama and other contemporary philosophers of biology[496] are thinking about the relationship between nature and culture in a manner that avoids viewing these as separate streams. This involves, for example, changing the image of what is self and not-self; challenging the idea that there is a strict, fixed boundary between them; and undermining the idea that they are manipulated by a central controlling mechanism.

Battersby and Oyama write from within completely different areas of philosophy and do not discuss each other's work. However, they share common ground regarding their treatment of the question of agency, an area that is relevant to the law of obligations. Both describe the way that the self develops in a manner that is active but not dependent upon a supposed autonomous will of the subject. So, Oyama[497] stresses that development should not be viewed in terms of genes that can organise 'raw materials' into human beings nor by describing an environment that shapes and selects, but by thinking about organisms that manipulate and seek out particular environments, just as they are shaped by them.

Similarly, Battersby[498] talks in terms of 'feedback loops' between the environment and the self. In common with the work of Andy Clark, Battersby's model should not be viewed as a simple feedback between an individual and environment. As Battersby argues, both self and not-self are carved out gradually through their modes of relationality. For Clark, this is demonstrated by the way in which it becomes impossible to separate the self from the environment which is part of its cognitive process, just as a dolphin *creates* eddies in order to swim faster than it would otherwise be able to do.

This image of what it is to be a self, or to develop as an organism, illustrates the paucity of the image of the possessive individual, discussed in the last chapter. Of course, it would be open to those adopting a political theory based upon possessive individualism, such as that of Hobbes and Nozick, to make a normative claim that we should be treated as if we were possessive individuals. It is then necessary to look at the contradictions produced by such a claim when the position of women is highlighted by political theorists such as Pateman[499] and Okin.[500] I will return to Pateman and Okin below.

Oyama and Battersby, in very different ways, pay attention to the development and emergence of the self to challenge the way it is often viewed as constituted by a split from what is 'outside' it: either other selves or the environment. Battersby

496 Oyama et al (2001).
497 Oyama (2000a) p. 95.
498 Battersby (1998a) p. 12.
499 Pateman (1988).
500 Okin (1989).

poses the question of what it would be to think of women's bodies and lifestyles as the norm rather than as an aberration. From her radical rereading of Kant, she also suggests a different understanding of 'essence'. To rethink essence in this way allows feminists to talk about women as a group without committing themselves to the assumption that they are discussing a fixed underlying entity. In doing so, Battersby challenges the Aristotelian view of 'essence' as something fixed in the world that all of a universal group have in common. It is Aristotle's view of essence that is assumed by those feminists, such as Spivak,[501] who then need to employ 'strategic essentialism' to justify discussions about women as a category. Battersby avoids this move by arguing that the way in which we view this grouping alters with shifts in the schemata through which we understand the world. This assumes that there is more than simply discourse that constructs the world and our understanding of it – in a top-down manner – but recognises that the world is not divided into pieces that we simply perceive. Our schemata or frameworks – through which we understand the world – change the way in which we view it but can also be changed in a bottom-up manner by the world of which we are a part. This is relevant to law because it opens up the possibility of making claims on behalf of women which avoids the pitfalls of either employing a fixed idea of what it is to be a woman (as presupposed by Aristotelian essentialism) or of appealing to 'strategic essentialism'.

In Chapter 3, I discussed the way in which Cornell provides a different answer to the problem of making legal claims for women as a group. This time the focus was upon legal personhood rather than the self. For Cornell, what it is to be, or have, a self in this culture, is to have legal rights. Her answer to the equality/difference problem, that women have had to show that they are 'like men' in order to claim the same rights but that this approach neglects areas of difference, is to move beyond it. Cornell argues that women should be viewed as joining the legal community as *persons* but that the definition of what it means to be a person is to be kept open. She thereby aims to avoid the trap of seeing 'the person' as paradigmatically male. This is a more compelling argument than proposals that women should be treated in law as *women* with specific rights pertaining to being female, such as those suggested by Irigaray.[502] Cornell's aim is to keep open space in order to transgress 'who we are' rather than to appeal to what we have been.[503]

---

501 Spivak (1990) p. 12.
502 For example Irigaray (1993b).
503 She explains that she was attracted to Irigaray's earlier work because of its utopian move, which Irigaray labels as 'the feminine'. Cornell views this as doing the same work as the imaginary domain. Cornell is critical of Irigaray's later work on feminine rights which appeal to a historical feminine, which Cornell views as conservative. Cornell describes her attitude on this position as arising out of discussions with Butler in 1995. See Cornell (1998) p. 21.

Cornell's version of personhood allows her to attack liberals for their 'atomism', quoting Charles Taylor.[504] She adopts the liberal idea that the law should not define what it is to be a person – or adopt a perfectionist image of the good – which has tended to look back wistfully to earlier times when women were not even viewed as persons. Instead, Cornell's definition of personhood looks forward to the possibility of women being treated as free and equal persons. Cornell radicalises contractarian justifications of the state when she argues that, for the state to be legitimate, it must address the question of whether it acts in ways we *would* agree to if we *were* free and equal persons.

Whilst I am sympathetic to Cornell's stated socialist, feminist aims, one of my concerns with her work is with the efficacy of the legal test that has been derived from her philosophical framework. As her hypothetical legislator/judge I would find her arguments compelling. However, I would vote with her anyway. This is the problem; the test of what 'free and equal persons would agree to' is empty. Nozick, with his view of what it is to be free and equal would certainly evoke her test to vote against us.[505] Cornell is driven to add more content to her test, as she does when addressing particular torts. My main concern is that the openness of the image of the 'free and equal person' will mean that, in a capitalist society, such a person will be understood to be a possessive individual – a term the meaning of which I explored in Chapters 5 and 6.

Whereas Cornell claims that in our culture we view ourselves as persons with rights, Ewald argues that one aspect of our lives that is now central to 'who we are' is shaped, in part, by our daily employment of the techniques of risk analysis. This is related to 'government' in the broadest sense of the term, not only a technique employed by the state but a way of conducting one's life. In Chapter 4, I adapted Ewald's analysis of insurance and governmentality to English law to continue to address the question of the anomalous historical position of women. Rather than proposing a different way of thinking about the equality/difference debate, as in the previous two chapters, in this chapter I considered contemporary developments: the extent to which women are actually now treated as possessive individuals, owners of their abilities and owing nothing to society for them.

I argued that the image of the possessive individual, owner of his abilities, can now be viewed as someone who can safeguard his 'property in the person' through insurance and the technology of risk, upon which the operation of tort law is based. The owner of his abilities is to be compensated if these abilities are damaged and is to act in a prudent manner in order to safeguard such 'property', such as his ability to earn a living, through private insurance. By virtue of their increasing participation in paid work, increasing numbers of women are being treated as such possessive individuals (as workers) at a time when such insurance is viewed more

---

504 Taylor (1985).

505 I am assuming that Cornell and I would have a vote. Given that Cornell's test is to be applied by either the legislature or the judiciary this is too optimistic.

as a market decision than as social security provided by the state. For those without paid work or in low paid employment, the breakdown of the family has resulted in the feminisation of poverty.

Insuring against risk has traditionally been subject to a public/private split, with the risks associated with women's traditional lives, such as income upon divorce and the costs associated with childbirth generally being excluded. However, with the increase in women workers and the influence of feminism, it may be that there is a move to view women in terms of possessive individualism. This is not clear cut and remains an area of tension and struggle. The feminist attack upon the public/private divide is important at a time when the marriage and employment contracts are altering with the breakdown of the breadwinner/wife model (amongst other factors, such as the ability of global capital to move and the impact of a gendered workplace model of distinguishing between core workers and peripheral workers, who are on temporary and short term contracts).[506]

The anomalous position of women can be seen in the varied approaches of the different courts on the question of the award of damages for the cost of child care. I looked at the example of the 'wrongful birth' cases to illustrate this. The House of Lords[507] refused to view childbirth as anything other than 'a blessing' and hence refused to award damages for the care of children that are born as a result of negligent sterilisation. However, they were willing to quantify the pain and suffering associated with pregnancy and to award damages for this.

What these cases also highlight is the double bind that women find themselves in. If women claim property in their persons then areas of their lives are open to commodification. Alternatively, they are not paid at all. In the wrongful birth cases, for women to be treated as possessive individuals has the advantage that they would receive compensation. Child care would be treated as an extra job that had been imposed by another's negligence. To be treated as the owner of one's abilities appears to offer respect but, as Pateman points out, this has historically entailed a different type of *subordination*, that of the worker who is viewed as exchanging labour power for a wage.

For women to be treated as possessive individuals also opens up the possibility of commodifying areas of life that were previously resistant to such commodification. A stark example of this is Dickenson's argument that payment for surrogacy ('contract motherhood') entails the recognition of the woman's ability to birth in that she is being paid for it. She claims that:

> The 'good news' about contract motherhood is that it implies a recognition that the mother has *something* to transfer or sell.[508]

However, she gives a more nuanced discussion on this point to illustrate the limitation of contract whilst advocating that surrogacy is viewed in terms of

---

506 Deakin (2002).
507 *McFarlane v Tayside Health Authority* (1999) 3 WLR 1301; (2000) 2 AC 59.
508 Dickenson (1997) p. 162.

payment for the woman's pain and suffering in pregnancy and labour. I am pointing out women's ambivalent position with regard to possessive individualism rather than giving a full analysis of the arguments for and against payment for surrogacy contracts.[509] In contrast to Dickenson, Radin[510] has pointed out that in the case of child surrogacy the possibility of payment for a child does raise the question of what a child is worth.[511] She asks an empirical question: at what point does the introduction of an area of commodification start a slippery slope effect whereby members of the population then view human abilities or bodies in terms of money, and hence view themselves as having a common measure?[512] She raises the spectre of a society in which children could grade themselves in accordance with the price they would have achieved on the open market. This is particularly relevant in law, given the influence of the school of law and economics which views all abilities in terms of commodities in a market place.

To distribute wealth does not necessarily involve the treatment of human attributes as objects. So, for example, the award of money to help with child care in the 'wrongful birth cases' could be viewed in terms other than those of commodifying aspects of human life. It could be viewed as questioning the way in which the burden of child care falls upon women. This would be better administered through the welfare state rather than through the litigation lottery, not merely because of efficiency but because the tort system would calculate an award in inverse proportion to need, by basing their calculations upon what the parents would be expected to spend on their child.

In terms of commodification, there is a huge difference between distribution of resources through welfare and a surrogacy contract. The 'wrongful birth cases' could be viewed ambiguously in this context. They were only seen in terms of commodification within the analysis of individual cases rather than as part of welfare scheme based upon loss distribution.

In Chapters 5 and 6, I then drew out the ambivalent historical position of women with regard to possessive individualism by returning to the work of Hobbes. Hobbes is unusual as a social contract theorist in his consistent application of possessive individualism to women as well as men. He is therefore a useful theorist to consider when discussing the developments and tensions in the current relationship between women and possessive individualism. So, for example, in Hobbes' hypothetical state of nature women can decide what to do with their children, who are then assumed to consent to obey them if they have been helped to survive.

509 For pragmatic arguments see, for example, M. Freeman, 'Does Surrogacy Have a Future After Brazier?', *Medical Law Review*, Vol. 7, Spring, 1999, pp. 1-20.
510 Radin (2001).
511 Note that it is not the ability to work that is exchanged and hence the surrogate mother is not told what to do on a daily basis – save with regard to issues relating to risk to the foetus, such as smoking. On this point see Lupton (1999).
512 For a discussion of how different items come to be viewed as having a common measure see Marx (1954) pp. 43-96.

Hobbes' attempt to think about the behaviour of 'free and equal persons' in the state of nature must import his views about how individuals *actually* behave to avoid simply being an empty abstraction. In this respect there are similarities to Cornell's analysis, save that she aims to avoid evoking individualism within her conception of personhood. Macpherson argues that Hobbes actually describes the behaviour of men within Hobbes' own emerging capitalist society. This is the image of the possessive individual that I am concerned will be read into Cornell's image of personhood. Whilst Macpherson's work has been subject to sustained attack for his historical analysis,[513] and whilst he ignores the position of women, his work is useful for focusing criticism upon possessive individualism, self-ownership or property in the person.

Pateman's work can be viewed as taking up Macpherson's analysis to consider the way in which the possessive individual, the owner of his labour and the fruits of his labour, has been understood as paradigmatically male. Pateman's analysis serves as a warning against a legal fiction, that an ability to work can be separated from a person. Hence, she attacks workplace subordination, as well as a different type of subordination within the traditional marriage contract. Importantly, her work stresses the historical relationship between these contracts in a manner that is now discussed by a few labour lawyers[514] but does not feature within much contemporary analyses of 'self-ownership' within political theory.[515]

The sexed body of the person concerned may be relevant to the contract, as is clear in the examples that Pateman uses, such as marriage, the prostitution contract, etc. The caselaw on sexual harassment in the workplace and the position of

---

513 See, for example, Miller (1982); Tully (1993).

514 For example, L.A. Williams, 'Beyond Labour Law's Parochialism: A Re-envisioning of the Discourse of Redistribution' in Conaghan et al (2002) pp. 93-114. However, this is exceptional. For the argument that issues that traditionally affect women workers are still viewed as 'specialised topics which do not touch the "essence" of labour law' see J. Conaghan, 'Feminism and Labour Law: Contesting the Terrain' in A. Morris and T. O'Donnell, *Feminist Perspectives on Employment Law* (London: Cavendish Publishing, 1999b) p. 14.

515 For example, Cohen (1995). Whilst Cohen does not bring together the marriage contract with the employment contract, he does provide a useful sustained attack on self-ownership. Many commentators simply accept self-ownership as meaning something akin to autonomy, rather than possessive individualism or property in the person. See Pateman (2002) p. 20. For example, Pateman cites Will Kymlicka in W. Kymlicka, *Contemporary Political Philosophy: An Introduction* (Oxford: Oxford University Press, 1990) p. 112 cited Pateman (2002) p. 23. This is kept in the updated edition: W. Kymlicka, *Contemporary Political Philosophy: An Introduction*, 2nd edition (Oxford: Oxford University Press, 2002) p. 116. To be fair, in his later edition he does outline Okin's arguments against Nozick, commenting favourably upon them, Kymlicka (2002) p. 126. This is an interesting example because, between 1990 and 2002, Kymlicka integrates feminist theory into arguments on self-ownership, rather than dealing with it mainly in the chapter dedicated to feminist political philosophy. He does not discuss Pateman (1988) but will have to discuss Pateman (2002) in any next edition.

gendered work such as the role of the secretary[516] also strengthens her point. Pateman's analysis of contract, the central theme of her work, does not rely upon an assumption of the natural vulnerability of women, which appears occasionally in *The Sexual Contract*. Pateman provides a critique of possessive individualism (and of contract) based upon the subordination it produces. As she does not rely upon an alternative view of the self, I believe that Pateman's critique of individualism is consistent with the analysis of the self discussed in Chapter 2.

The criticism of a 'male sex right' with respect to women's labour is also of relevance where there is no marriage contract but cohabitation takes place on the same terms. As Conaghan[517] points out, there has been recent recognition of the extent to which the marriage contract (or now cohabitation) and employment contracts interrelate in government concerns regarding the 'work/life balance'. There is still a struggle over whether women's unpaid labour in the home is to be acknowledged or to be viewed in terms of women's 'special needs' and 'dependency'. Given that middle-class women 'outsource' housework, this also raises questions of differences between women.

In the workplace, part of this struggle is played out in the discourse of 'human resource management' in which there has been a shift in language from 'equal opportunities' to 'managing diversity'. Although the conceptual positions differ, this resonates with the broad call to 'respect the other' within aspects of poststructuralism. I am not suggesting a simple causal relationship but am detecting approaches which conflate the term 'otherness' or 'diversity', meaning anyone who is not white, male, middle-class, able-bodied and heterosexual.[518] There have been arguments that 'managing diversity' tends to individualise issues of gender and race which were previously viewed as social issues.[519]

In Chapters 5 and 6, I discussed the ways in which consideration of women's position undermines the philosophical frameworks premised upon an image of possessive individualism. Pateman's rereading of Hobbes and the social contract theorists and Okin's rereading of Nozick both show the difficulties that arise for claims based upon possessive individualism when women's position is considered. The concept of the possessive individual, self-ownership or 'property in the person' evokes, as its paradigm case, the position of the employee in a capitalist society. The (male) worker was the owner of his ability to work that is viewed as a commodity for which he is paid a wage. Women under traditional marriage contract were not paid, did not alienate their abilities by the hour and were not always juridically equal with men hence they could not be described as possessive individuals. They were viewed as exchanging their persons upon marriage rather

---

516 Pringle (1989).

517 Conaghan (2002).

518 See Brown (1995) pp. 65-66.

519 For a critical appraisal of 'managing diversity' see, for example, J. Webb, 'The Politics of Equal Opportunity', *Gender, Work and Organisation*, Vol. 4, No. 3, 1997, pp. 159-169.

than as exchanging their ability to work. In keeping with this analysis, Deakin[520] outlines the way in which the employment contract had two aspects: to limit the extent of the employer's right of command and to regulate a relationship that worked as a vehicle for channelling risk, by the welfare state, for (male) employees.

The attacks upon possessive individualism by Pateman and Okin greatly strengthen the arguments of Cohen,[521] who points to the impact of an unrestrained capitalism on the working class, and of Charles Taylor,[522] who argues that Nozick's position is based upon an acceptance of freedom as an ideal and yet would undermine the social possibility of any such shared ideals flourishing in any future society. Indeed, the position of women produces such additional ammunition for these arguments that its omission now appears curious in recent debates about self-ownership.[523]

With the breakdown of the breadwinner/housewife model, any successor to Pateman's analysis of *The Sexual Contract* would be concerned with the developments within state provision of welfare. Here, the arguments of Yeatman and Hindness provide a sequel to the discussions about women's ambiguous position with regard to possessive individualism. In particular, Hindness describes the use of 'contract' as a technique of governance, operating such that the so-called consumer or customer of welfare is assumed to enter into a contract with state agencies. This new 'sexual contract' is then viewed as a contract between the state and the woman who is then trained to view herself as the owner of her ability to work and to 'take advantage' of training to be a 'job seeker'. This is a training in viewing oneself as a possessive individual, the owner of one's abilities.

---

520 Deakin (2002) p. 181.
521 Cohen (1995).
522 Taylor (1985).
523 See Pateman (2002).

Bibliography

Adler, Z. (1987) *Rape on Trial*, London: Routledge and Kegan Paul.

Adorno, T.W. and Horkheimer, M. (1995) *Dialectic of Enlightenment*, London: Verso.

Alcoff, L.M. (1996) 'Dangerous Pleasures: Foucault and the Politics of Pedophilia' in Hekman, S.J., *Feminist Interpretations of Michel Foucault*, Pennsylvania: Pennsylvania State University Press, pp. 99-135.

Alcoff, L.M. (2000) 'Review Essay: Philosophy Matters, A Review of Recent Work in Feminist Philosophy', *Signs: Journal of Women in Culture and Society*, Vol. 25, No. 3, pp. 841-882.

Arendt, H. (1958) *The Human Condition*, London: University of Chicago Press.

Atiyah, P.S. (1970) *Accidents, Compensation and the Law*, London: Weidenfeld.

Atiyah, P.S. (2000) *The Rise and Fall of the Freedom of Contract*, Oxford: Oxford University Press.

Atkins, S. and Hoggett, B. (1984) *Women and the Law*, Oxford: Blackwell.

Axelrod, R. (1990) *The Evolution of Co-operation*, London: Penguin.

Barron, A. (2000) 'Feminism, Aestheticism and the Limits of the Law', *Feminist Legal Studies*, Vol. 8, pp. 275-317.

Barry, A. Osbourne, T. and Rose, N., eds., (1996) *Foucault and Political Reason: Liberalism, Neo-Liberalism and Rationalities of Government*, London: UCL Press.

Bartky, S.L. (1988) 'Foucault, Femininity and the Modernization of Patriarchal Power' in Diamond I. and Quinby, L., eds., *Feminism and Foucault: Reflections on Resistance*, Boston: Northeastern University Press, pp. 61-88.

Bartky, S.L. (1990) 'Feeding Egos and Tending Wounds: Deference and Disaffection in Women's Emotional Labour' in *Femininity and Domination: Studies in the Phenomenology of Oppression*, London: Routledge, pp. 99-119.

Battersby, C. (1989) *Gender and Genius: Towards a Feminist Aesthetics*, London: The Women's Press.

Battersby, C. (1994a) 'Antinomies: the Art of Evelyn Williams', in *Antinomies: Works by Evelyn Williams*, Catalogue of a Mead Gallery Exhibition, The University of Warwick, pp. 25-37.

Battersby, C. (1994b) 'Unblocking the Oedipal: Karoline von Günderode and the Female Sublime' in Ledger, S., McDonagh, J. and Spencer, J., *Political Gender: Texts and Contexts*, London: Harvester Wheatsheaf, pp. 129-143.

Battersby, C. (1996) 'Her Blood and His Mirror: Mary Coleridge, Luce Irigaray and the Female Self' in Eldridge, R., ed., *Beyond Representation: Philosophy and Poetic Imagination*, Cambridge: Cambridge University Press, pp. 249-272.

Battersby, C. (1998a) *The Phenomenal Woman: Feminist Metaphysics and the Patterns of Identity*, Cambridge: Polity.

Battersby C. (1998b) 'Stages on Kant's Way: Aesthetics, Morality and the Gendered Sublime' in Zack N. et al, *Race, Class, Gender and Sexuality: The Big Questions*, Oxford: Blackwell, pp. 227-247.

Battersby, C. (2000) 'Learning to think Intercontinentally: Finding Australian Routes', *Hypatia: A Journal of Feminist Philosophy*, Vol. 5. No. 2, pp. 1-17.

Beck, U. (1992) *Risk Society: Towards a New Modernity*, London: Sage.

Beck, U. (1999) *World Risk Society*, Cambridge: Polity.

Bell, D. and Binnie, J. (2000) 'Sexual Citizenship: Law, Theory and Politics' in Richardson, J. and Sandland, R., *Feminist Perspectives on Law and Theory*, London: Cavendish, pp. 167-186.

Bell, V. (1993) *Interrogating Incest*, London: Routledge.

Benhabib S. et al, (1995) *Feminist Contentions: A Philosophical Exchange*, London: Routledge.

Beveridge, W. (1942) *Social Insurance and Allied Services*, Cmnd. 6404, London: HMSO.

Bock G. and James, S. (1992) *Beyond Equality and Difference: Citizenship, Feminist Politics and Female Subjectivity*, London: Routledge.

Bordo, S. (1990) 'Feminism, Postmodernism and Gender-Scepticism' in Nicolson, L.J., ed., *Feminism/Postmodernism*, London: Routledge, pp. 133-156.

Bottomley, A. (2000) 'Feminism is a Process not an End: A Feminist Approach to the Practice of Theory' in Richardson, J. and Sandland, R., *Feminist Perspectives on Law and Theory*, London: Cavendish, pp. 25-51.

Bottomley, A. and Conaghan, J. (1993) 'Feminist Theory and Legal Strategy' in Bottomley, A. and Conaghan, J., *Feminist Theory and Legal Strategy*, Oxford: Blackwell, pp. 1-5.

Brace, L. (2000) 'Not Empire, but Equality': Mary Wollstonecraft, the Marriage State and the Sexual Contract', *The Journal of Political Philosophy*, Vol. 8, No. 4, pp. 433-455.

Brazier, M. and Murphy, J. (1999) *Street on Torts*, 10th edition, London: Butterworths.

Brennan, T. and Pateman, C. (1979) 'Mere Auxiliaries to the Commonwealth', *Political Studies*, Vol. 27, No. 2, pp. 183-200.

Brenner, J. and Ramas, M. (2000) 'Rethinking Women's Oppression' in Brenner, J. *Women and the Politics of Class*, New York: Monthly Review Press, pp. 11-58.

Bridgeman J. and Millns, S. (1998) *Feminist Perspectives on Law: Law's Engagement with the Female Body*, London: Sweet and Maxwell.

Brophy, J. and Smart, C., eds. (1985) *Women in Law*, London: Routledge and Kegan Paul.

Brown, W. (1995) *States of Injury: Power and Freedom in Late Modernity*, Chichester: Princeton University Press.

Burchell, G., Gordon, C. and Miller, P., eds. (1991) *The Foucault Effect: Studies in Governmentality*, Chicago: University of Chicago Press.

Burke, C. Schor, N. and Whitford, M., eds. (1994) *Engaging with Irigaray*, New York: Columbia University Press.

Burke, E. (1998) *A Philosophical Enquiry into the Origin of Our Ideas of the Sublime and the Beautiful*, Oxford: Oxford University Press.

Butler, J. (1990) *Gender Trouble: Feminism and the Subversion of Identity*, London: Routledge.

Butler, J. (1993) *Bodies that Matter: On the Discursive Limits of 'Sex'*, London: Routledge.

Butler, J. (1997) *The Psychic Life of Power*, Stanford: Stanford University Press.

Calvino, I. (1979) *Invisible Cities*, London: Picador.

Cane, P. (1999) *Atiyah's Accidents, Compensation and the Law*, London: Butterworths.

Castel, R. (1991) 'From Dangerousness to Risk' in Burchell, G., Gordon C. and Miller, P., eds., *The Foucault Effect: Studies in Governmentality*, Chicago: University of Chicago Press, pp. 281-298.

Cavarero, A. (1984) *La teoria politica di John Locke*, Padova: Ed. Universitarie.

Cavarero, A. (1987) 'Pace e libert nel pensiero politico di Thomas Hobbes', *Per la filosofia*, Vol. 9, pp. 73-79.

Cavarero, A. (1995) *In Spite of Plato*, Cambridge: Polity.

Cavarero, A. (1996) *Rethinking Oedipus: Stealing a Patriarchal Text*. Paper at the UK Society of Women in Philosophy Conference.

Cavarero, A. (2000) *Relating Narratives: Storytelling and Selfhood*, London: Routledge.

Caygill, H. (1995) *A Kant Dictionary*, Oxford: Blackwell.

Chapman, R.A. (1975) 'Leviathan Writ Small: Thomas Hobbes on the Family', *American Political Science Review*, Vol. 69, pp. 76-90. Reprinted in King, P. (1993) *Thomas Hobbes: Critical Assessments III*, London: Routledge, pp. 629-656.

Cheah, P. and Grosz, E. 'The Future of Sexual Difference: An Interview with Judith Butler and Drucilla Cornell', *Diacritics*, Vol. 28. No. 1, pp. 19-42.

Clark A. (1997) *Being There: Putting Brain, Body and World Together Again*, Massachusetts: MIT.

Clark, A. (1999) 'Where Brain, Body and World Collide', *Journal of Cognitive Systems Research*, Vol. 1, pp. 5-17.

Clark, A. (2001) *Mindware: An Introduction to Philosophy of Cognitive Science*, Oxford: Oxford University Press.

Cohen, G.A. (1995) *Self-ownership, Freedom and Equality*, Cambridge: University of Cambridge Press.

Cohen, G.A. (1998) 'Once more into the Breach of Self-Ownership: Reply Narveson and Brenkert', *The Journal of Ethics*, Vol. 2, pp. 57-96.

Cohen, G.A. (2001) *If You're an Egalitarian, How Come You're So Rich?*, Harvard: Harvard University Press.

Collins, H. (1999) *Regulating Contracts*, Oxford: Oxford University Press.

Collins, H., Ewing, K.D. and McColgan, A. (2001) *Labour Law: Tests and Materials*, Oxford: Hart Publishing.

Conaghan, J. (1993) 'Harassment and the Law of Torts: *Khorasandjian v Bush*', *Feminist Legal Studies*, Vol. I, No. 2, pp. 189-197.

Conaghan, J. (1996) 'Equity Rushes in Where Tort Fears to Tread: The Court of Appeal Decision in *Burris v Asadani*', *Feminist Legal Studies*, Vol. IV, No. 2, pp. 221-228.

Conaghan, J. (1999a) 'Enhancing Civil Remedies for Sexual Harassment: s3 of the *Protection from Harassment Act 1997*', *Feminist Legal Studies*, Vol. 7, pp. 203-214.

Conaghan, J. (1999b) 'Feminism and Labour Law: Contesting the Terrain' in Morris A. and O'Donnell T., *Feminist Perspectives on Employment Law*, London: Cavendish Publishing, pp. 13-41.

Conaghan, J. (2000) 'Reassessing the Feminist Theoretical Project in Law', *Journal of Law and Society*, Vol. 27, No. 3, pp. 351-385.

Conaghan, J. (2002) 'Women, Work and Family: A British Revolution?' in Conaghan, J., Fischel, R.M. and Klare, K., *Labour Law in an Era of Globalisation: Transformative Practices and Possibilities*, Oxford: Oxford University Press.

Conaghan, J. and Mansell, W. (1998) 'From the Permissive to the Dismissive Society: Patrick Atiyah's Accidents, Compensation and the Market', *Journal of Law and Society*, Vol. 25, pp. 284-293.

Conaghan, J. and Mansell, W. (1999) *The Wrongs of Tort*, 2nd edition, London: Pluto Press.

Coole, D. (1986) 'Re-reading Political Theory from a Woman's Perspective', *Political Studies*, Vol. 34, pp. 129-148.

Coole, D. (1990) 'Patriarchy and Contract', *Politics*, Vol. 10, No. 1, pp. 25-29.

Cornell, D. (1992) *The Philosophy of the Limit*, London: Routledge.

Cornell, D. (1995) *The Imaginary Domain: Abortion, Pornography and Sexual Harassment*, London: Routledge.

Cornell, D. (1998) *At the Heart of Freedom: Feminism, Sex and Equality*, Chichester: Princeton University Press.

148   *Selves, Persons, Individuals*

Cornell, D. (2000a) *Just Cause: Freedom, Identity and Rights*, Oxford: Rowman and Littlefield.
Cornell, D., ed. (2000b) *Feminism and Pornography*, Oxford University Press.
Cruikshank, B. (1996) 'Revolutions Within: Self-Government and Self-Esteem' in Barry, A. Osbourne T. and Rose, N., eds., *Foucault and Political Reason: Liberalism, Neo-Liberalism and Rationalities of Government*, London: UCL Press, pp. 231-251.
Dahl, T. (1987) *Women's Law: An Introduction to Feminist Jurisprudence*, Oxford: Oxford University Press.
Davidoff, L., Doolittle, M., Fink J. and Holden, K. (1999) *The Family Story: Blood Contract and Intimacy 1830-1960*, Harlow: Addison Wesley Longman Ltd.
Davies, M. (1998) 'The Proper: Discourses of Purity', *Law and Critique*, Vol. IX, No. 2, pp. 141-173;
Davies, M. (1999) 'Queer Property, Queer Persons: Self-Ownership and Beyond', *Social and Legal Studies*, Vol. 8, No. 3, pp. 327-352.
Davis, G., Sullivan B., Yeatman, A., eds. (1997) *The New Contractualism?*, Melbourne: Macmillan Education.
Deakin, S. (2002) 'The Many Futures of the Contract of Employment' in Conaghan, J., Fischel, R.M. and Klare, K., *Labour Law in an Era of Globalisation: Transformative Practices and Possibilities*, Oxford: Oxford University Press, pp. 177-196.
Deakin, S. and Morris, G.S. (2001) *Labour Law*, 3rd edition, London: Butterworths.
Dean, M. (1995) 'Governing the Unemployed Self in an Active Society', *Economy and Society*, Vol. 24, No. 4, pp. 559-583.
Dean, M. (1999) *Governmentality: Power and Rule in Modern Society*, London: Sage.
Dean, M. and Hindess, B. (1998) *Governing Australia: Studies in Contemporary Rationalities of Government*, Cambridge: Cambridge University Press.
Defert, D. (1991) '"Popular life" and Insurance Technology' in Burchell, G., Gordon C. and Miller, P., eds., *The Foucault Effect: Studies in Governmentality*, Chicago: University of Chicago Press, pp. 211-233.
De Lauretis, T. (1994) 'The Essence of the Triangle or Taking the Risk of Essentialism Seriously; Feminist Theory in Italy, the U.S. and Britain' in Schor, N. and Weed, E., *The Essential Difference*, Bloomington and Indianapolis: Indiana University Press, pp. 1-39.
Deleuze, G. (1995) 'A Postscript on Control Societies' in Deleuze, G., *Negotiations*, New York: Columbia University Press, pp. 176-182.
Deutscher, P. (1997) *Yielding Gender: Feminism, Deconstruction and the History of Philosophy*, London: Routledge.
Deutscher, P. (2000a) 'The Declaration of Irigarayian Sexuate Rights: Performativity and Recognition' in Richardson, J. and Sandland, R., eds., *Feminist Perspectives on Law and Theory*, London: Cavendish, pp. 71-87.
Deutscher, P. (2000b) '"Imperfect Discretion": Interventions into the History of Philosophy by Twentieth-Century French Women Philosophers', *Hypatia: A Journal of Feminist Philosophy*, Vol. 15, No. 2, pp. 160-180.
Dickenson, D. (1997) *Property, Women and Politics: Subjects or Objects?*, Cambridge: Polity.
Dickenson, D. (1998) 'The New Contractualism?', *Women's Philosophy Review*, No. 20, pp. 108-111.
Dine, J. and Watt, B. (1995) 'Sexual Harassment: Moving Away From Discrimination', *Modern Law Review*, Vol. 58, pp. 355-362.
Diprose, R. (1994) *The Bodies of Women: Ethics, Embodiment and Sexual Difference*, London: Routledge.

Di Stefano, C. (1990) 'Dilemmas of Difference: Feminism, Modernity and Postmodernism' in Nicolson, L.J., ed., *Feminism/Postmodernism*, London: Routledge.

Dobash, R.E. and Dobash, R., eds. (1998) *Rethinking Violence Against Women*, London: Sage.

Drakopoulou, M. (2000) 'The Ethic of Care; Female Subjectivity and Feminist Legal Scholarship', *Feminist Legal Studies*, Vol. 8, pp. 199-226.

Dworkin, A. and MacKinnon, C.A. (1988) *Pornography and Civil Rights: A New Day for Women's Equality*, Minneapolis: Organising Against Pornography.

Edie, A., Grigg-Spall, I. and Ireland, P. (1992), 'Labour Law: From Master and Servant to the Contract of Employment' in Grigg-Spall, I. and Ireland, P., *The Critical Lawyers' Handbook*, London: Pluto.

Edwards, S. (1981) *Female Sexuality and the Law*, Oxford: Martin Robertson.

Ewald, F. (1991a) 'Insurance and Risk' in Burchell, G., Gordon, C. and Miller, P., eds., *The Foucault Effect: Studies in Governmentality*, Chicago: University of Chicago Press, pp. 197-210.

Ewald, F. (1991b) 'Norms, Discipline and the Law' in Post, R., ed., *Law and the Order of Culture*, California: California University Press, pp. 138-161.

Ewald, F. (2002) 'The Return of Descartes's Malicious Demon: An Outline of a Philosophy of Precaution' in Baker, T. and Simon, J., *Embracing Risk: The Changing Culture of Insurance and Responsibility* (Chicago: University of Chicago Press) pp. 273-301.

Feminist Legal Studies Special Issue: Law of Obligations (2000) Vol. 8, No. 1.

Fine, R. and Rai, S. (1997) eds., *Civil Society: Democratic Perspectives*, London: Frank Cass.

Finer, M. *Report of the Committee on One Parent Families* (1974), Cmnd. 5629, London: HMSO.

Florence, P. (1997) 'Towards the Domain of Freedom: Interview with Drucilla Cornell', *Women's Philosophy Review*, No. 17, pp 8-29.

Foucault, M. (1975) *Birth of the Clinic: An Archaeology of Medical Perception*, New York: Vintage/Random House.

Foucault, M. (1980a) *Power/Knowledge: Selected Interviews and Other Writings 1972-1977*, Gordon, C., ed., Sussex: Harvester Press.

Foucault, M. (1980b) 'On Popular Justice: A Conversation with Maoists' in Foucault, M., *Selected Interviews and Other Writings 1972-1977*, Gordon, C., ed., Sussex: Harvester Press.

Foucault, M. (1981a) *History of Sexuality Volume One: An Introduction*, London: Penguin.

Foucault, M. (1981b) *Remarks on Marx: Conversations with Duccio Trombadori*, trans., Goldstein, R.J. and Cascaito, J., New York: Semiotext(e).

Foucault, M. (1982) 'The Subject and Power' in Dreyfus H.L. and Rabinow, P., eds., *Michel Foucault: Beyond Structuralism and Hermeneutics*, Sussex: The Harvester Press, pp. 208-226.

Foucault, M. (1991a) 'Omnes et Singulatim: Towards a Criticism of Political Reason' in McMurrin, S. ed., *The Tanner Lectures on Human Values, Vol. II*, Salt Lake City: University of Utah Press, pp. 225-254.

Foucault, M. (1991b) 'What is Enlightenment?' in Rabinow, P. ed., *The Foucault Reader*, London: Penguin, pp. 32-50.

Foucault, M. (1996) 'The Anxiety of Judging' in Foucault, M., *Foucault Live: Collected Interviews 1961-1984*, New York: Semiotext(e), pp. 241-254.

Foucault, (1997a) 'Technologies of the Self' in *The Essential Works: 1954-1984 Vol. 1, Ethics, Subjectivity and Truth*, Rabinow, P., ed., New York: The New Press, pp. 223-251.

Foucault, M. (1997b) 'The Punitive Society' in Foucault, M. *The Essential Works: 1954-1984 Vol. 1, Ethics, Subjectivity and Truth*, Rabinow, P., ed., New York: The New Press, pp. 23-37.

Foucault, M. (1997c) 'The Ethics of the Concern for the Self as a Practice of Freedom' in Foucault, M. *The Essential Works: 1954-1984 Vol. 1, Ethics, Subjectivity and Truth*, Rabinow, P., ed., New York: The New Press, pp. 281-301.

Foucault, M. (2001a) 'Governmentality' in Faubion, J.D. ed., *Michel Foucault: Power, The Essential Works 3*, London: Penguin Press, pp. 208-209.

Foucault, M. (2001b) 'About the Concept of the "Dangerous Individual"' in Faubion, J.D. ed., *Michel Foucault: Power, The Essential Works 3*, London: Penguin Press, pp. 178-200.

Foucault, M. (2003) *Society Must be Defended*, London: Penguin Press.

Foucault M. and Deleuze G., (1980) 'Intellectuals and Power: A conversation between Michel Foucault and Gilles Deleuze' in Bouchard, D.F., ed., *Language, Counter-Memory, Practice: Selected Essays and Interviews by Michel Foucault*, London: Cornell University Press, pp. 205-217.

Fraser, N. (1989) *Unruly Practices: Power, Discourse and Gender in Contemporary Social Theory*, Cambridge: Polity.

Fraser, N. (1997) *Justice Interruptus: Critical Reflections on the 'Postsocialist' Condition*, London: Routledge.

Fraser, N. (1998) 'Heterosexism, Misrecognition and Capitalism: A Response to Judith Butler', *New Left Review*, No. 228.

Fraser, N. and Gordon, L. (1997) 'A Genealogy of 'Dependency': Tracing a Keyword of the U.S. Welfare State' in Fraser, N., *Justice Interruptus: Critical Reflections on the 'Postsocialist' Condition*, London: Routledge, pp. 121-149.

Frazer, E. and Lacey, N. (1993) *The Politics of Community: A Feminist Critique of the Liberal-Communitarian Debate*, London: Harvester Wheatsheaf.

Freedman, M.D.A. (1994) *Lloyd's Introduction to Jurisprudence*, London: Sweet and Maxwell.

Freeland, C.A. (1994) 'Nourishing Speculation: A Feminist Reading of Aristotelian Science' in Bar On, B.A., ed., *Engendering Origins: Critical Feminist Readings in Plato and Aristotle*, New York: State University of New York, pp. 145-187.

Freeland, M. (1976) *The Contract of Employment*, Oxford: Clarendon Press.

Freeman, M. (1996) 'Divorce: Contemporary Problems and Future Prospects' in Freeman, M., *Divorce: Where Next?*, Aldershot: Dartmouth, pp. 1-8.

Freeman, M. (1999) 'Does Surrogacy Have a Future After Brazier?', *Medical Law Review*, Vol. 7, Spring, pp.1-20.

Freud, S. (1950) *Totem and Taboo: Some Points of Agreement between the Mental Lives of Savages and Neurotics*, London: Routledge and Kegan Paul Ltd.

Fricker, M. and Hornsby, J. (2000) 'Introduction' in Fricker, M. and Hornsby, J., *The Cambridge Companion to Feminism in Philosophy*, Cambridge: Cambridge University Press.

Furedi, F. (1999) *Courting Mistrust: the Hidden Growth of a Culture of Litigation in Britain*, London: Centre for Policy Studies.

Gatens, M. (1996) *Imaginary Bodies: Ethics, Power and Corporeality*, London: Routledge.

Gatens, M. and Lloyd, G. (1999) *Collective Imaginings: Spinoza Past and Present*, London: Routledge.

Genn, H. (1987) *Hard Bargaining: Out of Court Settlement in Personal Injury Claims*, Oxford: Oxford University Press.

Gilligan, C. (1982) *In a Different Voice: Psychological Theory and Women's Development*, Cambridge Mass: Harvard University Press.

Gordon, C. (1991) 'Governmental Rationality: An Introduction' in Burchell, G. et al, *The Foucault Effect: Studies in Governmentality*, Chicago: University of Chicago Press.

Griffiths, J.A.G. (1997) *The Politics of the Judiciary*, 5th edition, London: Fontana.

Grigg-Spall I., Ireland P. and Kelly D. (1992) 'Company Law' in *The Critical Lawyers' Handbook*, London: Pluto pp. 98-105.

Grosz, E. (1994) *Volatile Bodies: Towards a Corporeal Feminism*, Bloomington and Indianapolis: Indiana University Press.

Grosz, E. (1994) 'A Thousand Tiny Sexes: Feminism and Rhizomatics' in Boundas C.V. and Olkowski D., eds., *Gilles Deleuze and the Theatre of Philosophy*, London: Routledge, pp. 187-210.

Habermas, J. (1992) *The Structural Transformation of the Public Sphere: An Inquiry into a Category of Bourgeois Society*, Cambridge: Polity.

Hacking, I. (1986) *The Taming of Chance*, Cambridge: Cambridge University Press.

Hacking, I. (1991) 'How should we do the History of Statistics?' in Burchell, G. Gordon, C. and Miller, P., eds., *The Foucault Effect: Studies in Governmentality*, Chicago: University of Chicago Press, pp. 181-195.

Haraway, D.J. (1997) *Modest_Witness@Second_Millennium.FemaleMan_Meets_OncoMouse: Feminism and Technoscience*, London: Routledge.

Harris, A. (1990) 'Race and Essentialism in Feminist Legal Theory', *Stanford Law Review*, Vol. 42, pp. 581-616.

Harris, D., Campbell, D. and Halson, R. (2002) *Remedies in Tort and Contract*, London: Butterworths.

Harris, J.W. (1997) 'What is Non-Private Property?' in Harris, J.W. ed., *Property Problems: From Genes to Pension Funds*, London: Kluwer Law International Ltd., pp. 175-189.

Hartmann, H. (1981) 'The Unhappy Marriage of Marxism and Feminism: Towards a More Progressive Union' in Sargeant, L., ed., *Women and Revolution: A Discussion of the Unhappy Marriage of Marxism and Feminism*, London: Pluto Press.

Hay, D. (1977) 'Property, Authority and Criminal Law: Crime and Society in Eighteenth Century England' in Hay, D., Linebaugh, P., Rule, J.G., Thompson, E.P. and Winslow, C., eds., *Albion's Fatal Tree*, Harmondsworth: Penguin.

Heberle, R. (1998) 'Remembering the Resistant Object: A Critique of Feminist Epistemologies' in Bar On, B.A. and Ferguson, A., eds., *Daring to be Good: Essays in Feminist Ethico-Politics*, London: Routledge, pp. 114-126.

Hegel, G.W.F. (1967) *Hegel's Philosophy of Right*, trans. Knox, T.M., Oxford: Oxford University Press.

Held, V. (1994) 'Non-Contractual Society: A Feminist View' in Okin, S.M. and Mansbridge, J., eds, *Feminism: Volume One*, Hants: Edward Elgar Publishing Ltd.

Herzog, D. (1989) *Happy Slaves: A Critique of Consent Theory*, Chicago: University of Chicago.

Hindness B. (1997) 'A Society Governed by Contract?' Davis, G., Sullivan B. and Yeatman, A., eds., *The New Contractualism?*, Melbourne: Macmillan Education, pp. 14-26.

Hindness, B. (1996) *Discourses of Power: Hobbes to Foucault*, Oxford: Blackwell.

152 *Selves, Persons, Individuals*

Hinton, R.W.K. (1968) 'Husbands, Fathers and Conquerors', *Political Studies*, Vol. XVI, No. 1, pp. 55-67.

Hobbes, T. (1968) *Leviathan*, Macpherson, C.B., ed., London: Penguin Books.

Hobbes, T. (1994a) 'De Corpore Politico' in *The Elements of Law*, Oxford: Oxford University Press.

Hobbes, T. (1994b) *Leviathan*, Curley E., ed., Cambridge: Hackett Publishing Ltd..

Hobbes, T. (1998) *Man and Citizen*, De Homine *and* De Cive, ed., Gert B., Indiapolis: Hackett Publishing Company.

Hoggett, B., Pearl, D., Cooke, E. and Bates, P. (1996) *The Family, Law and Society: Cases and Materials*, 4th edition, London: Butterworths.

Honoré, A.M. (1961) 'Ownership' in Guest, A.G., ed., *Oxford Essays in Jurisprudence*, Oxford: Oxford University Press.

Howarth, A. (1996) *Textbook on Tort*, London: Butterworths.

Hutchings, K. (1996) 'The Death of the Sovereign Individual: Reflections on Feminist Analyses of Political and Moral Agency' in Griffiths, M. and Whitford, M., ed., *Women's Review Philosophy*, Nottingham: Nottingham University Press, pp. 1-25.

Hyde, A. (1997) *Bodies of Law*, Princeton: Princeton University Press.

Hypatia: A Journal of Feminist Philosophy, Special Issue: Going Australian Reconfiguring Feminism and Philosophy (2000) Vol. 15, No 2.

Ingram, A. (1994) *A Political Theory of Rights*, Oxford: Clarendon Press.

Irigaray, L. (1985a) 'Women on the Market' in *This Sex which is not One*, New York: Cornell University Press, pp. 170-191.

Irigaray, L. (1985b) 'Questions' in *This Sex which is not One*, New York: Cornell University Press, pp. 157-158.

Irigaray, L. (1985c) 'Commodities among Themselves' in *This Sex which is not One*, New York: Cornell University Press, pp. 192-197.

Irigaray, L. (1985d) *Speculum of the Other Woman*, New York: Cornell University Press.

Irigaray, L. (1993a) *An Ethics of Sexual Difference*, London: Athlone Press.

Irigaray, L. (1993b) *Je, Tu, Nous: Towards a Culture of Difference*, London: Routledge.

Irigaray, L., (1993c) *Sexes and Genealogies*, New York: Columbia University Press.

Irigaray, L. (1996) *I Love to You: Sketch of a Possible Felicity in History*, London: Routledge.

Jackson, E. (1992) 'Catherine MacKinnon and Feminist Jurisprudence: A Critical Appraisal', *Journal of Law and Society*, Vol. 19, No. 2, pp. 195-213.

Jackson, E. (2001) *Regulating Reproduction: Law, Technology and Autonomy*, Oxford: Hart Publishing.

James, S. (1997) *Passion and Action*, Oxford: Oxford University Press.

Jardine, A.A. (1985) *Gynesis: Configurations of Woman and Modernity*, Cornell University Press.

Jay, M, (1993) *Downcast Eyes: The Denigration of Vision in Twentieth Century French Thought*, California: University of California Press.

Johnson, C. (1996) 'Does Capitalism really need Patriarchy?: Some Old Issues Reconsidered', *Women's Studies International Forum*, Vol. 19, No. 3, pp. 193-202.

Johnson, M. (1987) *The Body in the Mind*, Chicago: University of Chicago Press.

Johnson, S. and Rubenstein, M. (2002) 'Sexual Harassment and the Law', *Equal Opportunities Review*, No. 102, pp. 16-17.

Jones, R. (1997) *Mosaics of the Self: Kantian Objects and Female Subjects in the Work of Claire Coll and Paula Ludwig*, Unpublished dissertation, University of Warwick, Res. Dis. 65-66.

Jones, R. (2000) 'Subverting the Sublime for a Female Subject', *Women's Philosophy Review*, No. 25, pp. 30-55.

Kant, I. (1960) *Observations on the Feeling of the Beautiful and Sublime*, trans. Goldthwaite, J.T., California: University of California Press.

Kant, I. (1974) *Anthropology from a Pragmatic Point of View*, trans. Gregor, M.J., The Hague: Martinus Nijhoff.

Kant, I. (1987) *Critique of Judgment*, trans. Pluhar W.S., Indianapolis: Hackett.

Kant, I. (1991) *The Metaphysics of Morals*, trans. M.J. Gregor, Cambridge: Cambridge University Press.

Kant, I. (1993) *Grounding for the Metaphysics of Morals: On a Supposed Right to Lie because of Philanthropic Concerns*, Indiana: Hackett.

Keller, E.F. (1992) *Secrets of Life, Secrets of Death: Essays on Language, Gender and Science*, London: Routledge.

Kemp, D. and Mantle, P. (1999) *Damages for Personal Injury and Death*, 7th edition, London: Sweet and Maxwell.

Kerruish, V. (1991) *Jurisprudence As Ideology*, London: Routledge.

King, P. (1974) 'Mother and Infant' in King, P., *The Ideology of Order: A Comparative Analysis of Jean Bodin and Thomas Hobbes*, London: George Allen and Unwin, pp. 200-212.

Kingdom, E. (1991) *What's Wrong with Rights? Problems for Feminist Politics of Law*, Edinburgh: Edinburgh University Press.

Kingdom, E. (2000) 'Cohabitation Contracts and the Democratization of Personal Relations', *Feminist Legal Studies*, Vol. 8, pp. 5-27.

Kymlicka, W. (1990) *Contemporary Political Philosophy: An Introduction*, Oxford: Oxford University Press.

Kymlicka, W. (2002) *Contemporary Political Philosophy: An Introduction*, 2nd edition, Oxford: Oxford University Press.

Lacey, N. (1997) 'On the Subject of Sexing the Subject' in Naffine, N. and Owens, R.J., eds., *Sexing the Subject of Law*, London: Sweet and Maxwell, pp. 65-76.

Lakoff, G. (1987) *Women, Fire and Dangerous Things*, Chicago: University of Chicago Press.

Landes, J.B., ed. (1998) *Feminism: The Public and the Private*, Oxford: Oxford University Press.

Lange, L. (1983) 'Woman is not a Rational Animal: On Aristotle's Biology of Reproduction' in Harding, S. and Hintikka, M.B., eds., *Discovering Reality: Feminist Perspectives on Epistemology, Metaphysics, Methodology, and Philosophy of Science*, Dordrecht: D. Reidel, pp. 1-15.

Laster, K. and Raman, P. (1997) 'Law for One and One for All: An Intersectional Legal Subject' in Naffine N. and Owens, R.J., *Sexing the Subject of Law*, London: Sweet and Maxwell, pp. 193-212.

Le Doeuff, M. (1989) *The Philosophical Imaginary*, London: Athlone Press.

Leiss, W. (1988) *C.B. Macpherson: Dilemmas of Liberalism and Socialism*, New York: St. Martin's Press.

Lessnoff, M.H. (1999) 'C.B. Macpherson: Possessive Individualism and Liberal Democracy' in Lessnoff, M.H., *Political Philosophers of the Twentieth Century*, Oxford: Blackwell, pp. 93-110.

Lister, R. and Callender, C. (1999) 'Income Distribution within Families and the Reform of Social Security', *Journal of Social Welfare and Family Law*, Vol. 21, No. 3, pp. 203-220.

Lloyd, G. (1984) *The Man of Reason: 'Male' and 'Female' in Western Philosophy*, London: Methuen.

Lloyd, G. (2000) 'No-One's Land: Australia and the Philosophical Imagination', *Hypatia: A Journal of Feminist Philosophy*, Vol. 15, No. 2.

Locke, J. (1969) 'Of the Names of Substances' in *An Essay Concerning Human Understanding*, London: Collins, pp. 283-296.

Locke J. (1999) *Two Treatises of Government*, ed. Laslett, P., Cambridge: Cambridge University Press.

Lukács, G. (1983) *History and Class Consciousness: Studies in Marxist Dialectics*, London: Merlin Press.

Lunney M. and Oliphant K. (2000) *Tort Law: Text and Materials*, Oxford: Oxford University Press.

Lupton, D. (1999) 'Risk and the Ontology of Pregnant Embodiment' in Lupton, D., *Risk and Sociocultural Theory: New Directions and Perspectives*, Cambridge: Cambridge University Press, pp. 59-85.

MacKinnon, C.A. (1979) *The Sexual Harassment of Working Women*, New Haven: Yale University Press.

MacKinnon, C.A. (1982) 'Feminism, Marxism, Method and the State: An Agenda for Theory', *Signs: Journal of Women in Culture and Society*, Vol. 7, No. 3, pp. 515-544.

MacKinnon, C.A. (1983) 'Feminism, Marxism, Method and State: Towards Feminist Jurisprudence', *Signs: Journal of Women in Culture and Society*, Vol. 8. No. 2, pp. 635-658.

MacNeil, I. (1980) *The New Social Contract*, Yale: Yale University Press.

MacNeil, I. (2000) 'Contracting Worlds and Essential Contract Theory', *Social and Legal Studies*, Vol. 9, No. 3, pp. 431-438.

Macpherson, C.B. (1962) *The Political Theory of Possessive Individualism: Hobbes to Locke*, Oxford: Oxford University Press.

Macpherson, C.B. (1965) 'Hobbes's Bourgeois Man' in Brown, K., *Hobbes Studies*, Cambridge: Harvard University Press, pp. 169-183.

Macpherson, C.B. (1977) *The Life and Times of Liberal Democracy*, Oxford: Oxford University Press.

Macpherson, C.B. (1978a) 'The Economic Penetration of Political Theory: Some Hypotheses', *Journal of History of Ideas*, Vol. 39, pp. 101-118.

Macpherson, C.B., ed. (1978b) *Property: Mainstream and Critical Positions*, Oxford: Basil Blackwell.

Macpherson, C.B. (1980) *Burke*, Oxford: Oxford University Press.

Macpherson, C.B. (1987) 'Hobbes's Political Economy' in Macpherson, C.B., *The Rise and Fall of Economic Justice and Other Essays*, Oxford: Oxford University Press, pp. 133-146.

Macpherson, C.B. (1993) 'Hobbes, Analyst of Power and Peace' in Mukherjee, S. and Ramaswamy, S., eds., *Great Western Thinkers: Thomas Hobbes*, New Delhi: Deep and Deep Publications, pp. 493-519.

Mahendra, B. (2001) 'Revisiting No Fault Compensation', *New Law Journal*, Vol. 151, No. 6987, p. 837.

Maine, H. (1917) *Ancient Law*, London: J.M. Dent and Sons.

Marcus, S. (1992) 'Fighting Bodies, Fighting Words: A Theory and Politics of Rape Prevention' in Butler, J. and Scott, J.W., eds., *Feminists Theorize the Political*, London: Routledge, pp. 385-403.

Martin, R. (1994) 'A Feminist View of the Reasonable Man: An Alternative Approach to Liability in Negligence for Personal Injury', *Anglo-American Law Review*, Vol. 23, pp. 334-374.

Martinich, (1995) *A Hobbes Dictionary*, Oxford: Blackwell Publishers.

Marx, K. (1954) *Capital: A Critique of Political Economy, Volume One*, London: Lawrence and Wishart.

Marx, K. (1975) 'The Holy Family' in *Collected Works, Vol. 4*, London: Lawrence Wishart.

Marx, K. (1988) 'Thesis on Feuerbach' in Marx, K., *The German Ideology*, New York: Prometheus Books, pp. 569-575.

Marx, K. (1992) *Early Writings*, London: Penguin.

Massumi, B. (1993) *The Politics of Everyday Fear*, New York: Semiotexte.

Mauss, M. (1985) 'A Category of the Human Mind: The Notion of Person; the Notion of Self' in Carrithers, M., Collins, S. and Lukes, S., *The Category of the Person*, Cambridge: Cambridge University Press.

Mauss, M. (1990) *The Gift: The Form and Reason for Exchange in Archaic Societies*, London: Routledge.

Mauss, M. (1992) 'Techniques of the Body' in Crary J. and Kwinter, S., eds., *Incorporations*, New York: Zone Books.

McGlynn, C. (1998) *Legal Feminisms: Theory and Practice*, Aldershot: Dartmouth.

McLean, I. (1993) 'The Social Contract in Leviathan and the Prisoner's Dilemma Supergame' in King, P., *Thomas Hobbes: Critical Assessments III*, London: Routledge, pp. 591-606.

Mill, J.S. (1970) 'The Subjection of Women' in *Essays on Sex Equality*, ed. Rossi A.S., Chicago: University of Chicago Press.

Miller, D. (1982) 'The Macpherson Version', *Political Studies*, Vol. XXX, No. 1, pp. 120-127.

Minson, J. (1993) *Questions of Conduct: Sexual Harassment, Citizenship and Government*, London: MacMillan.

Mohanty, C.T. (1993) 'Under Western Eyes: Feminist Scholarship and Colonial Discourses' in Williams, P. and Chrisman, L., *Colonial Discourse and Post-Colonial Theoretical Reader*, Columbia: Columbia University Press, pp. 196-220.

Montag, W. (1995) 'The Soul is the Prison of the Body: Althusser and Foucault, 1970-1975', *Yale French Studies*, Vol. 88, pp. 53-77.

Moss, L. (2001) 'Deconstructing the Gene and Reconstructing Molecular Developmental Systems' in Oyama, S., Griffiths, P.E. and Gray, R.D., *Cycles of Contingency: Developmental Systems and Evolution*, Massachusetts: MIT, pp. 85-97.

Mossman, M.J. (1986) 'Feminism and Legal Method: the Difference It Makes', *Australian Journal of Law and Society*, Vol. 3, pp. 30-52. Reprinted in Fineman, M.A. and Thomadsen, N.S., eds. (1991) *At the Boundaries of the Law: Feminism and Legal Theory*, London: Routledge, pp. 287-388.

Naffine, N. (1998) 'The Legal Structure of Self-Ownership: Or the Self-Possessed Man and the Woman Possessed', *Journal of Law and Society*, Vol. 25, No. 2, pp. 193-212.

Naffine N. and Owens, R.J. (1997) *Sexing the Subject of Law*, London: Sweet and Maxwell.

Neave, M. (1997) 'The Hands that Sign the Paper: Women and Domestic Contracts' in Davis G. et al, *The New Contractualism*, Melbourne: MacMillan, pp. 71-86.

Nedelsky (1991) 'Law, Boundaries and the Bounded Self' in Post, R., ed., *Law and the Order of Culture*, California: California University Press, pp. 162-189.

Nelson, J.A. and England, P. (2002) 'Feminist Philosophies of Love and Work', *Hypatia: A Journal of Feminist Philosophy*, Vol. 17, No. 2, pp.1-18.

Neumann-Held, E.M. (2001) 'Let's Talk about Genes: The Process Molecular Gene Concept and Its Context' in Oyama, S., Griffiths, P.E. and Gray, R.D., *Cycles of Contingency: Developmental Systems and Evolution*, Massachusetts: MIT, pp. 69-84.

Nietzsche, F. *On the Genealogy of Morality*, Cambridge: Cambridge University Press.

Norrie, A. (1992) 'Criminal Law' in Grigg-Spall I. and Ireland, P., *The Critical Lawyers' Handbook*, London: Pluto Press, pp. 76-83.

Norrie, A. (2000) *Punishment, Responsibility and Justice: A Relational Critique*, Oxford: Oxford University Press.

Nozick, R. (1974) *Anarchy, State and Utopia*, Bristol: J.W. Arrowsmith Ltd.

O'Donovan, K. (1997) 'With Sense, Consent or Just a Con?: Legal Subjects in the Discourse of Autonomy' in Naffine N. and Owens, R.J., *Sexing the Subject of Law*, London: Sweet and Maxwell, pp. 47-64.

O'Malley, P. (1996) 'Risk and Responsibility' in Barry, A., Osbourne T. and Rose, N., eds., *Foucault and Political Reason: Liberalism, Neo-Liberalism and Rationalities of Government*, London: UCL Press, pp. 189-207.

O'Malley, P. (2000) 'Uncertain Subjects: Risks, Liberalism and Contract', *Economy and Society*, Vol. 29, No. 4.

Okin, S.M. (1989) *Justice, Gender and the Family*, US: Basic Books.

Okin, S.M. (1997) 'Families and Feminist Theory: Some Past and Present Issues' in Nelson, H.L., ed., *Feminism and Families*, London: Routledge, pp. 13-26.

Owens, R.J. (1997) 'Working in the Sex Market' in Naffine N. and Owens, R.J. *Sexing the Subject of Law*, London: Sweet and Maxwell, pp. 119-146.

Oyama, S. (2000a) *Evolution's Eye: A Systems View of the Biology-Culture Divide*, Durham: Duke University.

Oyama, S. (2000b) *The Ontogeny of Information: Developmental Systems and Evolution*, Durham: Duke University Press.

Oyama, S., Griffiths, P.E. and Gray, R.D. (2001) *Cycles of Contingency: Developmental Systems and Evolution*, Massachusetts: MIT.

Pashukanis, E.B. (1989) *Law and Marxism: A General Theory*, Worcester: Pluto.

Pateman, C. (1980) 'Women and Consent', *Political Theory*, Vol. 8, pp. 149-168. Reprinted in Pateman, C. (1989) *The Disorder of Women*, Stanford: Stanford University Press, pp. 71-89.

Pateman, C. (1983) 'Defending Prostitution: Charges Against Ericsson', *Ethics*, Vol. 93, pp. 561-565.

Pateman, C. (1985a) *Democracy, Freedom and Special Rights*, Swansea: The University of Wales Swansea.

Pateman, C. (1985b) *The Problem of Political Obligation: A Critique of Liberal Theory*, Cambridge: Polity.

Pateman, C. (1988) *The Sexual Contract*, Cambridge: Polity Press.

Pateman, C. (1989a) 'Women and Consent' in *The Disorder of Women*, Stanford: Stanford University Press, pp. 71-89.

Pateman, C. (1989b) 'Feminist Critiques of the Public/Private Dichotomy' in Pateman, C., *The Disorder of Women*, Stanford: Stanford University Press, pp. 118-140.

Pateman, C. (1990) 'Contract and Ideology: A Reply to Coole', *Politics*, Vol. 10, No. 1, pp. 30-32.

Pateman, C. (1991) '"God Hath Ordained to Man a Helper": Hobbes, Patriarchy and Conjugal Rights' in Shanley M.L. and Pateman, C., *Feminist Interpretations and Political Theory*, Cambridge: Polity.

Pateman, C. (1996a) 'A Comment on Johnson's Does Capitalism Really Need Patriarchy?', *Women's International Forum*, Vol. 19, No 3, pp. 203-205.

Pateman, C. (1996b) 'Democracy and Democratization: Presidential Address, XVIth World Congress International Political Science Association', *International Political Science Review*, Vol. 17, No. 1, pp. 5-12.

Pateman, C. (1997) 'Beyond the Sexual Contract?' in Dench, G., *Rewriting the Sexual Contract: Collected Views on Changing Relationships and Sexual Divisions of Labour*, London: Institute of Community Studies, pp. 1-9.

Pateman, C. (1998) 'The Patriarchal Welfare State' in Landes, J.B., ed., *Feminism: the Public and Private*, Oxford: Oxford University Press, pp. 241-274.

Pateman, C. (2002) 'Self-Ownership and Property in the Person: Democratization and a Tale of Two Concepts', *The Journal of Political Philosophy*, Vol. 10, No. 1, pp. 20-53.

Phillips, A. (1989) 'The Original Contract?', *Radical Philosophy*, Vol. 52, pp. 38-40.

Phillips, A. (1993) *Democracy and Difference*, Cambridge: Polity.

Phillips, A. (1999) *Which Equalities Matter?*, Cambridge: Polity Press.

Polanyi, K. (1991) *The Great Transformation*, Boston: Beacon Press.

Posner, R.A. (1992) *Economic Analysis of Law*, Boston: Little Brown.

Pringle, R. (1989) *Secretaries Talk: Sexuality, Power and Work*, London: Verso Books.

Radin, M.J. (2001) *Contested Commodities: The Trouble with Trade in Sex, Children, Body Parts and Other Things*, Harvard: Harvard University Press.

Rawls, J. (1972) *A Theory of Justice*, Oxford: Oxford University Press.

Rawls, J. (2001) *Justice as Fairness: A Restatement*, Mass.: Harvard University Press.

Richardson, J. (1998a) 'Jamming the Machines: "Woman" in the work of Irigaray and Deleuze', *Law and Critique*, Vol. IX, No. 1, pp. 89-115.

Richardson, J. (1998b) 'Beyond Equality or Difference: Sexual Difference in the work of Adriana Cavarero', *Feminist Legal Studies*, Vol. VI, No. 1, pp. 105-120.

Richardson, J. (1999) 'A Burglar in the House of Philosophy: Theodor Adorno, Drucilla Cornell and Hate Speech', *Feminist Legal Studies*, Vol. VII, No. 1, pp. 3-31.

Richardson, J. (2000) 'A Refrain: Feminist Metaphysics and Law' in Richardson, J. and Sandland, R., eds., *Feminist Perspectives on Law and Theory*, London: Cavendish, pp.119-134.

Richardson, J. (forthcoming) 'Feminist Perspectives on the Law of Tort and the Technology of Risk', *Economy and Society*.

Roach Anleu, S.L. 'Critiquing the Law: Themes and Dilemmas in Anglo-American Feminist Legal Theory', *Journal of Law and Society*, Vol. 19, No. 4, 1992, pp. 423-440.

Rose, N. (1996a) 'Governing Advanced Liberal Democracies' in Barry, A., Osbourne, T. and Rose, N., eds., *Foucault and Political Reason: Liberalism, Neo-Liberalism and Rationalities of Government*, London: UCL Press.

Rose, N. (1996b) 'The Death of the Social? Re-figuring the Territory of Government', *Economy and Society*, Vol. 25, No. 3, pp. 327-356.

Rose, N. (1997) 'Assembling the modern self' in Porter, R., ed., *Rewriting the Self: Histories from the Renaissance to the Present*, London: Routledge, pp. 224-248.

Rose, N. (1999a) *Governing the Soul: The Shaping of the Private Self*, London: Free Association Books.

Rose, N. (1999b) *Powers of Freedom: Reframing Political Thought*, Cambridge: Cambridge University Press.

Royal Commission on Civil Liability and Compensation for Personal Injury (1978) Chair: Lord Pearson, Cmnd. 7054, London: HMSO.

Royal Commission on Criminal Justice (1993) Chair: Lord Runciman, Cmnd 2263, London: HMSO.

Rubenstein, M. (1992) 'Sexual Harassment: European Commission Recommendation and Code of Practice', *Industrial Law Journal*, Vol. 21, p. 70.

Sachs, A. and Wilson, J.H. (1978) *Sexism and the Law*, Oxford: Martin Robertson.

Sandland, R. (1995) 'Between "Truth" and "Difference": Poststructuralism, Law and the Power of Feminism', *Feminist Legal Studies*, Vol. 3, No. 1, pp. 3-47.

Scheper-Hughes, N. (2000) 'The Global Traffic in Human Organs', *Current Anthropology*, Vol. 41, No. 2, pp. 191-224.

Schochet, G.J. (1975) *Patriarchalism in Political Thought*, Bristol: Basil Blackwell.

Schor, N. and Weed, E. (1994) *The Essential Difference*, Bloomington and Indianapolis: Indiana University Press.

Schrift, A.D. (1997) *The Logic of the Gift: Towards an Ethic of Generosity*, London: Routledge.

Scott J.W. (1996) *Only Paradoxes to Offer: French Feminists and the Rights of Man*, London: Harvard University Press.

Sergeant, L., ed. (1981) *Women and Revolution: A Discussion of the Unhappy Marriage of Marxism and Feminism*, London: Pluto Press.

Simon, J. (1996) 'Review' in Barry, A., Osbourne T. and Rose, N., eds., *Foucault and Political Reason: Liberalism, Neo-Liberalism and Rationalities of Government*, London: UCL Press.

Skinner, Q. (1999) 'Hobbes and the Purely Artificial Person of the State', *The Journal of Political Philosophy*, Vol. 1, No. 7, pp. 1-29.

Slomp, G. (1994) 'Hobbes and the Equality of Women', *Political Studies*, Vol. 42, pp. 441-452.

Sommerville, J.P., ed. (1991) *Filmer: Patriarchia and Other Writings*, Cambridge: Cambridge University Press.

Spivak, G.C. (1990) 'Criticism, Feminism and the Institution: An Interview with Elizabeth Grosz' in Harasym, S., ed., *The Post-Colonial Critic: Interviews Strategies, Dialogues*, London: Routledge, pp. 1-16.

Spivak, G.C. (1993) 'In a Word: Interview' in *Outside in the Teaching Machine*, London: Routledge, pp. 1-23.

Steels, L. 'The Artificial Life Roots of Artificial Intelligence', *Artificial Life*, Vol. 1, No. 1-2, pp. 75-110.

Sterckx, S. (1998) 'Some Ethically Problematic Aspects of the Proposal for a Directive on the Legal Protection of Biotechnological Interventions', *European Intellectual Property Rights*, Vol. 4, pp. 23-128.

Taylor, B. (1983) *Eve and the New Jerusalem: Socialism and Feminism in the Nineteenth Century*, London: Virago.

Taylor, C. (1985) 'Atomism' in *Philosophy and the Human Sciences: Philosophical Papers 2*, Cambridge: Cambridge University Press, pp. 187-210.

Thompson, A. (1992) 'The Law of Contract' in Grigg-Spall, I. and Ireland, P., eds., *The Critical Lawyers' Handbook*, London: Pluto, pp. 69-76.

Thompson, E.P. (1977) *Whigs and Hunters: The Origin of the Black Act*, Harmondsworth: Penguin.

Thompson, E.P. (1991) 'Custom, Law and Common Right' in Thompson, E.P., *Customs in Common*, London: Penguin.

Thornton, M., ed. (1995) *Public and Private: Feminist Legal Debates*, Oxford: Oxford University Press.

Tully, J. (1987) 'Review of Grunebaum', *Ethics*, Vol. 98, pp. 851-854.

Tully, J. (1993) 'After the Macpherson Thesis' in Tully, J., *An Approach to Political Philosophy: Locke in Contexts*, Cambridge: Cambridge University Press, pp. 71-95.

Van Der Weele, C. (2001) 'Developmental Systems Theory and Ethics: Different Ways to be Normative with Regard to Science' in Oyama, S., Griffiths, P.E. and Gray, R.D., eds., *Cycles of Contingency: Developmental Systems and Evolution*, Massachusetts: MIT, pp. 351-362.

Van Mill, D. (2001) *Liberty, Rationality and Agency in Hobbes's Leviathan*, New York: State University of New York.

Walsh, P. (2003) 'Editorial', *Clinical Risk*, Vol. 9, No. 2, p. 66.

Webb, J. (1997) 'The Politics of Equal Opportunity' in *Gender, Work and Organisation*, Vol. 4, No. 3, pp. 159-169.

Weir, L. (1996) 'Recent Developments in the Government of Pregnancy', *Economy and Society*, Vol. 25, No. 3, pp. 372-392.

Whitford, M. (1991) *Luce Irigaray: Philosophy in the Feminine*, London: Routledge.

Whitford, M. (1994) 'Irigaray, Utopia and the Death Drive' in Burke C., Schor, N. and Whitford, M., eds., *Engaging with Irigaray*, New York: Columbia University Press, pp. 379-400.

Wightman, J. (1996) *Contract: A Critical Commentary*, London: Pluto Press.

Williams, L.A. (2002) Beyond Labour Law's Parochialism: A Re-envisioning of the Discourse of Redistribution' in Conaghan, J., Fischel, R.M. and Klare, K., *Labour Law in an Era of Globalisation: Transformative Practices and Possibilities*, Oxford: Oxford University Press, pp. 93-114.

Williams, P. (1991) *The Alchemy of Race and Rights*, Massachusetts: Harvard University Press.

Wittig, M. (1992) 'On the Social Contract' in *The Straight Mind and Other Essays*, London: Harvester Wheatsheaf, pp. 33-45.

Yeatman, A. (1997) 'Contract, Status and Personhood' in Davis, G., Sullivan B. and Yeatman, A., *The New Contractualism?*, Melbourne: Macmillan, pp. 39-56.

Yeatman, A. (1998) 'Interpreting Contemporary Contractualism' in Dean, M. and Hindess, B., *Governing Australia: Studies in Contemporary Rationalities of Government*, Cambridge: Cambridge University Press, pp. 227-241.

Young, I.M. (1990) *Throwing like a Girl*, Indiana: Indiana University Press.

Zaitchik, A. (1993) 'Hobbes's Reply to the Fool: The Problem of Consent and Obligation' in Mukherjee S. and Ramaswamy S., eds., *Great Western Political Thinkers: Hobbes*, New Delhi: Deep and Deep Publications, pp. 263-284.

Web Sites

http://cmmg.biosci.wayne.edu/asg/polly.html
http://www.dti.gov.uk/er/fairness/fore.htm
http://www.dti.gov.uk/er/g_paper/chap1.htm
http://law-crime.rutgers.edu/omalley1.html
http://www.nyu.edu/gsas/dept/philo/courses/concepts/clark.html
www.westlaw.co.uk

Cases

Legislation

Index